Crossroads in Time

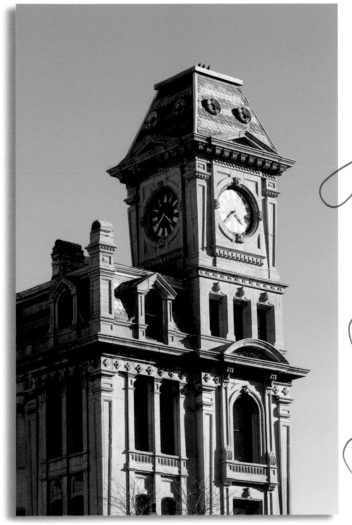

An Illustrated History of Syracuse

By Dennis J. Connors

Published by
Onondaga Historical Association
321 Montgomery Street
Syracuse, New York 13202
www.cnyhistory.org

Dennis J. Connors
Author
Curator of History
Onondaga Historical Association

Design
Marianne Mackey
Gina Mancini

Special Photographic Contributions
John Dowling Photography Library
www.JohnDowlingPhotography.com

Profile Writers
Bob Canino
John Doran
Cornelius J. Hannon
Lois Hickey

Published in cooperation with
Syracuse University Press
Syracuse, New York 13244
www.SyracuseUniversityPress.syr.edu

ISBN: 0-8156-8149-6

Printed in Hong Kong

LOOK
SET POT HOLDERS
FREE
WITH
IVORY FLAKES
☞ 20¢

IVORY
FLAKES
for safe washing
of fine things

GOOD-WILL SOAP

FARM CREST
CHERRY PIE

FARM CREST

FARM CREST
CAKES

FARM CREST

OHA Collection
Photo by Hal Silverman

TABLE OF CONTENTS

PREFACE 6

ACKNOWLEDGMENTS 10

CHAPTER *One* 12
Lines on the Land

CHAPTER *Two* 34
An Urban Center Emerges

CHAPTER *Three* 70
Syracuse Matures

CHAPTER *Four* 112
Meeting the Challenges
of a Changing Nation

EPILOGUE 138

PARTNERS IN SYRACUSE 146

BIBLIOGRAPHY 200

INDEX 202

INDEX OF PARTNERS
AND WEB SITES 208

Photo by John Dowling

PREFACE

"The Village of Syracuse is situated near the center of Onondaga County at the point where the Great Seneca Turnpike crosses the Erie Canal. The Onondaga Creek affording valuable water power, passes through it near the center of the Village. The Oswego Canal intersects the Erie, opening a direct channel of trade with the Canadas. The meeting of the Canals and Turnpikes at this point, renders it the great thoroughfare through which the immense travel from the East and West, and to and from the Canadas, must almost entirely pass."

From the border of an 1834 map of Syracuse

This lavish promotion reflects the promise of a young Syracuse. It also confirms and foretells a reoccurring theme in the story of Syracuse... the destiny of good transportation links.

Native Americans and Europeans used the natural river and lake systems. Early Syracusans enjoyed the crossings detailed above, which soon were joined by national railroad linkages going east and west, north and south. Even today, two great interstate highway arteries, Routes 90 and 81, intersect just at the edge of Syracuse. This long tradition of fortunate junctions inspired the title for this publication, *Crossroads in Time*. But more significantly, this work celebrates a diverse community with a rich heritage.

Assembling the history of any sizable locale is a monumental task. At first, it was thought that this book would encompass all of Onondaga County. The Onondaga Historical Association (OHA) is the book's sponsor, and that geography reflects its mission. But such a task quickly proved too ambitious. Narratives covering the heritage of the county's several towns, along with that of Syracuse, could not be given justice within the limitations of an illustrated history format. So this publication focuses primarily on Syracuse. The OHA will be considering a companion volume in the future to address the appealing history shaped in surrounding communities.

But even just the history of Syracuse could take volumes to chronicle. The story of this city is a profound one, often reflecting the great movements and eras of American life, but also possessing its own distinctive twists, idiosyncrasies and characters. One major history of the city, published in the 1920s, filled three volumes. In 2006, there are 80 more years to document and, in this instance, less space in which to do it. It is acknowledged, unfortunately, that a great deal had to be left out. And I apologize if a reader believes an important story or personality is not found among these pages.

Although this book cannot touch on every event nor person or place, it does offer a chronological journey that should shed some light on how Syracuse evolved through the years. Its form is a series of essays wrapped around some of the major trends in our city's evolution. It is intended both for those born here as well as for others who have adopted Syracuse as their home. I hope that newcomers will be delighted in learning more about their surroundings. And I think that even the old-timers might discover a few new revelations about our collective past.

This work does venture, on occasion, outside the strict boundaries of Syracuse. In the late 18th and early 19th centuries, there was not yet a Syracuse here. But the reader can sense the period flavor that the founders experienced in living on the land that would become the city. Later, the tale of Onondaga Lake's resorts are introduced. Although that shoreline was in a neighboring town, its amusements were a distinct part of living in Syracuse. And there is a discussion about suburban development following

World War II, since it has had such a major impact on the city's history.

Additionally, the text places an emphasis on the physical development of Syracuse. The city is a dynamic place, always changing and evolving. Generations come and go. People move about a great deal in American society. Neighborhoods transition. It is increasingly easy to avoid forming attachments to any place. Streets, buildings, green spaces and neighborhood corners with no meaning are too easily discounted.

But such meaning can often be imparted if residents gain some "presence of the past." Livable cities do not discount the historical significance contained in their neighborhoods. They celebrate it as a way to help enrich the lives of their citizens. Perhaps, in some small way, this book can help communicate a little presence of the past about Syracuse's streets and surroundings.

Hopefully, it will also demonstrate that who we are and what we have today is a direct result of actions and decisions made in the past. That

dynamic has to be understood. In large measure, we reap what we sow. The community that we and our children will occupy in the future is being decided every day.

I am not a native of Syracuse, although I have lived here longer than anywhere else. But the four most important people in my life, my wife and three children, are all Syracuse born. I hope this work will allow my three sons, Dan, Ryan and Neil, to better know the place that will always be a part of their biographies. I hope that it will assist their generation in making the right decisions that will shape Syracuse's fortunes throughout much of the 21st century.

Like most places where we live for a long time, we tend to think that all the significant history happened somewhere else. But the more we explore what transpired in our own backyard, learn the tales of the everyday people that walked our streets, enjoy the same views they experienced, realize that the neighborhoods where we live and work were homes to others, and understand that many past citizens struggled to make their small contributions to society — the more worthwhile our environment and circumstances become. I hope that this publication will make the daily lives of my fellow Central New York residents a bit more meaningful as they discover the past around them.

The Native Consideration

Onondaga County was formed in 1794 during the final decade of the 18th century. That era marks the first permanent, non-native settlement in what would become Syracuse. Therefore it was used as the chronological foundation for this text, which then proceeds to recount our community's evolution over the following 200 years. But much took place here during the prior decades. Some fascinating stories were played out on this region's stage during the colonial era.

It is common to begin histories of American communities by relating the presence of Native Americans. To 17th and 18th century European powers and colonial authorities, our hills and valleys were a remote wilderness. But this land was the traditional meeting place for the Iroquois Confederacy. Members of the Onondaga Nation, central Keepers of the Council Fire, and their ancestors had resided here for centuries. As the

Iroquois acted to maintain their own prerogatives and independence as a people, they exerted considerable influence on the affairs of European and colonial interests for more than two centuries. That made Onondaga a place of international notoriety. It was the locale for engaging lessons of cultural interaction as the two worlds maneuvered to both understand and influence each other.

And yet, when considering Native Americans in the eastern United States, it is too often only the adventures of colonial encounters that intrigue historians. But the Onondaga people still live here. The experiences, philosophies and struggles of that nation for the last two centuries to confront assimilation and endure as a distinct culture are also dramatic and notable topics for examination. The territory they occupy today, just south of Syracuse, has always been native land, well before Columbus stumbled into our hemisphere on his way to the Far East. The limitations of this publication, however, will not allow us to venture into their rich culture this time. But there are other sources that can be examined to discover Iroquois and Onondaga heritage. A sampling of reference titles are included in the bibliography.

Dennis J. Connors

OHA Collection

QHA Collection

ACKNOWLEDGMENTS

Certainly, no book about the history of Syracuse would be conceivable without the fertile holdings of the Onondaga Historical Association. As a community, we are fortunate that the OHA has dedicated itself to preserving the nearly one million items in its archive and artifact collections. These are available today for citizens to examine, enjoy and ponder. It is an incredibly diverse repository of amazing breadth. Almost all the resources necessary to compile this work were found at the OHA. And its ever-expanding museum is a treasure to explore.

Much of the labor in saving these materials was performed over the decades by countless volunteers and dedicated staff members. In recent memory, the tireless work of former president Richard Wright, his wife, Carolyn, and secretary, Violet Hosler, must be noted. And the ongoing financial assistance of Onondaga County and numerous other supporters, too extensive to list, is vital to maintaining this institution for the community.

The endorsement of the current Onondaga Historical Association Board of Directors, including presidents J. Warren Young and Christine B. Lozner, were essential in approving this project. OHA staff was most helpful and committed, especially Rebekah Ambrose, former research center coordinator, who dug out facts and figures, read drafts and made helpful suggestions. Greg Daily, past curator of exhibits, assisted with securing and reproducing images for illustrations. Thomas Hunter, curator of collections, aided in the photography of artifacts from OHA's collections. And executive director Paul Pflanz's support was invaluable.

Hank Schramm, longtime local historian and author, generously reviewed copy and offered useful comments and corrections. The publications that he penned over the years, sometimes in partnership with Bill Roseboom, offered enviable models of inspiration.

Thanks also are due to Craig Williams of the New York State Museum, Lou Nefflen of the Onondaga County Clerk's Office, local historian William Farrell, and to the staffs of the Fayetteville Free Library and the Beauchamp Branch of the Onondaga County Public Library for friendly and competent assistance in securing needed images. I am also in debt to the talented artist Len Tantillo and Key Bank for permission to use Len's powerful painting of a New York Central locomotive rumbling down Washington Street in the 1930s.

My grateful appreciation is also due John Dowling, Hal Silverman, Richard Kampas and Glenn Holloway for their cooperation, creativity and talent in drawing on their compelling contemporary photographs for use in this publication. The visionary cooperation of Syracuse University Press and the skilled experience of their staff were vital in assuring the completion of this project. And Jane Daily's professionalism and patience in preparing digital versions for the book's many images were outstanding. And readers should know that the book would not have happened without the financial commitment of many sponsors, especially that of CXtec executive William Pomeroy.

Finally, I salute my wife Amy's patience and support with the always lengthy trials of assembling a major publication. And as I candidly thank my sons for inspiration, I also honestly invite them and their generation to help preserve and esteem our community's past.

Dennis J. Connors

CHAPTER *One*

Lines on the Land

The land that nurtured the development of Syracuse and its surrounding communities has always been a fertile tract, valued by its inhabitants from the time the first Native Americans settled here. It has supported a variety of abundant agriculture. Its mineral resources, especially salt deposits, formed Syracuse's early economic foundations. Its waters are plentiful, excellent for fishing, recreation and travel.

Its central position, as well as the connections provided by its rivers and lakes, played critical roles in early relations among Indian peoples. These influences continued into the 17th and 18th centuries during dramatic contacts with recently arrived European powers.

And there is the allure of the land's natural beauty. Syracuse developed at the scenic head of a small lake, ringed with picturesque hills that stretch south to form the stately Onondaga valley. This territory had long been the home of the Onondaga people, central nation of the legendary Iroquois Confederacy. As America's successful revolution against Great Britain and her native allies concluded, most of this prized expanse would be handed to new landlords.

City. New York State's surveyor general leaned over the draftsman's table and watched his young map-maker begin to draw. A momentous transition was underway.

The 1792 map of New York State's Military Tract defines the instant when western society imposed a rigid grid of ownership boundaries across a broad swath of upstate land. For thousands of years it had been an open, expansive home to native peoples. This map began an ongoing story of change and dynamic human interaction.

The need to draft this map arose from the state's obligation to reimburse its soldiers who fought in the recent revolution against the British. It called for a survey of nearly 2 million acres stretching south from Lake Ontario. The territory was still occupied by members of the Cayuga, Onondaga and Oneida nations of the Iroquois League. But two centuries of conflict with European nations and their colonists had weakened the once invincible Iroquois. Some of

A Revolutionary Transformation

Simeon DeWitt gazed across the gabled townhouses of Albany, down to the **Hudson** River, busy with sloops headed to and **from** New York

the finishing touches were carried out by American troops during punitive expeditions known as the Clinton-Sullivan campaign in 1779.

One particularly harsh attack swung through what is today Syracuse in April 1779. Several hundred soldiers under Colonel Van Schaick destroyed the Onondagas' village, located near the present intersection of Valley Drive and Dorwin Avenue. Twelve natives were killed and more than 30 taken prisoner. The village, crops and livestock were destroyed. A small band of warriors tried to harass the troops as they withdrew. The brief skirmish occurred along Onondaga Creek, where Upper and Lower Onondaga Park meet today, Syracuse's only Revolutionary War site, albeit a dubious one.

Nine years later, representatives of New York and the Onondaga nation met to sign a treaty. That 1788 document called for the Onondaga to "cede" their lands to the state. Along with the Cayuga and Oneidas, they were to confine

themselves to "residence" reservations. New York could then divide the remainder into parcels that could be bought, sold and occupied by non-natives.

A Classical Demeanor

Today, names of communities like Lysander, Pompey, Cicero, or Marcellus are second nature to local residents. No one usually ponders their origin. But on occasion, an area student studying ancient history or literature will be surprised that the name of his or her town was being used by some Roman or Greek citizen centuries ago. In fact, classical history and localities formed the identity for many Onondaga County places.

Names for the Military Tract's 25 townships were decided by state officials. The late 18th century was an era when learned citizens were quite enamored with ancient Greek and Roman culture. Thomas Jefferson was inspired in his enthusiastic architectural pursuits by classical Roman buildings. And Americans, proud of their young democratic republic, readily accepted associations with ancient versions in Greece and Italy.

As populations increased in the late 1790s and early 1800s, local civil governments were formed within the Military Tract. Some of these first towns decided to carry on the names of the original survey designations.

Lysander, a naval commander and statesman of ancient Greece, was the inspiration for the name of the town comprising the northwest corner of Onondaga County. *William R. Farrell*

Lots were drawn and the corresponding land granted to the veterans, the quantity according to rank. These veterans already lived many miles to the east in the Mohawk and Hudson River valleys. A few decided new opportunities might lie in the frontier and relocated. But most readily sold their grants for immediate cash and continued their lives. The deeds sometimes passed through several hands until they were acquired by other adventurous souls, ready to start a new life. And so a stream of new settlers began.

There had been a handful of hardy pioneers who preceded them. Asa Danforth and his family arrived in 1788 along with Comfort Tyler. Others were drawn to carve out a living making salt from the area's famous brine springs. Like many early arrivals, Tyler and Danforth were industrious types. They made salt that first year and Danforth soon had a water-powered saw mill in operation on Butternut Creek. Tyler worked as a surveyor and operated a tavern along the first major turnpike.

Slavery was legal in New York at the time. Around 1790, Danforth purchased a slave named Jack Shoemaker in the Mohawk Valley. A few others brought one or two slaves with them to help clear land, do household tasks or begin all-important mill operations. A handful of free African-Americans also came. One such New Jersey family, the DeGroats, were purchasing farm land on Onondaga Hill by 1806.

A typical 19th-century surveyor's compass and measuring chain with a Military Tract survey book
OHA Collection

Simeon DeWitt's job was to survey and map the tract. One of his men in the field was 24-year-old Moses DeWitt, Simeon's cousin. Moses became enamored with the fertile and picturesque landscape he mapped during the early 1790s. He soon settled here, near today's Jamesville, invested in land and became a leader in forming Onondaga County.

DeWitt's map divided the Military Tract into 25 townships, geographical designations to organize the land. Each was subdivided into 100 numbered units of 600 acres each.

The Salt Lake

Onondaga Lake is not salt water. It is a fresh body. But French explorers surveyed its distinctive shoreline brine pools as early as 1654. The geological source was underground springs washing through buried salt beds.

In an era lacking refrigeration, salting of meat and fish provided a critical method for preservation. The Onondaga learned the value of salt making, copying the kettle boiling method shown them by the French. Onondaga salt became a colonial trade item. In 1774 a traveler observed that salt production was in the hands of two escaped slaves from the Hudson River valley, probably through an agreement with the Onondaga.

The 1788 treaty at Fort Stanwix mandated, "The Salt Lake and the lands for one mile round the same, shall forever remain for the common benefit of the people of the State of New York, and the Onondagoes and their posterity for the purpose of making salt...." Therefore Simeon DeWitt's map also shows a public tract, later known as the Onondaga Salt Springs Reservation, bordering most of the lake. It is the origin for much of the public ownership of Onondaga Lake's shoreline today.

As documented by this 1816 advertisement in the *Onondaga Register*, slave holding existed in New York until 1827. An 1814 census listed 49 slaves in Onondaga County, and another 187 free non-whites, among a total population of 30,801. *OHA Collection*

Unfettered native access to the lake did not last long. Recognizing that the most productive springs were within land assigned the Onondaga, new treaties in 1793 and 1795 reduced their territory to nearly its present size.

Salt production greatly expanded in the 1790s as families endured the aggravation of living next to mosquito-infested swamps to produce the "white gold." The state began to organize its salt reservation in 1797 with formal leases to private

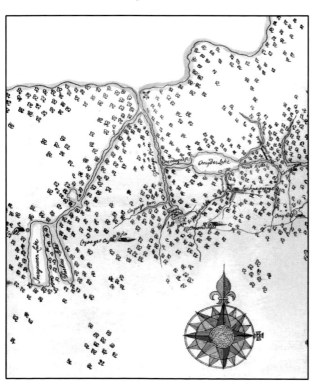

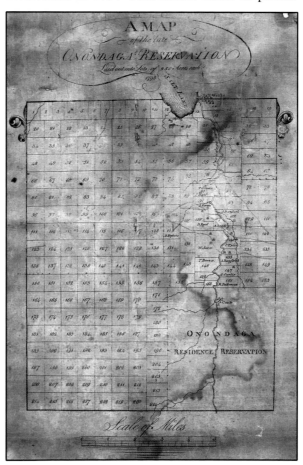

(Far left) Although not particularly large, the four-mile long body of water known today as Onondaga Lake regularly appeared on colonial maps, sometimes mistakenly labeled as a "Salt Lake." British Colonel Romer's 1700 map names it, unusually, "Cananda Lake," but does note the nearby brine springs as "salt pan." *OHA Collection*

This 1795 map documents the survey and laying out of lots on the original territory "reserved" for the Onondaga Nation. Most of the present city of Syracuse falls within these boundaries. Early white settlers in Onondaga Valley are identified. *OHA Collection*

Born of Salt

Salt nurtured three communities near Onondaga Lake. Geddes, on the west shore, was named after its first settler, James Geddes, a 1790s pioneer in the salt industry. Sometimes its village area, now Syracuse's west end, was called Geddesburgh.

Liverpool, to the east, also saw salt boilers in the 1790s. A c.1807 map shows it was first laid out with several streets named after fish, such as Salmon, Trout and Sturgeon. Later, they were changed to species of trees. Bass Street was the only one that stayed the same.

Huddled at the lake's southeast corner was the third settlement, first nicknamed "Salt Point," and a center for salt making. Village homes and stores for workers rose on higher land nearby, laid out in 1799 as Salina, and now Syracuse's far north side.

James Geddes (1763-1838) was a local salt maker who also served as one of the chief surveyors and engineers of the Erie Canal. *OHA Collection*

Salt blocks provided such a distinctive visual identity that Syracuse placed them on its original city seal in 1848. They remain on this version of the seal used today, along with salt evaporation sheds, railroad and canal representations, to symbolize the fundamental economic cornerstones of the Salt City. *OHA Collection*

manufacturers. It also decreed salt production rules for uniformity and quality and granted broad powers to an appointed state salt superintendent.

Modest wooden boxes were built around the springs to serve as small reservoirs. A hand-operated pump drew the brine. A single kettle over an open fire evolved into four kettles, suspended over a firing pit and fixed in a "block" built of stone. These soon grew to house eight, 12 or 16 kettles. There were nearly three dozen in operation by 1799. Covered with a protective timber "barn" and serviced by a tall chimney at one end to provide a flue for the firing pit, these "salt blocks" assumed their distinctive form by 1810. Eventually these "manufactories" stood by the hundreds.

At the beginning of the 19th century, the infant salt industry held great potential for economic wealth. But its product was a bulk commodity. Bateaux were used to bring some salt down the Oswego River, but the rapids and falls were a challenge. Roads to eastern markets often became muddy quagmires after heavy rains, swallowing the wheels of wagons loaded with heavy salt barrels. The future challenge lay in devising an efficient method to bring the salt to distant markets.

A County Named Onondaga

As Military Tract lots became populated, it was necessary to place the land under some formal local government jurisdiction. At first, it fell mostly within Herkimer County. For Moses DeWitt, Comfort Tyler and the others living in the area, legal business meant an inconvenient 50-mile trip east to the county seat at Whitesboro, near Utica.

Another issue was a desperate need for roads. Roads brought in supplies, sent out products to market and encouraged more settlement. The British still occupied forts at Niagara and Oswego. They posed a threat best countered by increasing America's population in upstate New York.

Locals felt such concerns were not being heard in the distant county seat and state capital. And in 1793, increased taxes to build a new courthouse at far off Whitesboro angered some. So in January 1794, 135 settlers signed a petition

James Geddes' 1810 map shows the early settlement at the south end or "Salt Point" of Onondaga Lake. It incorporated as Salina village in 1824. Salina's central village green still exists today as Washington Park. What became downtown Syracuse was directly south, where two roads crossed in a cedar swamp near Onondaga Creek. *New York State Office of General Services*

A 20th-century representation of the meeting where area settlers, led by Moses DeWitt, signed a petition asking the state to create Onondaga County. The original 1794 petition is in the collection of the Onondaga Historical Association. *Onondaga County Surrogate's Court*

(Next page top) When first established, Onondaga County extended much farther west, south and north than today. Just four town governments, Lysander, Marcellus, Manlius and Pompey, encompassed all of present Onondaga County. By 1848 these had split into 19 towns and a brand new city called Syracuse. Various villages also incorporated over time, from Manlius in 1813 to North Syracuse in 1925. *OHA Collection*

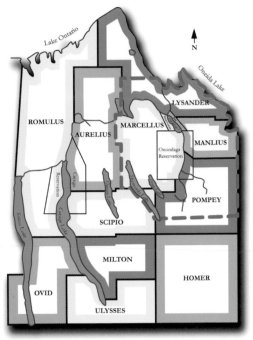

1794   2006

(Center)
Mickles promoted his foundry in the *Onondaga Register* of March 22, 1815. He also cast salt kettles and stove parts. Mickles' operation sat near a stream that today is still called Furnace Brook.
OHA Collection

(Below)
Typical tools used by 19th-century coopers to make barrels. Production of barrels to ship salt was once an extensive local trade. The state even issued regulations dictating barrel size and materials. This standardized its ability to inspect salt and maintain quality.
OHA Collection

A Man-made Landscape: Clearing Forests, Building Homes and Raising Mills

Removing trees with ax and hand saw was a back-breaking but necessary task to begin farms. Some lots, where the Onondaga had already cleared land for cornfields in decades past, were especially desirable. Clearing also served salt production. The salt block fires seemed insatiable for fuel and the common shipping container was a wooden barrel. Farmers made extra cash selling firewood to the salt boilers and timber to the cooper shops.

Early entrepreneurs scouted out advantageous sites for water-powered mills. Some featured the rhythmic up-and-down action of a six-foot vertical saw, ripping a season of cleared timber into planks for siding a barn or flooring a house. Others ground a bulky harvest of wheat, barley or corn into marketable flour and meal.

Dan Bradly and Samuel Rice placed a saw mill on Nine Mile Creek in Marcellus during the winter of 1795-96. The pattern was repeated wherever there were suitable streams. By 1813 Onondaga County was reported to have 34 grist mills and another 54 producing lumber. There were 31 tanneries in the county processing animal hides into leather. Other industries included distilleries for hard liquor and fulling mills for processing cloth.

tto the legislature calling on the state to create a new county. They also requested assistance in constructing six roads, most to help provide access to the salt springs. As might be expected from a society that did not let women vote, the petitioners were all men.

With what would be seen as remarkable speed today, the state acted by March 5, 1794, and Onondaga County was born. It was much larger then, almost 70 by 52 miles. The original boundaries covered most of the Military Tract, about four times the size of the present county. Over time, it was reduced piece by piece as adjacent counties like Oswego and Cayuga were created, each reflecting a process of making local government closer to its citizens.

From about 1802 until 1827, Nicholas Mickles operated the county's earliest foundry, producing iron from ore, limestone and charcoal. His Onondaga Furnace was located in what today is Syracuse's Elmwood park. Mickles also owned a few slaves. One, named Pomp, worked at the furnace.

Differing Visions in Central New York's Wilderness

William Vredenburgh was a wealthy merchant from New York City. He speculated in Military Tract lands and became impressed with their potential. He decided to move to Skaneateles in 1803, then part of Marcellus. At 43 his vision was to live in comfort as a landed gentlemen with a major estate overlooking the lake.

After relocating, he visited the more populated Mohawk Valley and purchased two African-Americans in March 1810. The 32-year-old woman, named Nancy, helped with household chores. The 27-year-old man, Harry Docksteder, was secured for manual labor.

But Harry had another vision of Central New York — a chance for freedom. That first summer, Harry made his bid. Vredenburgh put up a reward. A Pompey farmer named Heman Murray and a Mr. Badger of Cazenovia tracked Harry down near Cambria, New York. Harry had made it nearly 130 miles down the turnpike and was clearly headed for Canada, another 15 miles away across the Niagara River. Vredenburgh paid $35 to the two men as their reward and to cover expenses.

When Vredenburgh's estate was inventoried upon his death in 1813, only "1 Negro Wench" was tallied among the holdings, in the same column as wash tubs, old barrels and a 3-year-old colt. This entry was probably for Nancy, but there is no male slave listed. What became of Harry? It is documented that in the spring of 1811 Vredenburgh had 100 handbills printed seeking a "Negro Boy run away." It is possible this was Harry, making a second attempt. And perhaps he finally won his freedom.

20 Dollars Reward.

RAN away from the subscriber on Sunday the 5th inst. a black girl named JUDE, about 22 years old, middling statue, and thick set. The above reward and all necessary charges will be given to any person who will apprehend said girl and return her, or secure her in any jail in this state and give information of the same to the subscriber.

EB'R WILSON, Jr.

Onondaga, Nov. 14, 1815.   tf8

Another fugitive notice, *Onondaga Register*, March 20, 1816. OHA Collection

Mill sites often became the nucleus for a hamlet. The mill operators would build homes nearby. Farmers with business at the mill would enjoy a stop at a nearby tavern to socialize, hear the latest news and quench a thirst. A convenient general store could do a reasonable business.

Simple log construction represented the first architectural style. It provided humble shelter from notoriously harsh winters. But with the arrival of saw mills, frame houses were possible. Heavy timbers, hewed by hand, served as the structural frame. The exterior was covered with sawn planks. Shingles could be hand split from cedar logs for the roof. Such simple residences might be built by a talented farmer and his hard-working neighbors.

Those with adequate finances built homes that displayed the refined details of the Federal style, reflecting the architectural vogue of established places like Albany. Cash payment to a builder might be supplemented with compensation in produce, whiskey, or in one case, a $20 silver watch. And there were also utilitarian barns and outbuildings dotting the landscape.

(Previous page) This home, reportedly built in 1792 by early Manlius settler Conrad Lower, reflects a transition from log to frame construction. Logs or heavy planks filled spaces between the hewed timbers, which in turn, provided structural support. *OHA Collection*

(Above) Lucia Hutchinson (1800-1843) arrived in Central New York from Connecticut in 1802 with her family. She lived as a teen-ager in the stone house that her father, James, built in 1812 on his Seneca Turnpike farm. Lucia later moved to Syracuse with her husband, John Johnson, who was county sheriff. The Hutchinson home has long served as a local restaurant. *OHA Collection*

Crossroads in Time: An Illustrated History of Syracuse

Late 19th-century painter George Kasson Knapp re-created an 1803 scene along the Seneca Turnpike in Onondaga Hollow. It depicts Comfort Tyler's tavern, which stood where the road to the salt springs (Salina Street) crossed the turnpike. *OHA Collection*

This Federal style of architecture, rendered either in stone or brick, was popular by 1815. The prominent, stepped gables evolved from fashionable urban areas where they served as firebreaks. Homes like this still exist throughout the region.
OHA Collection

Vital Links: Waterways and Roads

The traditional colonial route linking Central New York to the east used rivers and lakes. Onondaga Lake connected with the Seneca River, then across Oneida Lake to sluggish Wood Creek, which reached east to the Mohawk River Valley. Some early pioneer commerce used that tortuous route. Others ran salt from the lake shore down the Oswego River and its rapids in boats. But area settlers also needed year-round connections that reached well beyond Onondaga Lake into the desirable, elevated lands to its south.

The task of road surveying was challenged by the region's varied terrain. But Moses DeWitt, James Geddes and others rose to the task. Some routes served local needs, but the most important were those that could connect to the population and markets of the east.

The first major route was called the "Great Genesee Road," running from the Mohawk Valley to Geneva and in operation by the 1790s. It was improved and realigned at various times and came to be known as the Seneca Road. The local portion roughly followed today's Seneca Turnpike through southern Onondaga County. By 1812 a "north branch" was completed that split off east of Chittenango and ran through what today is Fayetteville, Camillus and Elbridge before rejoining the main turnpike near Cayuga Lake. This route brought a closer connection to the salt works. In Syracuse it became the path of present-day Genesee Street and explains why that road cuts through the city's street pattern at an angle.

Wagons, stagecoaches, herds of livestock going to market, peddlers, postal riders and individual travelers on horseback used these turnpikes. In

Samuel Forman, the brother of Joshua, built his Seneca Turnpike residence in Onondaga Hollow in 1812. Its staircase reflected typically elegant Federal styling. The house still stands but is surrounded by modern commercial development.
Library of Congress — Historic American Buildings Survey

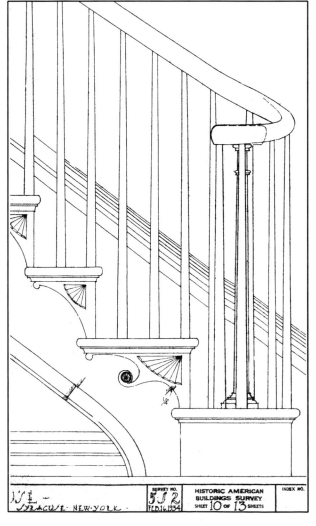

the winter, farmers transported their products to Utica and Albany by sleigh, the going often better on a frozen surface. Taverns dotted the route. Turnpikes were community lifelines.

A traveler named John Duncan crossed through Central New York in 1818. He and the other passengers were crammed into a typical coach. It had a roof but was open on all sides above the two bench seats. Large trunks were fastened to the top, but smaller boxes were packed inside, under seats and around the passengers' feet. The travelers bounced around, the coach suspended by leather straps. It was not unusual for the jarring surface to cause breakdowns. Duncan describes one repair between Chittenango and Manlius where every hand was needed:

" . . . the passengers got out, a stout rail from the nearest fence was thrust under the carriage, and up to [our] ancles in mud, we managed by dint of strength to sustain the waggon till the axle was replaced in its proper position, and the new bolt inserted."

They passed Manlius at 9 p.m. but continued west to Onondaga Hollow where they stopped and rested at a tavern around midnight. They resumed the journey at 4 a.m. and reached Skaneateles by 10 that morning.

In an era before canals and railroads, the major east-west turnpikes helped define settlement patterns. Places like Manlius, Pompey, Skaneateles and the town of Onondaga's settlements known as Onondaga Hollow and Onondaga Hill all straddled early turnpikes.

The population totals in 1810 confirmed that the towns in the hilly southern half of the county,

Town	*1810 Population*
Camillus	2,378
Cicero	252
Fabius	1,865
Lysander	624
Manlius	3,127
Marcellus	4,725
Onondaga	3,745
Otisco	759
Pompey	5,669
Salina	1,259
Tully	1,092

Source: *A Gazetteer of the State of New York* by Horatio Spafford, 1813

with available water power and turnpike access to the eastern markets, were attracting more growth.

Onondaga Hill won the honor as site of the first courthouse in 1801. The 2 1/2-story wood structure was in use by 1803. It energized growth on the Hill. Lawyers opened offices there. Court activities, especially those requiring lengthy orations, seemed to generate a fair amount of thirst as seven taverns were soon operating near the courthouse.

In addition to the usual deed filing, court proceedings and board of supervisor meetings, one occasional necessity required a man to prove his freedom because of the color of his skin. On April 28, 1814, James DeGroat and William Sisco, mulatto farmers on Onondaga Hill, had to appear before Judge James Geddes and show proof of their freeborn status.

Frederick Horner (1792-1860) came from Poughkeepsie about 1824 to operate a sawmill in Syracuse along Onondaga Creek. The Erie Canal was finished the following year. Horner prospered, along with Syracuse, and stayed. *OHA Collection*

(Right and below) The "Red Mill" was the first erected where Genesee Street bridged Onondaga Creek. Others soon joined it. A dam at Genesee Street created a mill pond upstream that encompassed much of today's Armory Square district. With its network of races, visible in an 1845 map, this mill area formed the village of Syracuse's first industrial precinct. *Onondaga County Clerk's Office/ OHA Collection*

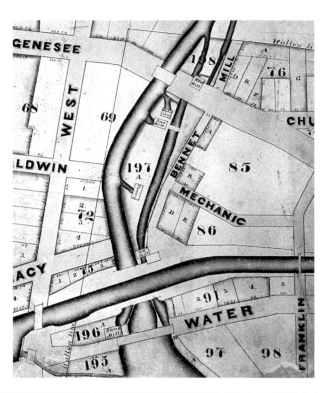

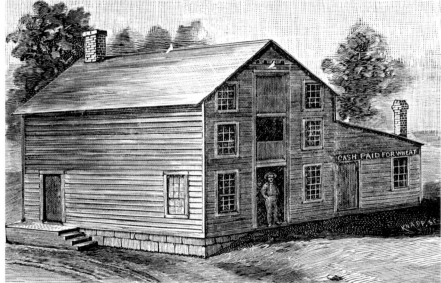

Syracuse Gets Its Start

Onondaga County's only city also owes its origins to a turnpike and a mill. Its beginnings centered near Clinton Square. But the land, at first, was not prized. It was low, dominated by an unhealthy, smelly and discouraging cedar swamp. Places like Manlius, Pompey and Geddes were well underway before anyone showed much interest in what would become downtown Syracuse.

The catalyst for change became the state's need to raise money for improving the Seneca Turnpike's connections to the salt works. In 1804 the legislature authorized selling 250 acres of the salt reservation for revenue. James Geddes surveyed the parcel and included a stretch of Onondaga Creek and its water power potential as an incentive. Residents at Salt Point and Onondaga scoffed at the thought of anyone investing in a swamp. But Abraham Walton, a land speculator and Utica attorney, bought the acreage. By 1805 he had a grist mill erected where the improved road, today's Genesee Street, spanned the creek. Another road, now Salina Street, crossed nearby on its way to the salt works.

Walton laid out a small settlement and sold a lot at the corner of Salina and Genesee to Henry Bogardus. The latter opened a tavern in 1806 and the intersection took on the appellation, Bogardus Corners. Soon a few simple houses joined the mill and tavern. After a few years, ownership of the inn passed to Sterling Cossitt of Marcellus, and the location was renamed Cossitt's Corners. The nucleus for Syracuse was being formed.

War on the Frontier

Onondaga County's population grew steadily, passing 7,500 in 1800 and reaching almost 26,000 by 1810. But worries about the nearby British nemesis remained. The state built a timber blockhouse at Salt Point in 1794, complete with a 6-pound cannon. Jay's Treaty, ratified in 1795, removed the English from Oswego to across Lake Ontario. The blockhouse was converted into a salt storehouse, but foreign relations remained strained.

Shipping Onondaga salt from Oswego, using Lake Ontario, would be severely hindered by open warfare. This concerned local residents. But world events brought war with the British in 1812 and New York's borders became a major front.

A number of Onondaga County's militia units were mobilized, some to Sackets Harbor, others to Niagara. Captain John Sprague's company, primarily from Pompey, served at Oswego. Records show some were given temporary furloughs to return home in the fall, perhaps to help with harvesting. A few also deserted. And there were always a handful listed as sick. A 21-year-old drummer, Calvin Hall, succumbed to his illness in October 1812. Two unnamed women were also on the rolls, perhaps wives who came to help with washing and cooking.

Mickles' Onondaga Furnace filled orders for cannon balls. A state arsenal was erected along the Seneca Turnpike in 1812 to store arms for defense

(Above)
The Niagara Frontier, 150 miles west of Onondaga, saw extensive action during the War of 1812 such as this assault at Chippewa. One local militia company, commanded by Captain Leonard Kellogg of Manlius, was engaged during an earlier but unsuccessful invasion of Canada at Queenston Heights.
OHA Collection

(Center/Below)
With the state arsenal standing nearby, area residents watch British prisoners marching along Seneca Turnpike in the artist's interpretation of an 1814 scene at Onondaga Hollow. The old stone arsenal, photographed about 1895, became a noted landmark after its abandonment. Periodic discussions about its preservation were never implemented. Only a corner of its limestone walls remain today.
OHA Collection

of the region. The location provided good access to dispense supplies as the road was regularly used for troop movement. Peace was declared in 1815 but local men continued to volunteer for the militia as a civic duty.

The Flavor of Early Commerce
"Will not pay cash ... will pay salt ...":

Most area residents in the early 19th century lived self sufficiently by farming on 100 to 300 acres. They made most of their own clothing. Over 1,000 hand looms were sprinkled around the county in 1810. Wheat and corn were cash crops. Vegetable gardens of potatoes, cabbages, beets, carrots and onions supplemented diets. Apple orchards were common. Farmers produced a few kegs of fermented hard cider for their own use and could trade an extra couple for other goods. Sheep were raised and their wool sold to mills for processing.

Manufacturing salt and related activities like making barrels, supported other families near Onondaga Lake. Some locals operated taverns. Homes and modest mercantile establishments clustered around crossroads and near mill sites.

Manlius village was the largest such community in 1810 with about 85 homes and 65 other structures. In 1813 it became the first incorporated village in Onondaga County.

Local newspapers were under way by 1806. One of the earliest surviving examples is the *Onondaga Register*, published from 1814 to 1829 at Onondaga Hollow. This location now falls within the city of Syracuse's Valley section. An examination of pages from an 1815 issue provides the flavor of daily life:

Noah Witney and Matthew Cadwell announce to area blacksmiths that they have established an "Anvil Factory" in Jamesville. Edward Smith and Hosea Hall are advertising their "Boot & Shoe Making Business" in the Hollow. Ephraim Webster, Agent for the Onondaga Indians, seeks help in locating four horses stolen from the Onondagas. Adam Ainslie is selling a 52-acre farm on a road to the salt works, complete with a log house and 100 fruit trees.

Joseph Swan is promoting his sign painting business in the Hollow and also notes he sells windsor chairs and drums. Nicholas Mickles cannot pay cash but is willing to pay with salt in exchange for iron ore to use in his furnace. In these early years, salt was often used as a standard for exchange. There were no banks in the immediate area but salt was plentiful and could be turned into cash once marketed.

S.P. Hawley is selling a pair of 5-year old oxen, "well broke for service." The state superintendent of the salt works reports 295,215 bushels produced in 1814. With a state duty of 3 cents per bushel, he notes the state used $5,200 to subsidize road building, and after other expenses, retained $2,103.87. James Mann and Caleb Johnson's store offers:

"handsome morocco Pocket books, Chintz Shawls, Irish Linen, Silk Parasols, Groceries, Hardware, Crockery" and, for tavern keepers, "a choice collection of Liquors." J. Swett of Elbridge is promoting his "Physic & Surgery" services and seeking, "A young man of talents and medical acquirements" as an apprentice partner. Mr. Bond plans to open a school at Onondaga for "instructing young Ladies and Gentlemen the polite and fashionable accomplishment of Dancing."

These were busy times in many pioneer settlements, but there is no mention in the *Onondaga Register* of 1815 of tiny Cossitt's Corners, down the creek near the cedar bog.

A Civil Society: Churches and Schools

Onondaga County's first generation of non-native settlers were mostly from eastern New York, Massachusetts and Connecticut. Their background was Protestant with a strong tradition of public education. They looked to establish parallel institutions as soon as feasible.

At first, Episcopalians, Methodists, Congregationalists or Presbyterians, and Baptists were the most numerous. Initially, services were sporadic, conducted in houses, one-room schools, taverns or even shops. Eventually, sufficient numbers allowed the erection of churches and the retention of regular ministers instead of traveling preachers.

The importance of religion to the community was reflected in its architecture. The meeting houses often were the most impressive buildings in the early settlements and their bell towers served as distinctive landmarks. Marcellus lays claim to the first church building in 1803. By 1825 most communities had at least one. Larger villages had more.

The first sufficient concentration of Roman Catholics did not occur until 1827, when Irish

Local Presbyterians built a distinguished Federal-style church at Onondaga Hollow in 1810. It was the first church erected inside what today is Syracuse and reflects the worshipers' New England roots. It burned in 1922. *OHA Collection*

salt workers at Salina organized and secured regular visits of a priest. They dedicated their first building in 1830. Syracuse's Society of Concord organized in 1841. For the next decade Jewish services were conducted in private homes until a temple was opened in 1850.

Physical needs for early schools were modest and teacher requirements almost non-existent. A small structure could be built easily and a single young man, perhaps a minister or other male without the responsibilities of a farm, hired. By 1813 the county had nearly 50 public school houses in as many districts. The earliest inside today's city borders were those at Geddes in 1804 and Salina in 1805.

School was a luxury few families could allow in the busy months that ran from spring planting

A Woman's Perspective

Women are rarely mentioned in the early records. Commerce and government were left to men in an era when women were considered second-class citizens. But with most farms functioning as family-run operations, women were busy night and day with a variety of essential household chores.

Between 1803 and 1814, Skaneateles resident Mary Vredenburgh offered some local female perspective on this era in a series of letters written to a friend in her former Long Island neighborhood.

Mary lamented the lack of companionship, especially in the early years when settlement was sparse, and noted the winters could be long and dreary. Before established churches, she longed for an occasional passing preacher to deliver a sermon.

But Mary praised the beauty of the region and took delight in her children. In one letter she proudly reported on her 11-year-old daughter's domestic skills. Evelina sewed a table cloth, wove a basket and was "making her papa a shirt."

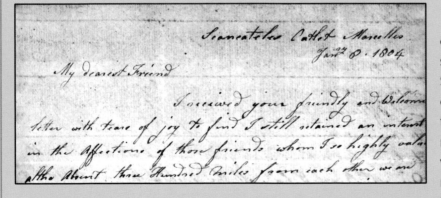

In April 1813, with two of her sons away at school, she asked her friend to visit. She predicted, that, "... while our gentlemen are amusing themselves with fishing, riding or smoaking [sic], we will amuse ourselves with reading, our needles or knitting ..." She asked her friend to purchase a bonnet in New York and forward it to her. With her home overlooking the turnpike, Mary was troubled in 1814 about the continuing war with England and wrote that, "... it makes my heart ach [sic] to see the number of men passing by here daily on their way to west and fear many of them will never return."

The death of Mary's husband, William, in 1813 cast a pall over her life. She missed him and especially worried about her "dear fatherless boys" and her ability to guide them into appropriate careers. She continued to live in the large Skaneateles house, although she only occupied two rooms, and, without William, admitted that , ". . .Skaneateles has lost all its beauty to me." With help from her son-in-law, Mary eventually relocated to Schenectady.

The Vredenburgh home in Skaneateles and one of Mary's letters
OHA Collection

This 1840 portrait of Ursula Ann Elliott Fitch (1818-1907) is by the noted local artist, Charles Loring Elliott, her brother. She was educated at academies in Owasco and Geneva, then married by age 16. Ursula was one of 32 women who founded the Syracuse Home Association in 1853, originally a residence for indigent females and their children. *OHA Collection*

to fall harvest. Pompey district #15 in 1819 was typical in conducting its school "year" for just 4 1/2 months from November to March.

One teacher's notebook of the period contains the following problems, demonstrating practical use for mathematical lessons:

"If 20 bushels of wheat are sufficient for a family of 8 persons, 5 months, how much will be sufficient for 4 persons, 12 months?"

"A certain quantity of pasture will last 963 sheep 7 weeks, how many must be turned out of it that it will last the remainder, 9 weeks?"

"Select" or private schools were also begun, usually by a traveling instructor who set up operations in rented rooms. Among other courses, a Mr. Marcelus was offering English, arithmetic,

Onondaga Academy evolved into Valley High School, which in turn was absorbed into Corcoran High School during consolidation in 1965. A Syracuse street called Academy Green bears the legacy of its original location.
OHA Collection

Onondaga Academy.
Onondaga Hollow,

moral philosophy, Latin, Greek, surveying, navigation and astronomy to Syracuse students in 1825.

In large communities, private academies were begun to offer more advanced curricula. Leading citizens of Pompey incorporated one in 1811 and added a female division in 1833. Another was chartered for Onondaga Hollow in 1813. More were started over the next 20 years. These places might be thought of as high school level today. The 1811 bylaws of the Pompey Academy included the following:

"no scholars shall frequent a tavern for the purpose of entertainment or amusement without permission of the preceptor . . ."

A book entitled, *Theory and Practice of Teaching*, was published in Syracuse in 1847. In the 22-page section on "Corporal Punishment," the author offers a thoughtful framework, but concludes some limited use is required of "a light rule for the hand, or a rod for the back or lower extremities ...," but cautions, "... on no account should a blow be given upon the head."

Some viewed formal education for girls as needless, at least much beyond the basics of reading and writing. They could learn all that was necessary in domestic skills at home from their mother. Young women from affluent families might be sent to a select school or later to a female academy. At such places, courses included feminine manners, fine needle work and music.

The Right Place at the Right Time
Plagued by the unhealthy nature of the surrounding low lands, anemic Cossitt's Corners grew very slowly. But a local visionary named Joshua Forman understood the potential of increasing talk in Albany about building a canal across the state. Forman pushed for the canal shortly after he was elected to the state Assembly in 1807. He knew any eventual canal would need to service the salt industry. If an inexpensive way could be found to transport the salt to market, the economic potential of that natural resource was staggering. But the leading citizens at Onondaga derided the

canal idea as impractical and Salina's salt manufacturers were either skeptical or reluctant to give up their precious production lands for canal construction. So Forman, a resident of Onondaga Hollow, set his sites on struggling Cossitt's Corners. He formed a land company, bought out Walton's remaining interests in 1814 and later moved down to a site at the "Corners."

Forman worked tirelessly to promote his adopted community. It needed a more formal name and Forman chose "Corinth." Forman continued to be a strong canal advocate and helped guide that revolutionary venture into being through his effective lobbying. Construction was begun in 1817 and the middle section completed by 1820. And sure enough, it flowed right past his doorstep.

In 1819 Forman had directed that the streets and lots for a village be surveyed. By 1820 community leaders sought establishment of a post office. But the name Corinth was already taken by another village. John Wilkinson, another newcomer from Onondaga and a lawyer protégé of Forman's, suggested

"Syracuse." It was the name of an ancient city in Sicily, another classical setting, but one also appropriately located near a lake and salt works.

In 1822 Forman was active in drafting the state legislation to dredge the outlet of Onondaga Lake. The lake level dropped, draining much of its surrounding wetlands, including the central area of Syracuse. A major hindrance to expanding settlement was removed. Three years later, with easy access to the completed Erie Canal, additional mills along Onondaga creek, a handful of stores and a busy branch turnpike still passing by, the upstart settlement of 1,000 incorporated as a municipality.

The canal sustained Syracuse's growth for the next several decades. Meanwhile, the salt workers of Salina, having incorporated their own village in 1824, worried that the upstart village a mile to their south might be a formidable competitor for economic activity and prestige. An often bitter rivalry began.

West Water Street – Clinton Square

Sketch by M. W. Hanchett 1899

CHAPTER *Two*

An Urban Center Emerges

The marriage of salt production with an advantageous position astride the state's wondrous new canal system set the stage for the 19th-century evolution of Syracuse into a bustling commercial center. New immigrants arrived from Ireland and Germany to lend their talents and labors. An expanding network of railroads linked the growing city with the rest of the nation's economy.

Syracuse radiated forth from Clinton Square. The city's civic heart boasted new architectural landmarks, such as the fashionable Second Empire-style Onondaga County Saving Bank with its impressive clock tower. Streets and buildings were lit by the latest manufactured gas and a public transit system of horse-drawn streetcars reached out to surrounding neighborhoods. Syracuse was poised to grow into one of New York State's leading industrial, cultural and financial centers.

(Previous page) Clinton Square and the Erie Canal are in the foreground of this 1871 view by artist Johann Culverhouse. Adjacent Hanover Square can be seen to the right as the surrounding buildings glow with gas illumination. *OHA Collection.*

Both the Erie and Oswego canals served the salt works. In 1878 these workers were loading barrels of salt at the Erie Canal in Geddes. This location is now part of Syracuse's west side. A short thoroughfare there still bears the name Harbor Street, even though the long-filled canal is nowhere in sight. *OHA Collection*

The Remarkable Ditch

When it opened in 1825, the Erie Canal was the great wonder of its age, a 363-mile long engineering marvel. It traversed all manner of terrain ... swamps, forests, rivers and right up the side of a 70-foot precipice at Lockport! More importantly, it was a tremendous engine for economic and social transformation. The "Grand Canal" changed all the rules for where commerce flowed and how people traveled in America. New York City replaced New Orleans as the main gateway to America's interior. Hoards of immigrants heading west used it. Goods flowing from as far away as Chicago poured east along its path. And sitting astride this new wonder was the promising village of Syracuse.

The canal also worked its metamorphosis on the land and people of Onondaga County. In 1820

local population and trade were strung along the vital Seneca Turnpike, across the county's southern half. By the early 1830s the action had shifted north, centered at Syracuse. Some towns would not see their population exceed 1830 levels until the second generation of suburban growth in the 1980s.

One of the turnpike localities, while smarting from the loss of residents and prestige, tried to place a positive perspective on the shift. A promoter of the Onondaga Academy, located in the Hollow, penned the following recruitment pitch:

"In consequence of a transfer for the most part of the mercantile business to the villages on the Canal, [this] place is now free from all those sources of annoyances and allurements to vice which are often found in a dense population."

With completion of the Oswego Canal in 1828, the Erie was also linked at Syracuse with Lake Ontario. Each waterway passed directly through the salt works. Together, they ignited an explosion in local salt production. That was appropriate since a duty collected on Onondaga salt by the state helped generate revenue used toward building the canal. Canals significantly dropped shipping costs. Bulky cargoes, like salt, that previously moved laboriously by wagon at a cost of $100/ton could now be shipped at $5/ton.

The growth of the salt industry brought wealth into Syracuse, seeding the establishment of banks whose capital financed other local industries. By 1835 Onondaga County ranked third in population out of New York State's 55 counties, with 60,908 inhabitants. The stage was set for Syracuse to become one of New York's largest cities.

But at the outset, village trustees had little time to dream as they handled more practical civic duties. One of the very first appointed public officers was Henry Young as "Poundmaster." His responsibility was to maintain a site for temporarily housing any livestock found wandering the dirt streets. There was special concern that rooting hogs be kept out of the burying ground established by 1824 at West Water and Franklin streets.

Protection against fires was also an ongoing concern. In 1833 any citizen could be fined $5 if he refused to help form a bucket brigade to fight fires. One of the more unusual village ordinances was one that made it unlawful,

> "... to bathe, at any time during day light in the Onondaga Creek or Mill Pond, within sixty rods of the Canal, or any Street, or Highway, or in the Race-way ... under the penalty of one dollar for each and every offence."

Clearly, trustees were trying to make sure that Syracuse appeared as a civilized community, demonstrating appropriate decorum in public.

Syracuse's population expanded continuously, from around 1,000 in 1825 to nearly 6,500 by

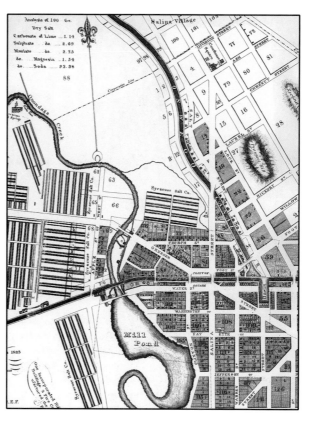

By 1834 Syracuse was expanding outward from Clinton Square. Salt production dominated but there also were manufacturing concerns turning out soap, furniture, carriages, leather and steam engines.
OHA Collection

In 1830 Syracuse village trustees ordered that leather fire buckets be kept in each dwelling and business. They often bore initials of the owner. Before a system of municipal hydrants were in place, such buckets carried water from wells, mill ponds and canals to fight fires.
OHA Collection

1840. An 1836 gazetteer listed 16 general stores, 11 physicians, 2 book stores, 3 fire companies, 2 weekly newspapers, 1 brewery, 4 clothing stores and 17 small manufacturing shops. The village also had a quantity of taverns, 16 lawyers and a bank.

A devastating setback struck in 1832 with a cholera epidemic. It was ravaging New York City and village officials tried to halt and quarantine suspected canal boats at the eastern edge of Syracuse, but to no avail. Packets arrived carrying dead passengers. By late July, residents were taking ill and dying within hours. It is estimated over 100 succumbed. Many more were bed-ridden with severe diarrhea and dehydration. The mood was somber as no one was immune. Rich and poor lost loved ones. The disease subsided in 1833 but did not completely withdraw until 1834.

But Syracuse quickly recovered. When the city was chartered in 1848 by

merging the villages of Syracuse and Salina, the population had reached an estimated 15,800. It passed 22,000 in 1850 and hit 25,226 by 1855, an increase of 60 percent in just 30 years.

A building boom reflected this growth, spreading across the landscape. The salt industry was a priority. In 1836 there already were 133 salt "manufactories" or boiling blocks with their distinctive long shed and tall chimneys. At first, most were in the village of Salina, Syracuse's north side rival. But by the 1860s they stretched from Liverpool, south along the Oswego Canal nearly four miles, to within a few blocks of Clinton Square. To the west, in the village of Geddes, they lined the route of the Erie Canal. Reaching an average capacity of 50 or more kettles each by 1850, the number of blocks eventually exceeded 300. Most salt blocks were individually owned, sometimes by women who inherited them from fathers or husbands. In 1841 Lovinia Hulin received half ownership of a 38-kettle block in Salina from her deceased husband, Jacob. She owned it until her death in 1881 at age 88.

The block fires roared for days at a time, evaporating brine and consuming wood at a furious pace. The state's canal system, with new branches stretching south toward Pennsylvania's mines, brought coal as an alternative. But fuel added expense.

(Above) Henry Gifford (1801-1872) helped introduce solar salt making to Syracuse. He used his profits to expand into real estate, lumber, banking, the gas works and the city's private water company. Gifford Street, on the city's west side, carries his name. *OHA Collection*

For generations, salt had been made in coastal areas around the world by solar evaporation of ocean water. There was such a tradition in Cape Cod. Syracusan Stephen Smith, an agent of the Onondaga Salt Company and a Massachusetts native, had acquaintances there. In 1820 he persuaded Henry Gifford, a 19-year-old Cape resident familiar with solar salt production, to move to Syracuse.

Setting up an operation that depended on sunshine must have appeared a daunting task in cloud-prone Central New York, but Gifford soon had a successful solar evaporation field opened in Syracuse west of Onondaga Creek. With the free effects of wind and sun, plus state land subsidies, solar production proved economically appealing and its use increased steadily. It overtook the boiling method in 1887 and by the 1890s was the only process employed locally to produce salt.

Railroads Roll Into Town

The first train drawn by a steam engine arrived in Syracuse in 1839, just 14 years after completion of the Erie Canal. By the 1840s Syracuse was joined by rail to Utica and Auburn, and a good run might hit 25 mph. Both speed and connections improved rapidly. By the 1860s rails superseded canals in shaping the destiny of communities.

The Syracuse & Utica Railroad entered Syracuse along a right-of-way down the center of Washington Street, granted in perpetuity by the village in 1837. Village officials were anxious to have this modern transportation system convenient to lodging and dining opportunities, and to allow travelers to easily make connections with the canal packet boats in nearby Clinton Square.

Many of the railroad's investors and its chief agent, John Wilkinson, were prominent Syracuse men. Their influence helped citizens see the interests of the railroad and village as similar. Eventually, all the small lines between Albany and Buffalo combined to form the New York Central. The Washington Street right-of-way remained part of its main line.

In 1838 village trustees granted the Syracuse & Utica permission to erect a depot on Washington Street between Salina and Warren Street. The railroad had to pave and widen the street in that block so that wagon and carriage traffic had room to pass along the south side of the station. The physical impact is still visible in

(Previous page bottom) During their peak use in the decades following the Civil War, nearly 50,000 solar salt evaporating vats lined the edges of Onondaga Lake. Each featured a movable roof, or shed, that prevented rain from diluting the brine.
OHA Collection

(Above) The DL&W's 1877 passenger station stood just south of the state armory at the corner of Jefferson and Clinton streets. It served Syracuse for over 60 years. The railroad's old right-of-way is presently used by the OnTrack rail shuttle.
OHA Collection

SYRACUSE MARBLE WORKS.
158 CANAL ST.
Sidney Stanton

what became Vanderbilt Square, named after New York Central Railroad baron Commodore Vanderbilt. The extra-wide sidewalk is a remnant of the old bypass.

Other lines soon arrived, one north to Oswego in 1848 and another south to Binghamton in 1854. By 1870 both were part of the Delaware, Lackawanna & Western or DL&W. It skirted the west side of downtown. Street-level trains would remain an inescapable downtown feature for 100 years, helping shape its national image and physical development.

Patterns of Development

The solar salt process required extensive acreage. Soon much of the territory stretching south from Onondaga Lake was blanketed with shallow wooden vats producing the distinctive large crystals of solar evaporation called "coarse" salt.

The canal routes dictated good locations for both salt blocks and other commercial activity. Barges serviced canal-side warehouses, brought factories raw materials and hauled out finished goods.

Downtown grew rapidly after completion of the Erie. Frame buildings went up in short order. But with streets that alternated between dust and mud, the overall appearance could be shabby. About the time that the canal was being dug, a visitor had commented that Syracuse's swampside, thrown-together appearance would, "Make an owl weep to fly over it." But the town was bustling now. Continuing expansion and prosperity brought grander structures.

Water Street, just south of the Erie and Oswego Canal junction and north of the first railroad depot, became an early commercial center, especially Hanover Square. A great inferno in 1834 cleared nondescript wooden buildings along its

north side. A group of new **brick** structures, called the Phoenix Buildings, rose from the ashes. After the Civil War, Clinton and adjacent Hanover squares sported a concentration of grand bank structures. The depot on Washington helped draw retail activity down **Salina** Street, where it held fast, even to the present day.

The area to the southeast of Hanover Square became residential. Fayette Park was ringed with several prominent mansions during the 1840s. Homes also spread south of the Salina Street retail area, which ended for many years at Jefferson Street. As more bridges were built to improve access across the canals, James Street became the elite residential district, in part because its rising topography afforded majestic views.

As Syracuse's population rose, several churches formed. Their steeples were the tallest structures, defining the landscape. Many, at first, built near Clinton Square. As growing congregations required bigger capacities, stone or brick

A concentration of hotels developed along the Washington Street railroad corridor in the 19th century. The Globe opened in 1847 at the corner of Salina, across from the New York Central's first depot. It hosted the likes of Horace Greeley, William Seward and Daniel Webster.
OHA Collection

The First Ward Methodist Church on Bear Street as it appeared in the 1860s. After the villages of Salina and Syracuse merged, most of the former's churches continued on, some maintaining a distinct identity by adopting the area's new political designation in their name.
OHA Collection

edifices replaced wood, and they relocated to established residential districts such as those along Montgomery, State or James streets.

Both the DL&W and the New York Central built new, bigger passenger stations in the 1870s on downtown's west side. This stimulated development of hotels and wholesale businesses around Franklin and Clinton streets. Many of these today form the architectural character of the Armory Square Historic District.

The railroads also served expanding industries. Factories located near rail lines and were often directly connected with track sidings. This especially became true on the city's west side, already earmarked as a working district by Onondaga Creek water power, solar salt production and the Erie Canal's route. A large swath in this quarter, south of the Erie, was also developed for railroad yards. A definite industrial district was in place by 1860. Over time, it expanded to produce a staggering variety of products from caskets to agricultural plows and from lanterns to automobiles.

Provincial Politics

Immediately north of Syracuse was its rival, the village of Salina. The latter was focused on salt making and related necessities like coopering. It had its own commercial district centered at the intersection of Wolf Street and the north end of Salina Street. There, merchants, tavern owners and shop keepers often had a hand in the salt business as it was a commodity of exchange.

Extensive salt works spread out on the low land toward Onondaga Lake. South and east of the business district were Salina's residential areas. The middle-class owners of salt blocks built a number of fine homes in the 1840s and 1850s along Park and other nearby streets. Scattered among them were modest residences of blacksmiths, salt inspectors, pump house mechanics and coopers. Several remain.

Salina residents started their own Methodist and Presbyterian churches.

This 1917 painting by Lillie Belle Dimond depicts the second county courthouse and nearby stone jail in an overly pastoral setting. It is based primarily on verbal descriptions since no detailed photographs were taken of the building before it burned in 1856. *OHA Collection*

And because the salt works drew a number of Irish laborers, the first Roman Catholic congregation in Onondaga County was formed at Salina in 1827, the roots of today's St. John the Baptist parish.

The two villages were linked by Salina Street and the parallel Oswego Canal. Between was an undistinguished expanse in the 1830s and 40s, occupied by buildings . . .

" *... of the poorer class, generally the homes of coopers, whose unattractive shops with the litter of hoops and staves, lined the streets. On the west the smoke from the salt blocks filled the air, while to the east arose abrupt hills, with deep gorges between them. Not a sidewalk in any direction was laid and in rainy weather the mud seemed to be without bottom.*"

This was an unlikely place to build a new courthouse, but that was exactly what happened in the late 1820s. Empowered by its location on the marvelous canal and led by the politically savvy Moses DeWitt Burnet and his real estate interests, Syracuse convinced the state to authorize a new county courthouse. The old Onondaga Hill facility was tired and its site no longer the center of activity.

Salina village, with population and business comparable to Syracuse, did not want to surrender this new advantage to its rival. A courthouse meant law offices, visitors, taverns and prestige. The County Board of Supervisors were to select the site. Syracuse thought it had a lock. But a clever argument by Salina officials proposed that the two villages might eventually merge and county offices needed to be centered.

MORNING EDITION.

CITY CHARTER!

THE ELECTION YESTERDAY !

THE PEOPLES' CHARTER TRIUMPHANT !

The election yesterday on the adoption of the proposed City Charter, was one of the most warm and spirited contests which have ever taken place in this village. The unprecedented number of 1849 votes were polled in this village, being full five hundred over the vote last May, at the Charter election, and some hundreds higher than any number ever before given.

The vote as declared by the Board, stood as follows :

Whole number of votes cast	1849
Charter	1072
No Charter	771
Rejected as duplicates,	6
Majority in favor of Charter	301

VILLAGE OF SALINA.

Whole number of votes cast	424
No Charter	39
Charter	385
Majority in favor of the Charter	346

Making a nett Majority of SIX HUNDRED AND FORTY SEVEN.

So Syracuse and Salina are the CITY OF SYRACUSE.

The event of our union with our sister village, and assuming the title of City, was signalized by all sorts of demonstrations of rejoicing last evening. Firing of Cannon, Bonfires, Illuminations, &c. &c , continued until a late hour. KELLOGG's Brass Band were out, and constituted one of the principal attractions of the evening.

In common with the great mass of our citizens, we are heartily gratified with the result. We believe the union of Salina with Syracuse, and the corporation of both, under an efficient local government, will tend to the promotion of their mutual growth and prosperity. It will require but the experience of a few years to vindicate the wisdom of the step.

That carried the day. A site midway along Salina Street, at aptly named Division Street, became home in 1829 to a handsome brick edifice. Nobody, however, appreciated the location, inconvenient and far removed from the business centers of either place.

Consolidation — 19th-century Style

The rivalry evidenced in the courthouse skirmish was genuine. It was part civic pride, and part economic self-interest, such as arguing over bank locations or access to brine. Sometimes, it was just an excuse to launch a rowdy debate. One got out of hand on January 1, 1844, when a gang of Salina salt boilers and some Syracuse ruffians engaged in a major brawl at Warren and Washington Street. The militia was needed to regain control. After that, officials from each village began to think seriously about growing up and becoming a city.

Many animated meetings and investigative committees followed. Getting a handle on the final boundaries proved tricky. Some thought Geddes and Liverpool should be included. In the end, it came down to the two original rivals. The formal reasons for merger were presented in a December 1847 pamphlet:

1. Secure better representation in the County's legislative body, the Board of Supervisors, especially to resist what was felt to be "unreasonable" county taxation forced on Syracuse by surrounding towns. (The village of Syracuse was part of the town of Salina and the whole town had

only one representative. Under the new city charter, Syracuse would have four of its own.)

2. Provide the ability to organize a more effective police force.

3. Provide an elected Common Council with the authority to raise money in a responsible manner for municipal expenses, instead of needing to hold inefficient and sometimes emotional meetings of the residents.

4. Improve statewide name recognition for Syracuse to increase the city's chances to become a new state capital.

5. Increase efficiency of local government by consolidating two sets of village officers into a single set of city officials.

6. Allow municipal taxation of the extensive solar salt works inside Syracuse that were exempt under the village charter.

A referendum was held on January 3, 1848. The totals were 1,457 in favor and 810 against. One of the factors that helped convince the salt folks to join in was the charter's designation of their old village as the First Ward, since the name Salina would be extinguished. It is a distinction that the north side neighborhood retains to this day.

This merger would not be Syracuse's last. In 1886 the village of Geddes gained entry, evolving into Syracuse's far west side and Tipperary Hill neighborhoods. The following year, the town of Onondaga's Danforth village joined, centered around South Salina and Kennedy streets.

Danforth, named after the 18th-century settler, had only been incorporated since 1874. It was an early suburb of Syracuse, developing as a residential district and linked with the city's business center by horse-drawn streetcars. Becoming part of the city's school system was a primary motivation for Danforth's mating.

The life of Charles Ashley Baker (1799-1881) reflects local settlement patterns. Born in Massachusetts, he arrived in LaFayette as a young child with his pioneer parents. At age 20 he apprenticed at law at Onondaga Hollow, then the county seat. After marrying in 1827, he relocated to Salina, then Syracuse. He moved in the 1840s to quieter outskirts and became a leading figure in adjacent Danforth village. *OHA Collection*

One of the earliest known images of Frederick Douglass, former slave turned abolitionist leader, shows his appearance about the time he first spoke in Syracuse in 1843 at Fayette Park. *OHA Collection*

The Great Dilemma

At the time Syracuse became a city, a boiling controversy was increasingly consuming American society. How could a nation that proclaimed, "all men are created equal" justify the slavery of nearly 3 million inhabitants? Throughout the 1830s and early 1840s, a small but growing number of reformers had been calling for change. Their philosophies ranged from simply opposing the spread of slavery to advocacy for its immediate and universal abolition.

Upstate New York was a caldron of debate and a crucible for leadership in the cause of anti-slavery, much stemming from a fiery religious revival that had recently surged through this "Burned Over District." Some Syracusans opposed slavery with words. Others used actions, reasoning if all slaves could not yet be released, maybe some could be aided in escaping. The courageous journey of many fugitives toward freedom often passed directly through Syracuse.

Syracuse's anti-slavery forces drew renewed inspiration with the 1845 arrival of Samuel May, a Boston abolitionist associated with William Lloyd Garrison. May came to minister for the local Unitarian congregation. Another towering figure was Jermain Loguen, himself an escaped Tennessee slave. By the 1840s he led a small African-American

congregation at Syracuse's AME Zion Church. Loguen lectured and wrote passionately for the abolitionist cause.

And both May and Loguen were active in the Underground Railroad. They assisted fugitive slaves into Canada or, sometimes, helped them settle in Syracuse. Loguen's own narrative states that he and his wife, Caroline, had a direct hand in the successful passage of over 1,500 fugitives, many through their home at the northeast corner of Pine and East Genesee. Some came on foot, some rode through on canal packets and others on the iron rails of real steam-powered trains.

Many other residents, both white and black, worked less conspicuously but bravely for this "freedom train." In 1839 African-American Thomas Leonard was employed in the Syracuse House, a local hotel. In late September, guests included a couple from Mississippi, the Davenports, who were traveling with a servant named Harriet Powell. Harriet was their slave. Leonard and another black, William H. Livingston, made arrangements for her escape, along with William Clarke, deputy county clerk, and John Owen, a marble dealer. She was spirited away by carriage, leaving Mr. Davenport furious. A reward poster soon appeared in town and vigilantes roamed the back roads. But Harriet found safety in Kingston, Ontario. She later married and had eight children.

In 1845 Harriet expressed sadness at not being able to see her mother or sister again, but vowed never to return to slavery. She consoled herself with the knowledge that, "The greatest desire of my mother's heart was that her children might be free, and for that she prayed."

The stakes became higher after the 1850 passage of the federal Fugitive Slave Law. It not

Helen Amelia Loguen (1843–1936) was the daughter of anti-slavery leader Jermain Loguen. She grew up in Syracuse, often helping her parents and siblings to harbor fugitive slaves. She became a teacher and in 1869 married Frederick Douglass' son, Lewis, at her family's East Genesee Street home.
OHA Collection

The site of the 1851 Jerry Rescue was a commercial building along the west side of Clinton Square. At the time, it also housed the offices of the city's police justice. "Jerry" Henry was freed from a room on the raised first floor. The building's foundations are believed to survive beneath the surface. OHA Collection

only made it a serious crime to help fugitives but essentially obliged all citizens to actively aid federal authorities in the capture of runaways. Recognizing that the law would be unpopular in abolitionist strongholds like Syracuse, Daniel Webster visited in May 1851 to denounce any citizen that would disobey the law of the land.

Southern politicians wielded a great deal of control in Washington. Even in Northern cities, like Syracuse, some of the established commercial interests had financial ties with the South. They worried that abolitionist agitation would lead to a great national schism. As one New York City businessman explained to Reverend May in 1835,

> *"There are millions upon millions of dollars due from Southerners to the merchants and mechanics of this city alone, the payment of which would be jeopardized by any rupture between the North and the South. It is a matter of business necessity ... We cannot afford to let you succeed."*

In fact, a group of prominent local men had gathered at the Division Street courthouse in 1836 and adopted a series of anti-abolition resolutions. In part, they stated that, "the people of the North

rest under the most solemn obligation of duty to their southern brethren, to adopt the most efficient measures to arrest the mad course of the Abolitionists." Among the meeting's authors were James Geddes of Camillus, along with Syracusans Hiram Putnam, Elias Leavenworth, John Wilkinson and B. Davis Noxon.

But abolitionists won over many locals during the next 25 years, including Putnam, Wilkinson and Leavenworth. The Fugitive Slave Law played a major role, especially during the arrest of William Henry, a former slave from Missouri working in Syracuse as a cooper. He was seized under its provisions by federal authorities on October 1, 1851, less than five months after Webster's challenge. During the afternoon, there was an unsuccessful escape attempt by Henry, commonly called "Jerry." After a short sprint down Water Street through Clinton and Hanover squares, the fugitive was recaptured by marshals. The episode was violent and brutal, leaving Jerry bloodied. The site of a man hounded and beaten simply because of his race might have been familiar in the South but shocked Syracusans, even those ambivalent to the general racism prevalent in the North. Many eventually decided that they could not support a law that abetted such treatment.

That evening a crowd of supporters organized by anti-slavery leaders such as Loguen, May and Gerrit Smith, and including both black and white citizens of Syracuse, broke into the jail and rescued Henry, spiriting him away to Canada. It was electrifying news across the country, cheered by abolitionists and condemned in the South. President Fillmore ordered a swift prosecution of the lawbreakers. Some local fugitives who had settled in Syracuse fled to Canada. James and Mary Baker, along with George and Phebe Carter, resigned from Syracuse's Wesleyan Methodist

Church on October 20, its membership roles recording, "Removed to Canada to escape from the slave catchers!!"

But the local Underground Railroad continued to function, even more openly after 1853 when the federal government failed to mount an effective case against the rescuers. And Syracuse continued to host boisterous and often nationally prominent conventions advocating the end of slavery. These meetings were usually held in the Congregational church on East Genesee Street or at city hall.

Frederick Douglass, a resident of nearby Rochester, was a frequent participant. One rally was held in 1854 at Wieting Hall commemorating the third anniversary of the Jerry Rescue. Douglass advocated active resistance to the forces of slavery and, holding aloft the manacles that once shackled Jerry, thundered forth on their symbolism, "These fetters will live, they will speak, they will act."

National and local passions escalated throughout the 1850s. Radical abolitionist John Brown communicated with Loguen, seeking him or other Syracusans to recruit for his ill-fated 1859 assault on Harpers Ferry. Loguen wisely declined. Abraham Lincoln's 1860 election forced the issue. By December, South Carolina had withdrawn from the Union. Some Syracusans blamed the abolitionists. During a January 1861 anti-slavery convention in Syracuse, a crowd of 200 protesters disrupted proceedings. Carrying banners that proclaimed "The Jerry Rescuers Played Out," they burned effigies in Hanover Square representing two of the meeting's leaders, Samuel May and Susan B. Anthony. But the crusade for freedom hardly winced. Soon a violent

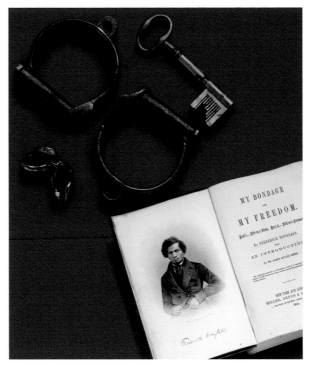

civil war did erupt, a ghastly but apparently inescapable conflict that ended the tragic dilemma. Loguen summed up his feelings by pronouncing it, "God's war with this guilty nation."

Syracuse and Onondaga County responded with great patriotic fervor to restore the Union. Five regiments were formed in the locality, and

The manacles that once restrained fugitive slave William "Jerry" Henry were later used by Frederick Douglass in an impassioned anti-slavery speech in Syracuse. They are now on display at the Onondaga Historical Association Museum along with the key to Henry's jail cell.
OHA Collection

(Below left) Colonel Augustus Dwight was the highest-ranking Syracusan killed during the Civil War. The popular commander of the 122nd New York Volunteers was struck by a cannon ball at Petersburg, just two weeks before Lee surrendered at Appomattox.
OHA Collection

Syracuse-native Hiram Foote served as a drummer in two area regiments. With the 185th New York, he saw considerable action in Virginia. He lived to march up Salina Street in 1917, helping send other local men off to World War I in Europe.
OHA Collection

over 12,000 men from Onondaga County served. Hundreds never returned. Area residents fought in a number of major battles. The 149th New York Volunteers helped mount a tenacious defense of Culp's Hill at Gettysburg, seize Lookout Mountain at Chattanooga and march with Sherman to the sea. The 122nd New York assisted in chasing Confederate General Jubal Early away from the very gates of Washington in July 1864 and then advanced with Phil Sheridan to sweep the Shenandoah Valley of Rebels.

Twenty local African-Americans responded to Frederick Douglass' call in 1863 to join the 54th Massachusetts, the north's first all black regiment. Several, like Syracuse barber Jacob Carter, waiter Andrew DeForest and machinist Charles Willis were in the ranks when they stormed the walls of Battery Wagner in Charleston. Two of the local

men died. Charles Highgate, another Syracuse black, enrolled in the locally raised 185th New York Volunteers in September 1864, even though it was not a "Colored" unit. He died from wounds received in action at Quaker Road, Virginia, in 1865.

And Syracusans served with distinction in the Union Navy. Irish-born James Tucker, a U.S. Marine, helped man one of the guns on the *USS Kearsarge* when it sank the dreaded Confederate raider, *CSS Alabama*, off Cherbourg, France, in 1864. His grave in St. Agnes Cemetery proudly features a miniature of *Kearsarge's* cannon in stone.

The City Comes of Age

The 1848 transformation of Syracuse into an official city sparked a number of civic initiatives. The combined village populations gave the new municipality a unified, critical mass of nearly

The city of Syracuse's first mayor, Harvey Baldwin, set up offices in the old village hall, which once housed a public market on its first floor. It was built in 1845 and modified over the years. City government outgrew and replaced it in 1889.
OHA Collection

16,000 citizens. The legislative city council and executive mayoral structure provided a stronger focus for city functions. Those entities set up shop in Syracuse's old village hall.

A public school board was formed immediately in April 1848. It had responsibility for 3,724 pupils, but Syracuse's 10 school buildings had seating for just 1,460! Four had only one room. An ambitious construction program began.

The first faculty consisted of just nine men and 15 women. The male teachers averaged $35/month in wages; the women received between $15 and $18. High school classes were offered for the first time in 1855. By 1868 the first true high school building was completed on West Genesee. Other schools were built or expanded throughout the rest of the 19th century as Syracuse's population maintained its upward climb.

Annual city directories were published beginning in 1851. Their listings over the next several decades show a maturing city with an ever increasing number of churches, clubs, businesses, charitable institutions, entertainment venues, musical societies and city offices.

The directories show the state's prominent role in maintaining the area's valuable salt works and canals. It engineered and maintained brine wells, log pipe systems, stone pump houses and a salt superintendent's headquarters. In addition to servicing several lift locks, New York also erected a new Syracuse weighlock in 1850 to help calculate tolls. The unique structure still stands as the Erie Canal Museum. In 1854, through the influence of Elias Leavenworth, New York also opened in Syracuse the first American facility designed to educate mentally disabled youth, as an alternative to simply housing them. Dr. Hervey Wilbur was one of America's pioneers in this field and, until his death in 1883, supervised this innovative forerunner of the Syracuse Developmental Center.

The county needed a new center of operations after its isolated Division Street courthouse burned in 1856. The suspicious fire was a blessing. It

Situated on the northwest corner of Park and Court streets, Jefferson School was the first erected by the new city of Syracuse in 1848. This 1890s view shows a third floor, added in 1874. A new Jefferson School opened on this site in 1918 and remains in use today as apartments. *OHA Collection*

A Capital Location for a Beer Garden

As development spread west across New York, many believed it was inevitable that the state capital would have to be moved from Albany to a more central location. In 1846 and 1851, legislation was introduced proposing Syracuse or Utica.

One of the reasons that local leaders decided in 1848 to reorganize Syracuse and Salina villages into a bigger city was their dream of attracting the capital. The north side's prominent Prospect Hill was the preferred location. It was graded down in 1849, in preparation for the capitol building. The soil was used to fill the old Onondaga Creek mill pound, whose stagnant waters had become a loathsome source of disease. A small park was built on the pond site and then, in 1858, the first version of the state armory.

But back on Prospect, the anticipated capitol building never came. Albany would not let it go. So with an increasing German population nearby, the prominence became home to the Prospect Hill Brewery, complete with adjacent beer garden. It is visible above the three chimneys in this c.1865 photo. Eventually the site did host a more virtuous use. St. Joseph's Hospital, the city's first, opened there in 1869 where it remains today.

OHA Collection

ended acrimonious debate about whether a new courthouse was required and made it a necessity. A grand, new limestone structure, designed by Horatio Nelson White, was opened on Clinton Square the following year. By then, the square had become the recognized public center of the barely 10-year-old city. This new architectural landmark served as a 19th-century symbol of Syracuse's rising prominence.

Canals, steam railroads and stagecoach lines connected Syracuse to other communities. But as the city itself expanded, the need for an internal

An 1852 view of Syracuse shows a young, prosperous community centered on the salt works that wrap around the southern half of Onondaga Lake. Church steeples, although exaggerated here, were the tallest structures. *OHA Collection*

transit system arose. Privately operated, horse-drawn coaches called "omnibuses" ran from Clinton Square to the First Ward in the 1850s. In 1860 streetcar rails were laid along Salina Street linking the two centers, with cars pulled by horses. Other routes soon joined it.

By 1889 there were 11 separate and distinct streetcar lines operating, carrying nearly 6 million passengers annually in a city with less than 90,000 residents. The first electric-powered line went into operation in 1888. Called the Third Ward Railway, it ran through the west side, terminating at Solvay.

Water is a necessity for any town. In village days, natural springs were tapped and public wells dug. Some residents drilled their own. In 1849, one year after the city was chartered, the private Syracuse City Water Works Company was formed.

Over the next 30 years, this company expanded into additional springs, built reservoirs and installed a network of pipes in attempts to keep up with the city's growing needs. Its last major project, Wilkinson Reservoir, opened around 1879. It still exists as the reconfigured Hiawatha Lake in upper Onondaga Park. The company even built a stone pump house along the banks of Onondaga Creek to draw water. Unfortunately, it sat downstream from a tannery's wastewater discharge!

Ultimately, the privately run system was unable to maintain a clean and adequate supply to the city's citizens, industries and fire hydrants. Fighting major fires could be disastrous if the water ran short, as it did with one major north-side inferno in 1870. Agitation grew stronger in the 1880s for a new arrangement and water source. When the private sector stalled, the city took the initiative in the 1890s. Syracuse constructed the present municipally owned system that draws, by gravity, from the pure waters of Skaneateles Lake, 20 miles away. The opening of the new system in 1894 was one of the city's major municipal achievements and is still used today.

The Danforths, Tylers and other early arrivals used the dim light of animal fat candles to see around Central New York after dark. In the 1830s the brighter-burning oil derived from sperm whales was used in lamps and street fixtures. By the 1840s a new technology to light cities employed gas manufactured from coal. New Orleans and Baltimore had gas lamps by 1816. Syracuse's turn came when the Gas Light Company of Syracuse was organized in 1849 and secured exclusive rights from the city council.

To allow boats to conveniently unload the required coal, production facilities were built along the Erie Canal at Franklin Street, just west of Clinton Square. This district already was home to other industries. Pipes were laid below ground to service gas lamps along streets or mounted inside public buildings. Individual homes and businesses could also be hooked up.

B. Austin Avery (1814-1882), a Connecticut native, came to Syracuse in 1838 to manufacture salt. But he also served as founder and general manager of the Central City Railroad, which in 1860 became Syracuse's first street railway. He was killed in a winter sleighing accident in 1882.
OHA Collection

Horse-drawn streetcars were operated in Syracuse until 1900. This one is being pulled down Gifford Street on the city's west side in March 1893.
OHA Collection

War of 1812 veteran, canal contractor and real estate investor, Oliver Teall (1788–1857) was the force behind Syracuse's first privately run water system. He lived in a grand home which was demolished in 1990, despite its listing on the National Register of Historic Places, a tragic loss for the community.
OHA Collection

By the 1860s, downtown glowed at night as the warm color of gas lighting shone from windows and street corners. Such lighting was evidence of a progressive community, but there were complaints about the monopoly held by the local gas company.

In 1874 a disgruntled consumer sent a poem to the *Syracuse Journal* that contained the following passage:

Gas man! Gas man!
Are you made of brass man -
Heart, and brain, and conscience -
All as brazen as your pipes?

The 1880s saw the arrival of electric lighting across the country. Manufactured gas illumination faded from the scene, along with the quaint lamplighters, who once walked the streets of Syracuse igniting or extinguishing each fixture. Syracuse's

first electrical light companies organized in 1882. Steam from coal-fired boilers powered the dynamos. In 1886 consolidation occurred under the Syracuse Electric Light & Power Company. From then on, electricity revolutionized all aspects of life.

Protecting the Populace

The villages of Salina and Syracuse used a handful of hired constables to provide public security. But the community grew so rapidly after completion of the Erie Canal that they proved inadequate. The canal, and later railroads, brought many strangers and travelers through town. Some were unsavory types, looking for criminal opportunities. Syracuse had a reported 75 locations where liquor was sold in 1841, often with limited controls. This fostered fights, illegal gambling and assaults.

Once a city, Syracuse sought a larger police force. But various improvements were not particularly effective until 1869. A police commission was formed that year with an allowance for 30 patrolmen. Thomas Davis became first chief of police under the new system.

An 1882 map documents the Onondaga Creek pumping station and nearby concentration of private reservoirs built to supply Syracuse with water. These were superseded in 1894 by a system fed from Skaneateles Lake.
OHA Collection

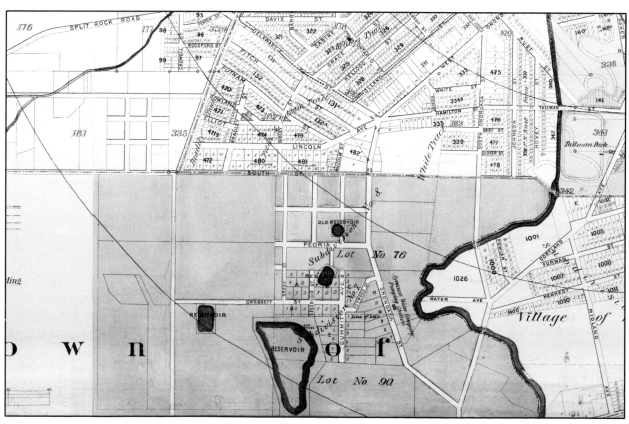

For years, officers had little training. Political or family connections often determined appointments. Size and endurance were useful, however, as police did not always carry firearms. Neither did most criminals. So the ability to physically subdue a ruffian was a measure of the officer's effectiveness.

One day in the 1880s, officer Billy O'Brien chased a member of the Earll gang for almost four hours. They ran through, around and under north side salt sheds before the thief was caught. Back-up patrol cars and radios did not exist. It was O'Brien's singular toughness that mattered.

Crime statistics in 1866 show that the majority of arrests involved petty larceny or drunk and disorderly conduct. Officers worked on foot and often resorted to wheelbarrows to remove the excessively inebriated to jail. Later, horse-drawn police wagons became standard equipment.

Sometimes, well-dressed Syracusans were the targets of pickpockets at train stations. In 1881 there was a rash of burglaries in the mansions around Fayette Park. Criminal gangs were a reoccurring problem. One, nicknamed the "Chain Gang," used Daggett's saloon at West Fayette and

There have been four legal executions carried out in Onondaga County, all hangings. Three took place between 1873 and 1881 at the first county penitentiary, a castle-like brick structure built to the designs of architect Horatio Nelson White. Sections of each rope have been preserved.
OHA Collection

Otisco Streets as headquarters. In one month, police suspected its members broke into over 30 safes, mostly of small businesses. Eventually, authorities broke the gang's back.

A red-light district of saloons, catering to prostitution and gambling, developed in the mid-19th century along East Washington Street near Townsend. The increasing railroad traffic on Washington made the area undesirable for residences but handy for promoting the oldest profession to passing male travelers. The police kept things from getting out of hand by breaking up common fights. But they only periodically moved to clean up the area, with temporary effects, when pushed by reform-minded citizens.

An unknown artist has left this 19th-century image of Syracuse's early gas works, the present site of the National Grid headquarters. A large "gas holder" storage tank occupies the center.
OHA Collection

Gone and Too Often Forgotten

Syracuse's first true municipal cemetery, established by 1824, was located at the southwest corner of Water and Franklin. But the expanding village soon hemmed in the simple Water Street Burying Ground. A new, larger site was sought, one that some citizens hoped could be handsomely landscaped. In 1841 the village opened the 22 acres of Rose Hill Cemetery at Lodi and Highland. It sufficed for a time but lacked the necessary size for creative landscaping.

In 1859 private Oakwood Cemetery was dedicated. Brought about by local civic proponents like Elias Leavenworth, Syracuse's second mayor, it was a masterpiece of romantic 19th-century rural cemetery design. Woodlawn Cemetery was incorporated in 1881, servicing north side neighborhoods located too distant from Oakwood.

The only known city burial ground once segregated for Americans of African descent exists in Rose Hill. As the municipal cemetery, Rose Hill had a "potters field" for indigents. It was divided into sections for "English," "German," "Irish," "Americans" and "Africans." It reflected both the prejudices and ethnic concentrations of mid-19th-century Syracuse.

Within its borders, Syracuse holds many other historic graveyards. Some were early cemeteries that were annexed, like the west side's Myrtle Hill, opened in 1855 to serve the village of Geddes or the oldest, Valley Cemetery. Others are linked to Catholic congregations such as picturesque St. Agnes, opened in 1873, or associated with Jewish synagogues. Many remain active. Some, sadly, are often forgotten. The Water Street site today lies under a parking lot, although records indicate several bodies may still rest there.

A section of Syracuse's Rose Hill Cemetery, *OHA Collection*

Luther Gifford (1811–1847) was a 30-year old Syracuse architect and volunteer fireman who was severely injured in the 1841 gunpowder explosion. He later wrote that the process of suturing his deep wounds, ". . .was no trifling job, the needle seemed to me like a crowbar running through my flesh." *OHA Collection*

The city had a jail inside the original city hall. It was replaced by one, used until 1908, in the basement of the present city hall. But those were holding cells, usually for minor offenders until seen by a justice. Sentenced criminals were sent to the county jail, traditionally located near the courthouse. In 1850 the county built a penitentiary at Pond and Alvord streets, about three blocks north of the second courthouse. Later courthouses were downtown, but the 100-cell pen stayed on the north side until replaced in 1901 by a facility in more rural Jamesville. The original penitentiary site became the location for North High School in 1908.

As the population increased, more tragic crimes appeared. In 1872, during a domestic feud, Henry Fralich stabbed and killed Peter Schaffer, a cooper, in a north side Syracuse tavern. His was not the only murder of that era, but came at a time when capital punishment was increasingly looked to as a deterrent. Found guilty, Fralich was hanged by County Sheriff William Evans in the yard of the original penitentiary. He lies buried in the Potter's Field section of Rose Hill Cemetery.

From its beginnings as a village, Syracuse encouraged the formation of volunteer fire fighting companies. Young lads joined up, motivated by civic duty, but also seeking adventure and camaraderie. Village trustees purchased hand pumpers and ladders for them. By 1853 there were six companies; a proud lot, full of rivalry and sporting distinctive names like the "Salina Blues," "Rough and Ready," "Deluge" and "Cataract."

One early tragedy that remains the most deadly in Syracuse history occurred on August 20, 1841. A fire broke out that evening in building contractor Charles Goings' carpentry yard, situated along the Oswego Canal behind the corner of Willow and North Salina. As expected, the village's volunteer fire companies rushed to the scene along with hundreds of spectators drawn by the excitement. But unknown to all, a gunpowder consignment totaling 625 pounds in 27 kegs was temporarily stored in Goings' shop. Within a few minutes, just as the firemen were starting their hoses, a shattering explosion ripped the night. Wooden pieces of the building became lethal missiles. Bystanders were blown into the canal. Others were buried under debris. The blast, heard as far as 26 miles, snuffed out the fire. There was darkness and momentary silence, then the chilling screams from dozens of injured filled the air.

Twenty-five citizens were killed outright, some literally beheaded by flying timbers. The dead included three volunteer firemen; two left grieving widows and children. Another 64 residents were injured, some horribly and ultimately, some mortally. Almost everyone in the village knew a killed or wounded victim. An inquest censured Goings and the gunpowder owners,

Syracuse's second steam-powered pumper arrived in 1866 and was assigned to the "Empire" Company, reorganized as Central City Number 2. Its mostly German members sported a uniform of black pants, red shirts and black hats with white crest. *OHA Collection*

hardware merchants A.A. Hudson and William Malcom, but no further legal action was taken. Malcom was wrought with guilt and provided funds for the victims, but never recovered emotionally.

The earliest paid firefighters were hired to man the first steam pumpers acquired by the city in 1865-66. The entire department became professional in 1877. They faced death on numerous occasions, fighting roaring infernos like the 1890 Leland Hotel fire, which claimed seven lives, and an 1891 conflagration which, whipped by high winds, could have leveled most of downtown.

The second-most lethal day in Syracuse occurred 33 years after the 1841 explosion. On June 23, 1874, during a social inside Central Baptist Church at Jefferson and Montgomery, a poorly designed structural support gave way under the weight of numerous guests. Over 250 men, women and children plunged to the floor below in a mass of broken timber and bodies. Nearly 90 were injured, 14 fatally, including Minnie Collins of Burnet Avenue who was celebrating her 13th birthday. *OHA Collection*

Helmet from Chemical Number 2. This late-19th-century fire fighting company was privately financed by affluent Hamilton S. White through special arrangement with the city. *OHA Collection*

The Leland Hero

One of Syracuse's greatest 19th-century calamities was the October 16, 1890, Leland Hotel fire. Flames broke out just after midnight in the 139-room structure at East Fayette and Franklin and spread rapidly. Portions of the hotel were collapsing within 45 minutes. Dozens of guests and employees were trapped. Many had to escape by jumping from upper-story windows or using emergency ropes to lower themselves. Seven individuals perished, but it would have been many more if not for 21-year-old Henry Rucker, the elevator operator.

Rucker lived on Irving Avenue and was of African-American descent. When the inferno blocked the stairways he kept running the elevator despite surrounding flames and choking smoke, bringing terrified patrons to safety then returning for more. Finally, the elevator itself ignited and with blistered hands, Rucker was forced to surrender it. He was credited with saving at least 20 people that night. The Leland was considered the city's worst fire in 50 years.

Henry Rucker and an 1890 view of the Leland Hotel, *OHA Collection*

Entertaining and Intellectual Pursuits

Watching local firefighters race to put out all-too-frequent blazes might have enthralled citizens, but by the 1850s Syracuse began offering a greater variety of opportunities for public entertainment and enlightenment. These continued to expand throughout the rest of the 19th century, especially as formal theaters and concert halls were built.

Music was always popular, with local bands of many types offering concerts in parks or at picnics. As the population rose there was a surge in fraternal, religious and ethnic clubs that sponsored such outings. Special trains were chartered and bands hired.

Minstrel shows were in their prime during the mid-19th century. Troupes followed a circuit from city to city. Their mixture of song, humor and dance, performed in black face makeup, both ridiculed African-American culture while at the same time popularizing black musical traditions. In cities like Syracuse, which had a relatively small population of African Americans in the 19th century, minstrel images perpetuated racist impressions. These stereotypes lasted for decades.

Additional traveling entertainment featured outlandish circuses, amazing magicians, Shakespearean dramas and light-hearted operettas. In 1851, the famous "Swedish Nightingale," Jenny Lind, performed to a packed throng at the National Theater on West Genesee near Franklin Street. Considered Syracuse's first true theater, it was a crude affair converted from a Baptist church. Two years later, the anti-slavery melodrama, *Uncle Tom's Cabin*, was also staged there.

Famous actors made stops. The renowned thespian stars, Edwin Forrest and Edwin Booth (brother of assassin John Wilkes Booth) appeared here. In the 1870s and 1880s, traveling wild west shows joined the circuit. Syracuse saw the oddities and daring feats of P.T. Barnum's original "Greatest Show on Earth" and the "shoot-em-up" offerings of the real Buffalo Bill, William F. Cody.

Some residents preferred milder, more intellectual pursuits. Various lectures were available, some espousing the serious reform movements of abolition and temperance, others literary in nature, and several offering discourses on various natural phenomenon or spiritual philosophies.

The third national Woman's Rights Convention was held in Syracuse in 1852, four years after the landmark Seneca Falls gathering. The local meeting drew a young wife and mother from nearby Manlius named Matilda Joslyn Gage. She excited the audience and leaders like Susan B. Anthony with her passion for equality. Gage would become a vital and often radical figure in the national woman's rights movement.

In 1868 Charles Dickens stopped by to tender readings from his *Pickwick Papers* and *A Christmas Carol*. He performed on the stage of Clinton Square's Wieting Hall, a space that predated the famous opera house. Local reviewers were surprised by his small stature, but generally complimentary of his "power of expression."

Dickens, however, was less than enthused about the community. He had the misfortune of

arriving in Syracuse in early March, when lingering winter temperatures created gray skies, cold mud and a shivering dampness. Dickens huddled in the nearby Syracuse House hostelry and later complained that it was, "the worst inn that ever was seen." He grumbled on that Syracuse was, "a very grim place in a heavy thaw." He expressed great interest in visiting the salt works, a point of notoriety for many 19th-century tourists, but declined to venture out in the raw weather. Nevertheless, he was pleased with the attendance and ticket sales.

During an 1873 stop in Syracuse, Phineas T. Barnum's advertising defined his boastful approach to promotion. *OHA Collection*

(Both photos below) The Hutchinson Family specialized in inspirational music with spiritual overtones. Their circuit in the 1840s and 50s included performances in Syracuse. This original sheet music was owned by Syracusan Frances Amelia Clarke, pictured here. *OHA Collection*

Theatrical Rivalry

Early productions in Syracuse were staged in "halls," usually just an open, upper floor in a business block. These were multi-purposes spaces, used for any large gathering. After the Civil War, Syracuse grew out of its frontier era of converted churches or dance halls. The year 1870 saw the opening of two venues that claimed true theatrical status, popularly called opera houses in their time. One, variously known as the Barton, Wild's, the Park and then the Grand Opera House stood on East Genesee Street, just south of city hall. Its rival was called the Wieting Opera house, prominently holding forth on the south side of Clinton Square. In 1893 the Bastable Theater in Hanover Square became a third competitor.

Interestingly, each played a role in the rise of the Shubert theatrical dynasty. The Shubert brothers, Sam, Lee and J.J., grew up in Syracuse's inner-city Jewish community during the late 19th century. Raised in poverty, Sam made the family's first theatrical connection around 1887 by selling programs at the Grand Opera. He quickly worked his way up, becoming house manager at the Wieting in 1891, producer of his first play about 1896 and then executive of the Bastable by 1897. He expanded to New York City in 1900 and with his brothers created one of America's leading theatrical empires.

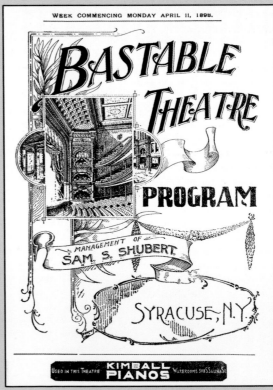

(Top photo) The Wieting Opera House went through three variations, rebuilding after fires in 1881 and 1896. This 1878 view shows the first version, seating 1,017 and reflecting the typically ornate environment of late 19th-century theaters. It tended to host the big stars in traveling productions. The last Wieting was demolished in 1930. (Above left) The first incarnation of the Grand Opera House, seen here about 1880, sat 1,400. It was extensively rebuilt following an 1888 fire but eventually torn down in the 1920s. It became noted for vaudeville offerings.(Above right) The Bastable initially specialized in featuring stock companies and melodramas. After the Shuberts left it, burlesque was offered. The Bastable was lost during a spectacular fire in 1923. *OHA Collection*

With no radios, TVs, stereos or internet, popular music was brought into homes by live instruments. Sheet music for Stephen Foster's "Oh Susanna" was a hot item in local music stores at the time Syracuse became a city. Throughout the 19th century, one symbol of a civilized, middle-class home was a piano, melodeon or small organ. Syracuse's business community in the second half of the 19th century included both dealers and manufacturers of these instruments.

For artistic interests, the acquisition of a painting or perhaps just a visit to a local artist's studio were possible. Sanford Thayer, John D. Barrow, Levi Wells Prentice and James Cantwell were notable 19th-century Syracuse painters. All did landscapes. Prentice, although self-taught, established a following in the 1870s with his detailed, realistic Adirondack scenes. Barrow preferred a softer mood, one associated with the Luminism school. Cantwell, by 1887, was moving toward a more Impressionistic style.

Small exhibitions by a single artist might be held in a local store or the artist's own studio since no formal art museums yet existed. But there were art clubs, which fostered interest in painters and sculptors. And Syracuse University established a College of Fine Arts in 1873, just two years after its founding.

Sporting Times

Early versions of baseball were common in Syracuse by the 1850s. The 1859 city directory lists four amateur clubs. The **Salt Point Baseball Club** played in Washington Park, the old Salina village green. In the late 19th century, many schools fielded teams, as did fraternal associations and ethnic clubs. Neighborhood rivalries revolved

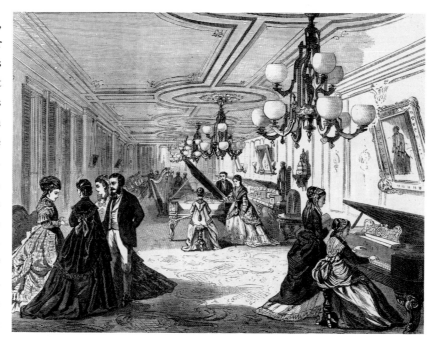

In 1869, George Ellis' showroom at Warren and Salina streets was one place where Syracuse's middle class could purchase the pianos, organs and melodeons that were a fixture in many Victorian homes. *OHA Collection*

ARTISTS.

FINE ART GALLERY.

"A thing of Beauty is a Joy Forever!"

TO THOSE AMONG US OF TASTE and refinement, who may desire work done in my particular vocation, I would most respectfully offer my services and invite their attention to my

Studio in the Pike Block

And all who may feel any interest in what my pencil may be about, are invited to call on any day and at any hour. I make no parade day, but submit my work to the public alike at all times.

Ever the same,
oct. 14   SANFORD THAYER.

(Left and following page) Sanford Thayer's 1861 advertisement appeared in the *Syracuse Journal*. His painting, *The Connoisseurs*, includes a self-portrait with Thayer looking directly at the viewer. Perhaps he is wondering if those depicted in his studio have sufficient "taste" to appreciate his work. *OHA Collection*

around the game as teams like St. Cecilia's Foresters, from the north side, challenged the Shamrocks from Geddes.

In 1866 the first Syracuse Stars club was formed. From 1876 until 1929, this name would represent local professional baseball. As a result, various wooden stadiums were known as Star Park. One was located at the northwest corner of Salina and Taylor streets in the 1880s. Others were out among the solar salt fields near Onondaga Lake. The last stood in the 1400 block of West Genesee Street.

Crossroads in Time: An Illustrated History of Syracuse

During the 1879 season, the Stars played in the National League but generally spent most of their years in the upper minors. They won the International League pennant in 1888, fielding two African-American players at a time when the growing influence of Jim Crow was ending integrated ball clubs. When Stars catcher Moses Fleetwood Walker was released during the 1889 season, the International League would not see another black player until 1946 when Jackie Robinson joined the Montreal club on his way to the Brooklyn Dodgers.

Bowling was gaining a small following by 1879, with lanes installed below the Wieting Opera House. Its popularity expanded in the next two decades nurtured by alleys at various Onondaga Lake resorts.

Billiards attracted many disciples in the 1870s. Millionaires on James Street built elaborate billiard rooms in their mansions. Pool tables were found in dozens of taverns and common billiard halls, frequented by working-class souls. The first such parlor was opened by Joel Owen during the 1850s on Hanover Square, in a building still standing at 122 East Genesee Street. Owen manufactured cue sticks and ivory billiard balls on the upper floors. By 1879 Syracuse had is own billiard table factory where Gifford Street bridged Onondaga Creek.

Pool came under attack in 1881 when an alliance of Syracuse clergy, politicians, temperance advocates and worried mothers condemned the

Of Hopes for Better Times

Moses Fleetwood Walker and fellow Syracuse Stars pitcher Bob Higgins suffered racial threats and intimidation during the 1887 season from other squads and, occasionally, an intolerant teammate. Although they had a popular following locally, their high profile could bring trouble.

Higgins had enough by the middle of the next season and quit. Walker was not renewed in August 1889, but stayed in Syracuse. Although he had gone to college, Walker could only secure a job as a railroad postal clerk and settled on Green Street. In 1891 he was drawn into a fatal brawl by local ruffians, reportedly baiting him with racial slurs, and Walker was arrested for murder. He claimed the stabbing occurred as self-defense. The all-white jury eventually agreed and the courtroom erupted in celebration. The trial had been closely followed in the community, especially by the city's small black population, to whom Walker was a local hero.

Walker, however, could not reconcile that, although innocent, he had served two months in a Syracuse jail. He moved his family to Ohio. His later writings as a journalist despair that America could ever be completely integrated. He died in 1924, 23 years before Jackie Robinson put on his Dodgers uniform.

The champion International League Syracuse Stars of 1888. Pitcher Conny Murphy, seated second from left, threw 34 wins that season. Catcher Moses Walker, back row at left, and pitcher Robert Higgins, on floor at left, were among the last African-Americans to play in the League until Jackie Robinson in 1946. *OHA Collection*

T. WM. MEACHEM, Prop'r.   H. A. BENEDICT, Sup't.
The Benedict Billiard Table Factory.
OUR TABLES
CANNOT BE EXCELLED
—FOR—
BEAUTY OF DESIGN
—AND—
PERFECT ACTION.
—OFFICE AND WAREROOMS—
3 and 5 Gifford Street,
SYRACUSE, N. Y.
A complete Stock of Superior Billiard Supplies New and Second Hand Pool Tables. Old Tables Remodeled and Repaired.

pastime. Rev. O'Reilly of St. John the Evangelist Church, sounding like professor Harold Hill, warned a large rally that young boys, "... cheat their mothers and fathers by spending their money at the pool table gambling for drinks."

There was some crackdown, but the "pestilence" of pool was not "crushed" in Syracuse. While gambling and drinking continued to be

An advertisement from the 1879 Syracuse City Directory. *OHA Collection*

An 1891 artist's depiction of the famous late 19th-century sleigh competitions held on West Onondaga Street. *OHA Collection*

The racing bill for an early summer afternoon in 1881. *OHA Collection*

(Below) The grandstand in Kirk Park was packed almost exclusively with men during this 1890 race. *OHA Collection*

first Catholic bishop, Rev. Patrick Ludden, was reported to have "a fine billiard room at his house" in 1899.

Boxing provided other diversions, with exhibitions between national figures staged in Syracuse, along with local matches. Football in the late 19th century was primarily a collegiate sport. Basketball, tennis and golf were in their infancy. But horse racing had long been an American favorite and Syracuse was no exception.

Formal racing tracks developed after the Civil War. The first of any consequence, called Driving Park, opened in 1868. Its half-mile oval sat east of Westcott Street where Beech intersects. Tallman Park, on the south side, featured a track beginning in 1877. These were superseded by Kirk Park in the 1890s. Kirk's track facilities burned in 1902 and its grounds became a city park in 1909. Racing activity then shifted to the New York State Fairgrounds in Geddes.

Those early tracks were the site of hotly contested races, drawing many fans, and featuring central New York's stable of impressive trotters. Owning a fast, spirited steed

frowned upon, billiards enjoyed increasing acceptance by the late 1890s. Prominent men's clubs added billiard rooms. Leading citizens played the game. Even Syracuse's

in the 19th century was a point of pride, especially for the wealthy. Their horses competed in the formal surroundings of these various parks, with professional drivers riding the high-wheeled sulkies. In the winter, owners themselves gravitated to an informal winter tradition of racing sleighs along city streets. West Onondaga Street was the preferred course. Hundreds of spectators would line the route to enjoy these contests, watching the fast cutters driven by their famous owners, like typewriter king L.C. Smith or merchant prince Milton Price.

New Patterns of Immigration

The pioneer settlers of Onondaga County were mainly from New England and eastern New York. Their ethnic roots were in Britain, Scotland and Ireland. Others were of Dutch lineage from the Hudson Valley, New York City and New Jersey. There were also a sprinkling of Germans, a few arrivals of African descent plus a modest number of Irish Catholic salt workers at Salina.

But the 1840s brought a rapid change as a flood of immigrants from Germany and Ireland arrived in Syracuse, part of a larger flight to America. The former were escaping from political unrest and the latter fleeing the great potato famine. By 1865 native German and Irish far exceeded any other foreign-born residents of Syracuse. There were over 4,000 of each. French-Canadian and English immigrants were next, totaling 1,659, then a drop to where arrivals from France, Poland and Scotland were counted by the dozens. If one includes the first generation of children born to the German and Irish, their numbers comprised about a third of the city's 31,784 citizens at the end of the Civil War.

Although first seen as outsiders, citizenship brought voting privileges and sheer numbers helped both groups gain political clout. As they achieved positions in city government they could integrate more Germans and Irish into municipal employment. Syracuse saw its first German-born

mayor, cigar manufacturer George Hier, take office in 1875.

Most Germans settled along North Salina Street and nearby side streets like Butternut and Prospect. The city's first Lutheran church was organized there in 1838. By 1891 there were nine Syracuse churches serving the city's German community. Assumption parish was established in 1843 to serve German Catholics.

A third group of German immigrants were Jewish. They settled east of downtown, along Jefferson, Madison and Harrison streets and cross streets like McBride and Townsend. Their first

(Top)
These north side cottages stood on Schneider Street in 1910 when this block was populated with names like Hundshamer, Strauss, Eitzenberger and Wurth. Their occupations included cigar-packer, carpenter, brewer, cooper and tinsmith. Many of these homes remain but today's residents reflect a broader ethnic diversity.
(Center)
Haberle Brewery workers, c.1880.
OHA Collection

St. Peter's Kirche, erected in 1860, was one of three Lutheran churches that once stood at the corner of Butternut and Prospect streets, in the heart of Syracuse's German community.
OHA Collection

(Below) Stores run by fellow countrymen created a supportive network for recent arrivals, where a foreign language was understood and temporary employment might be found. Philip Paulus, a German immigrant, became a hardware merchant at 319 North Salina Street.
OHA Collection

(Right) The Syracuse Liederkranz, a social club and singing society, was formed by German immigrants in 1855.
OHA Collection

boilers, laborers and teamsters. A number of Germans joined them but others became coopers, making the thousands of barrels required annually to ship salt.

Some new industries had their origin in the German community. This included candle making, cigar manufacturing and brewing "lagier bier," all concentrated on the north side. While the latter two have faded away, some candle production still remains centered there. The Germans formed many social organizations. A few were oriented toward sports, others to music. Among the more famous and long-lasting were the Turn Verein and the Liederkranz.

As with most immigrants, extended families, ethnic churches, stores or taverns run by former countrymen, native-language newspapers and fraternal clubs formed an altruistic and comforting network. These also offered new arrivals connections for obtaining work and housing.

The Irish first congregated on Syracuse's far north side, Salina, and the villages of Liverpool and Geddes, all locations for salt industry jobs. The latter area is still known for its Irish moniker, Tipperary Hill.

As with the Germans, the Irish were greeted with a combination of suspicion and fascination.

synagogue, Temple of Concord, was consecrated in 1851 at the site of the present Everson Museum. They worked primarily as peddlers, dry goods merchants and grocers. The neighborhood retained a Jewish presence through the 1940s.

The growing salt industry was a lure for the Irish and Germans. Wages were good and the primary requirement was a strong back. The Irish gravitated to the boiling blocks and solar fields as

1881   JULY 4th.   1881
GRAND OPEN-AIR
CONCERT AND PICNIC
GIVEN BY THE
SYRACUSE   LIEDERKRANZ
AT
DANFORTH PARK

PROGRAMME:

Procession at 9 a. m., headed by Maurer's Full Brass Band, through the principal streets to Danforth Park. From 2 till 4 p. m., GRAND CONCERT at the Park by Maurer's Orchestra, assisted by the Liederkranz and Concordia Glee Club, after which dancing and merry-making will rule supreme. The management will leave nothing undone to make this the most enjoyable affair of the season.

Admission to the Park - - - 15 Cents

june28deod2

The Irish had the advantage of knowing the language, which allowed for more rapid assimilation. But their Roman Catholic faith initially set them apart from a community leadership that had always been Protestant. Early Catholic pastors were often of Irish background and served as recognized leaders in that community.

An almost forgotten presence were French-Canadians. In the 19th century, many emigrated south in search of employment. Most headed to New England, their objective provided by numerous textile mills. But enough reached Syracuse by 1869 to allow the organization of St. Joseph's French Catholic Church, a converted Baptist structure on West Genesee near Townsend. In 1897, it was estimated that as many as 2,500 former Canadians lived in Syracuse, many near Green and Gertrude streets. Some worked as carpenters, others as shoemakers. By the time urban renewal razed St. Joseph's in 1967, this group's presence had faded, mostly through assimilation.

By the 1890s Syracuse had come a long way from its humble beginnings as the muddy crossroads with tavern, mill and odorous swamp. It had captured a big piece of the Erie Canal action, capitalized on its salt production, overcome rivalries to form a city, built up its municipal infrastructure, produced an impressive array of new institutions and accumulated a hard-working population of over 90,000.

CHAPTER *Three*

Syracuse Matures

As Syracuse approached the end of the 19th century, it was a dynamic, growing community. Its population reached 88,000 in 1890, 70-percent greater than 1880's 51,792. By 1900 it had more people than Atlanta. The canal and salt works were still present but no longer the mighty engines of development. Syracuse's ever-expanding base of heavy industry was the source of its wealth, tied to the rest of the country by rail.

As the city moved into the 20th century, a new flood of immigrants added their muscle and spirit to its expansion. Sons and daughters of Italy, Poland, Russia and the Ukraine filled homes and apartments, sent their children to city schools, started new churches and churned out a variety of goods in noisy city factories.

Electricity improved the mass transit system, and homes boasted appliances that would have amazed early Syracusans. Civic leadership added parks, monuments, museums, bigger schools and better libraries to the landscape. Buildings soared past the usual five or six stories that dominated local 19th-century streets and approached 20 floors by 1927.

By the late 1920s the city reached over 200,000 residents and considered itself headed for half a million.

(Previous page) In the 1920s downtown was Syracuse's bustling commercial core, providing the essence of local entertainment and retail. Its economic foundations were the city's burgeoning factories, like the Franklin auto plant, manned by hardworking laborers and managed by enterprising local executives. *OHA Collection*

(Above) Today's Columbus Circle was called both St. Mary's Circle and Library Circle when this 1910 photo was taken. The old Baptist church, center, was replaced in 1912 with a new, larger structure. Its addition helped enclose and complete the circle as downtown's second major civic space. *OHA Collection*

The site of the present county courthouse about 1903. *OHA Collection*

A New Civic Look

Syracuse's public library system dates to 1848, when the city's school system was established. The Board of Education created a central library collection in 1852, housed in the old city hall. In 1869 the nearly 6,000 volumes were moved to the first high school. To improve access, the library was relocated in 1894 to the former Putnam grammar school at Jefferson and Montgomery streets in a

pleasant residential neighborhood near downtown. The library's arrival encouraged the city gardener to landscape the unadorned triangle in front of the building into an attractive circle of grass and flowers. The Common Council christened it Library Circle.

Book circulation doubled, but the old school building was nearly 40 years old. And despite a large addition in 1898, conditions were spartan. This troubled Syracuse's youthful mayor, 30-year old Jimmy McGuire. In an early example of municipal grantsmanship, McGuire lobbied millionaire philanthropist Andrew Carnegie. It worked and the steel baron committed $200,000 for a new library if a suitable site could be found.

The mayor wasted no time. The Putnam site was already owned by the city and, McGuire reasoned, "also fronts on a park, and on three of the adjacent corners stand churches, which insure the permanency of the character of the surroundings." The old school came down and the cornerstone of the new library was laid in 1902. (Carnegie would later help fund libraries in Solvay and at Syracuse University.)

In 1904 the county **began** work on a new courthouse, its fourth. **Library** Circle was again chosen. Initially, many **could not** fathom building the courthouse anywhere **but** on the location of the old one, in prominent **Clinton** Square. But a larger site was needed. Circle proponents argued that the new cour**t**house, along with the library and churches, would bestow the site with its own "conspicuous" personality.

By 1906 both new buildings were completed, magnificent monuments in the Beaux-Arts style of classic architecture that was redefining American cities. The circle's west side already boasted two large churches, St. Mary's and Central Baptist. In

The "Boy Mayor"

He was only 27 when elected mayor in 1895, the youngest in Syracuse's history. A first-generation Irish-American, James Kennedy McGuire was called a "natural politician." His schooling never included college but he commanded attention as an orator.

McGuire worked his way up from a newsboy to become partner in a local hardware business by age 23. When 24, he worked on the national presidential campaign of 1892 for fellow New Yorker, Grover Cleveland. The following year, he was made a trustee of the Syracuse library. An avid reader, McGuire had a passion for Irish history, Shakespeare and politics.

In 1895 he captured the Democratic nod for mayor. Local GOP kingpin Francis Hendricks was being challenged for control of the Republican Party by James Belden. The feud resulted in a split and two Republicans wound up running against McGuire. One, Charles Baldwin, actually lived next door to McGuire in attached houses still standing at 201-203 Green Street. With his opposition divided, McGuire pulled a 3,000 vote plurality and broke the 20-year Republican hold on city hall.

He was re-elected twice, a populist who moved aggressively to secure new schools, more teachers, improved streets and six additional fire stations. He sponsored picnics and dinners for thousands of city youth, attracting widespread affection. Hendricks got his revenge, however. As a

state senator, he had the legislature change the rules for municipal debt, driving Syracuse's tax rate from $13 to over $21, just as McGuire sought his fourth term in 1901. The boy mayor lost and retired to the private sector. McGuire died in 1923. His tombstone in St. Agnes Cemetery bears a quote from Shakespeare, attesting to his love of literature. But his most notable monument is the grand Carnegie Library building, which he helped secure for his cherished city in 1902.

James Kennedy McGuire, Syracuse's "Boy Mayor" *OHA Collection*
Construction of the Carnegie Library, Mayor McGuire's dream, was well underway by the fall of 1902. *OHA Collection*

This ornate original facade of the downtown YMCA was covered when a major addition was added in 1956. *OHA Collection*

1907 the YMCA opened a new facility nearby, with another powerful facade of classical revival. And in 1912, the Baptists replaced their Victorian home with a soaring Gothic landmark. In a remarkably busy decade, the once unrefined intersection had been transformed into a major public space. The change symbolized Syracuse's maturity as an urban community.

A Productive Era

From 1890 to 1915, an astounding number of projects reflected this coming of age. In 1892 Syracuse dedicated a new city hall, replacing one that dated to village days. In 1894 an impressive new water system flowed from Skaneateles Lake. And in 1902 an architecturally stunning new Central High School opened.

It was also an era when electrical use soared. Between 1888 and 1900 all horse-drawn streetcars succumbed to ones powered by electricity. The city had its first crude arc circuit lamps suspended over intersections in 1886. By 1910 it began installing attractive ornamental street poles. Power came from steam-run generators at a Fulton Street plant, opened in 1893 and still standing. The steam was produced from water drawn off the adjacent Oswego Canal.

Leavenworth Circle was landscaped in the late 1880s. Its elaborate cast iron fountain and Victorian design was a symbol of the importance of civic spaces to a maturing community. The fountain was removed in 1934 during the Great Depression as too costly to maintain. *OHA Collection*

George Fisk Comfort, former dean of Syracuse University's College of Fine Arts, dreamed about another trait of a mature city — an art museum. He steered the Syracuse Museum of Fine Arts to incorporation in 1896, then through temporary quarters and finally into the new Carnegie Library in 1906. Comfort stayed as the museum's first director until his death in 1910. Noted local artist Fernando A. Carter replaced him. By 1915 the museum occupied the library's entire top floor.

This period saw a flowering of intellectual and cultural organizations. The Onondaga Historical Association, founded in 1862, drew new energy from the county centennial celebration in 1894. Bolstered by a bequest from salt baron William Kirkpatrick, it opened a new museum and headquarters at 311 Montgomery Street in 1906. Civic Morning Musicals was started in 1890 by a group of visionary women to increase the community's access to quality performances by classical musicians. And in 1903, the concentration of science and engineering minds in the city organized the Technology Club to present lectures and programs. All three still exist, and there were others.

The city had a few small parks from its village days. Fayette Park was one, made over into a densely ornamental retreat in the 1870s. But Syracuse started a modern parks system in 1886 when John B. Burnet donated the sprawling acreage on the west side that bears his name.

In 1899 the farmers' market moved from Clinton Square to a North Salina Street site and the square was given its first landscaping. The same year, use of Hanover Square as a disheveled wagon rental staging area was ended and a small Veterans Park dedicated there. Syracuse's most ambitious monument-building era occurred in the early 20th century. In 1905 statues to fallen fire chief Hamilton S. White and local Civil War hero General Gustavius Sniper were erected. In 1908 a memorial to early newspaper pioneer Lewis Redfield was dedicated in Forman Park. Three years later, the north side received a statue of German cultural stars, Goethe and Schiller.

And in 1910, the massive Soldiers and Sailors Monument was completed in Clinton Square. The long-delayed honor for Civil War veterans formalized the square's role as the city's primary civic space.

Encouraged by the 1906 creation of the city's first parks commission, greater park improvements occurred in the following decades with development of Thornden and Onondaga parks. And in 1914, the tumultuous-looking town that a visitor once said would make an "owl weep to fly over it," created its first planning commission. In 1910 Syracuse's population had passed 137,250 making it the 34th-largest city in America. It was bigger than Memphis or Dallas.

A Manufacturing Giant

Civic improvements required wealth, whether private or public. And a growing population needed jobs. By the early 1900s Syracuse had developed a variety of manufacturing to create both. Numerous plants and mills, mainly brick with

Seen here at its 1911 installation, the monument to Goethe and Schiller commemorates the city's rich German heritage. *OHA Collection*

75

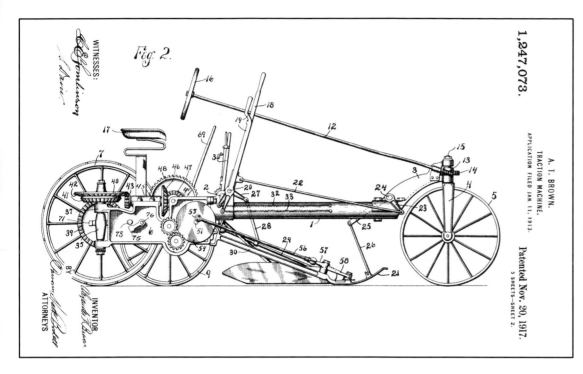

1,247,073.

A. T. BROWN.
TRACTION MACHINE.
APPLICATION FILED JAN. 11, 1913.

Patented Nov. 20, 1917.
5 SHEETS—SHEET 2.

Fig. 2.

Syracusan Alexander T. Brown was a prolific mechanical innovator. He was awarded patents for numerous products including one on this 1913 "Traction Machine" for agricultural mowing. *OHA Collection*

imposing smokestacks, stood along canal and railroad routes, providing convenient movement for raw materials and products. Working-class residential neighborhoods surrounded factories, offering proximity for immigrants who owned neither carriages nor autos. There was a large manufacturing corridor running west from downtown toward Geddes and into Solvay. Another was a district between Onondaga Creek and the Oswego Canal. Both were expansions of the old village industrial sector born along the creek.

Some firms began modestly. Syracuse's candle industry started in Bavarian-native Anton Will's small north side kitchen in 1855. By 1914 the value of the several local candle companies totaled nearly $2 million. In the early 1870s John Marsellus began producing a line of wooden products, including coffins. By 1890 he had a large factory by the Erie Canal making caskets. Syracuse China evolved from the single 1871 kiln of Onondaga Pottery. John Robinson leased a small facility in 1876 to produce an improved agricultural plow. By 1911, when it was bought out by the John Deere Company, Syracuse Chilled Plow operated a complex of over 500,000 square feet on Wyoming Street. Specialty steel giant Crucible has its roots in Syracuse's west

side industrial corridor, when Sanderson Brothers of England established a modest American division in 1876.

Other manufacturers rose more quickly, hitting the market at the right moment with a timely new product. Syracuse got a fast start with the auto business thanks to local proponents like John Wilkinson, Willard C. Lipe and Alexander T. Brown. Wilkinson's air-cooled engine concept impressed local aluminum die cast producer Herbert H. Franklin. With Brown and others, Franklin began car production on the west side. Franklin auto became Syracuse's largest employer by the 1920s.

Bicycle manufacturer E.C. Stearns turned out a line of "steam carriages" in 1901. Moyer Carriage produced autos between 1908 and 1914. But only Franklin truly succeeded, earning a national reputation for its engineering. Models were found from Alaska to Florida. A Franklin's high price, however, would prove catastrophic when the stock market crashed in 1929.

The Franklin car and several other products were nursed into reality at a modest machine shop on South Geddes Street. It was established around 1880 by Charles E. Lipe, a local mechanical engineer. Over the next three decades, creative minds worked out the details for numerous inventions, many the basis for new local industries.

The Straight Line Engine Company of John Sweet was located adjacent to Lipe's shop. Its specialty was a high-speed steam engine for generating electricity. Kemp & Burpee, manufacturer of agricultural machinery, developed new products at the shop, as did Engleberg-Huller, maker of rice and coffee-processing machinery. Brown-Lipe Gear started with a two-speed bicycle sprocket, perfected at the shop, and grew to a

This Franklin "Touring-Car" sold for $2,800 when it rolled out from the Geddes Street factory in 1907, an expensive but well-engineered vehicle.

A Diverse Industrial Legacy

Period catalogs in the Onondaga Historical Association collection provide a fascinating sampling of products produced in Syracuse around the start of the 20th century.

Bradley & Company built horse-drawn wagons, carts and agricultural implements at its Wyoming Street factory.

Model B.
1894 Pattern.

E. C. Stearns built a national reputation in the 1890s based on its bicycles. Later, it focused on hardware, tools and lawn mowers.

Price, $125.00.

The Syracuse Arms Company was formed in 1893. In 1902 it was producing shotguns that ranged in price from this $60 model to one topping out at $475 featuring a Damascus steel barrel and stock of Circassian walnut.

In 1902 the Syracuse Stove Works was turning out cast iron units for both heating and cooking purposes. The Water Street firm was especially proud of its stoves' ornamentation, highlighted with polished nickel finishes.

SYRACUSE CHILLED PLOWS.

CHILLED WEARING PARTS. STEEL BEAM.

SYRACUSE CHILLED PLOW CO.,
SYRACUSE, N.Y., U.S.A.

The Syracuse Chilled Plow Company operated a sprawling factory along West Fayette Street. The name referred to the process for hardening the plow blade.

DIETZ "KING"
FIRE DEPARTMENT LANTERN

Dietz oil and kerosene lanterns were shipped all over the world from its west side plant. They provided light for factory interiors, carriages, autos, fire departments and many of America's railroad lines.

The factory producing the Monarch was just one of several typewriter plants in Syracuse during the first half of the 20th century. This building now houses upscale condominiums in the revitalized Franklin Square district. *OHA Collection*

"No first class farmer can afford to do without one"

"SUCCESS" Manure Spreader

FERTILIZES THE EARTH
A SOIL BUILDER
FOR HUNGRY CROPS

KEMP & BURPEE MFG. CO.
SYRACUSE, N.Y. U.S.A.

Catalog cover, OHA Collection

Perhaps one of the more infamous commodities associated with Syracuse's industrial heritage was the "Success" manure spreader, built by the Kemp & Burpee Manufacturing Company. The device was developed in 1878 by Joseph S. Kemp, a Canadian native, to help farmers efficiently apply the natural fertilizer. In 1880 a partnership with William Burpee led to the establishment of a plant on West Fayette, near Geddes Street, a center of local industry.

By 1904 the company was building 12,000 spreaders annually. They were shipped by rail to places diverse as Minnesota and Florida. Eventually, in a story often repeated in Syracuse manufacturing, the business was purchased in 1911 by distant interests, Deere & Company of Illinois, and production was shifted out of town.

major auto parts producer. There were others. A century later, several of those industries are gone, but the little shop still stands, one of Syracuse's most significant but overlooked landmarks.

New Process Gear also took advantage of the booming auto industry. Formed in 1888, it machined laminated rawhide to produce gears commonly used on streetcars. The firm expanded into auto components and by 1915 ran a complex of factories along Onondaga Creek. This company exists today as suburban New Venture Gear, but still manufactures transmission parts. Its old facilities, along with former plants of the Bradley forging hammer, O.M. Edwards railroad windows and Monarch typewriters, help make up the revitalized historic district known as Franklin Square.

Prolific inventor Alexander T. Brown worked for gun-maker Lyman C. Smith. One day he showed Smith a sample typewriter that he had developed. That led to the 1890 organization of the Smith Premier Typewriter Company, later purchased by Remington. Before the buyout L.C. and his three siblings (Wilbert, Monroe and Hurlbut) broke off and founded L.C. Smith & Brothers Typewriter in 1903. Their new plant on East Washington became Syracuse's largest. Monarch also entered the scene that year.

Typewriters inherited the dominant role that salt once held in the local economy. Some suggested that Syracuse's new nickname be the "Typewriter City." Production of the writing machines was the city's most valuable industry in 1914. By 1923 nearly 150,000 typewriters were being made here annually, many with keyboards carrying Greek, Japanese or Arabic characters for customers across the globe. In 1929 the Remington plant alone employed 1,350.

Social Progress

The working conditions in many Syracuse plants of the late-19th and early-20th centuries would be considered harsh today. For immigrants, such jobs were keys to the American dream. But it was a time of labor unrest and organization for social reform. Capitalists were making huge profits, evidenced in Syracuse by the growing number of opulent mansions on James Street. By comparison, working wages were extremely low and days long.

Following the national trend, local unions formed along trade lines and were a growing factor by the 1890s. Some companies developed paternalistic social programs, classes, clubs and sports teams as benefits for employees. This was altruistic, but also served to maintain worker loyalty and

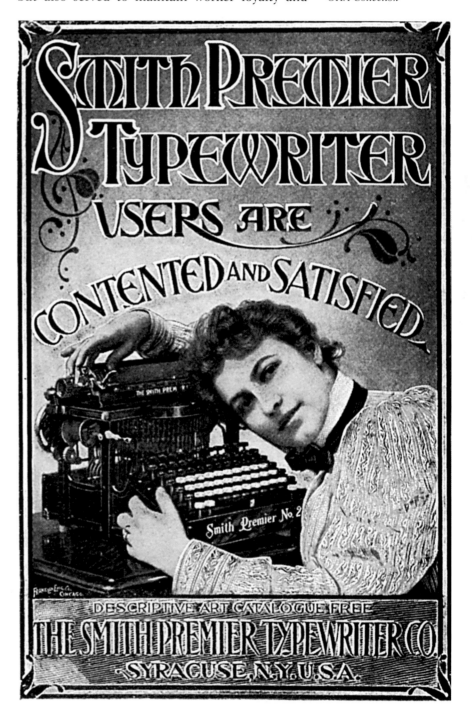

An 1898 magazine advertisement marketed Syracuse's Smith Premier to be appealing for women. By the late 19th century, females were a growing presence in clerical office positions, previously an all-male domain. *OHA Collection*

preclude union organization. Onondaga Pottery and Solvay Process were two practitioners.

But labor activism occurred in plenty of places. During 1890, 100 members of the local Stone Cutters' Union struck several quarries and yards, demanding a raise in daily wages from $3 to $3.50. They held up construction of Syracuse's city hall for a short time.

In July of that year, state labor inspector Margaret Gibson reported that Syracuse contained a number of hazardous sweatshops. Some employed small children and overworked women, "sunken-cheeked and hollow-eyed" from the "stuffy" and "dingy" conditions. Many shops produced clothing, but one of the worst was that of J.P. Hier, a cigar-maker. Others were in the district along Adams and Harrison Street, populated by Eastern European Jews and a number of the city's African-Americans.

In 1899 the Journeymen Horseshoers Union had Bert Dodge, a reported strikebreaker, arrested because he was not officially registered as a farrier.

In both 1913 and again in 1919 major local strikes hit the building trades. There were many Italian immigrants employed in that field seeking higher wages.

In 1899 Syracuse had nearly 10,000 men and a number of women in 76 unions, including cigar makers, brewers, milk peddlers, theatrical workers, printers and mincemeat workers. The last, no doubt, were employed by Merrell-Soule, a company that later produced powdered milk and became part of the Borden empire. The number of unionized females was small, concentrated in the garment and typographical trades. Their involvement reflected the growing number of young, urban women who were beginning to pursue work outside the home, before marriage, or even as a lifetime career.

As a new century dawned, women sought expanded roles in society and they continued their half-century search for voting rights. Some women found that the opportunities and education that came with wealth could be used to

Members of the local painters, decorators and paperhangers union, which included their own band, posed proudly on the steps of the Willow Street County Clerk's office around 1900. *OHA Collection*

In 1910 the women's suffrage movement was in full swing. In Syracuse, Harriet May Mills led the local efforts of the National Woman Suffrage Association. Mills' parents had been fierce abolitionists and their West Genesee Street home hosted the likes of Frederick Douglass. Mills still lived there when she became the first female candidate nominated by a major party to run for statewide office in 1920. Fortunately, the home was saved from demolition in 2001.

Philanthropist Dora Sedgwick Hazard and retired actress Blanche Weaver Baxter (niece of 19th-century feminist Matilda Joslyn Gage) were prominent in the more militant Women's Political Union. But both groups marched together in 1920 when the 19th Amendment was ratified.

Dora Hazard and other women associated with the Commonweal Club helped nurture the start of the Dunbar Center in the early 1920s a social organization for African-Americans. Dunbar became more independent by 1929, and grew under the direction of Golden Darby in the 1930s. Led by members of the African-American community, Dunbar advocated progress in the

improve the community, even if cultural restrictions kept them from traditional positions of influence. Aria Huntington, daughter of Syracuse's Episcopal bishop, was the first female elected to the Syracuse School Board in 1897. She was a tireless worker for labor, women and the poor, helping found the forerunner of Memorial Hospital in 1887.

> *"While women do as good work they should receive the same pay as men receive."*
> — Aria Huntington, speaking at a women's labor rally in Syracuse on February 12, 1891

Blanche Weaver Baxter (1856–1947). An 1892 photo records Baxter in her thespian days. She became locally active in the women's suffrage movement after retiring from the stage. She also helped organize an amateur acting troupe to raise money for St. Joseph's Hospital. Local hospitals owe much to Syracuse women. Roman Catholic nuns organized St. Joseph's in 1869. Thirteen ladies incorporated the Hospital for Women and Children, forerunner of Memorial Hospital, in 1887. And Mary Emma Jenkins, publisher of the *Syracuse Herald,* chaired its 1929 building committee. *OHA Collection*

areas of housing, employment, recreation and education. It remains a vital center for Syracuse's black community today.

The year 1930 also saw the completion of Percy Hughes Elementary School, which housed innovative facilities especially designed to service the recreational and educational needs of physically disabled students.

A Growing Ethnic Diversity

One of the expanding industries of the early 20th century was Oberdorfer Foundries, a firm specializing in aluminum and brass castings. It opened a new facility on Thompson Road in 1922 and enjoyed a successful relationship with Franklin, Pierce-Arrow and General Motors in supplying auto parts. The firm was developed by Moses Oberdorfer, a second-generation Jewish German-American.

By the 1890s Syracuse's early German-Jewish community had established several temples and its second and third generations were successfully expanding into a number of trades and businesses. That decade also witnessed an influx of new Jewish arrivals, from Russia, Poland and other Eastern European nations. They gravitated to the old Jewish district southeast of downtown and established their own synagogues. The earlier Jewish population moved east, past Irving Avenue, along the Genesee Street corridor, toward Euclid and beyond. Temple Concord built a new synagogue in 1911 at Madison and University, the first outside the traditional quarter. Temple Adath Yeshurun followed in 1922.

Neighborhood churches often provide a system of landmarks for following immigration patterns. Syracuse's first Italian-American church was St. Peter's, at North State and Burnet, organized in 1895, and used until 1957 when the congregation moved to a new edifice on James Street. St. Peter's was near the enclave of Italians first attracted in

In 1901 this building at the southeast corner of Adams and McBride streets, in the heart of the city's Jewish district, housed a grocery run by Issac and Celia Heiman. The family, including a son, Marcus, who became an associate of the Shuberts and eventually executive vice-president of RKO theaters, lived above.
OHA Collection

Crossroads in Time: An Illustrated History of Syracuse

the early 1880s by construction opportunities for a new railroad line called the West Shore. They settled north of downtown, not far from the railroad route, replacing German-Americans who moved east. Holy Trinity church on Park Street, an offspring of Assumption, was built in 1891 to serve the latter group.

By 1899 it was estimated that there were 5,000 Italian-born residents in Syracuse, second only to German and Irish natives. Their community spread north on Salina and State streets. A second church, Our Lady of Pompeii, was necessary by 1924. By the 1930s immigration from Italy had virtually ended, but over 30,000 residents of Syracuse were then first-, second- or third-generation Italian-Americans. The north side still reflects a hint of its "Little Italy" character, although it is a more diverse area today.

A few Italian-Americans found work in the shrinking yards of the declining solar salt industry. Some worked as railroad laborers. Others focused on building trades as masons and plasterers. Some became contractors, using their native language skills to recruit their countrymen. An Italian language newspaper, *L'Union,* reported news from the homeland and helped Italian businesses advertise services to their community.

Thomas Mainelli arrived around 1883. He worked as a railway foreman, later as a saloon-keeper and then contractor and private banker in the 1890s. He became a leader of the city's Italian-American community, helping them assimilate and assisting with financial needs. He became an ardent Republican and is credited with that party's strength among many of Italian ancestry.

The dedication of a downtown monument to Christopher Columbus in 1934 was a significant event for local Americans of Italian descent. Its prominent location at the former "Library" Circle, since renamed Columbus, reflected the success that many Italians had achieved in their adopted city.

During the 1920s, the Americanization League of Syracuse conducted classes in the homes of foreign-born women. The lessons helped them prepare for the literacy test required to obtain U. S. citizenship. *OHA Collection*

Eastern European immigration to Syracuse was dominated by Poles, numbering an estimated 1,500 by 1897 and 10,000 by 1924. These new arrivals were drawn to the west side and nearby Geddes, where numerous factories and railroad yards offered employment. Sacred Heart parish was formed in 1892 and its members built a magnificent limestone edifice in 1909. Its twin towers at West Genesee and Park Avenue remain landmarks for the community. A Polish-language mass is still offered, more than a century after its founding,

SYRACUSE'S FOREIGN BORN POPULATION—SOME STATISTICS.

This interesting "chart" was published in 1897. Not only does it provide an insight into Syracuse's ethnic mix a century ago, but it also reflects common stereotypes held in that era. *OHA Collection*

Temple Adath Jeshurun or "Rosenbloom's Shul" in the 700 block of South McBride Street was built in 1887. This congregation split from Temple Concord in 1864. The structure later housed Hopps Memorial Church, an African-American assembly.
OHA Collection

But Poles weren't alone in the neighborhood. St. Stephen's Catholic Slovak Church opened on Geddes Street in 1915. Ukrainian immigrants organized an Eastern rite congregation in 1900 and erected the onion-domed St. John the Baptist church just a few blocks west of Sacred Heart in 1913. And Saints Peter and Paul Russian Orthodox was formed in 1916. Its present Byzantine-influenced edifice on Hamilton Street was consecrated in 1927. The Greek presence was small, but also dates to this period. St. Sophia's Orthodox was organized in 1916 and built a church in 1921 on the southwest edge of downtown.

Such churches helped immigrants feel comfortable in a new world. Customs and traditions were passed down to new generations. The first arrivals struggled with the English language, but the second generation mastered it quickly and soon integrated into the local economy. In 1969 Syracuse elected Lee Alexander as mayor, a first-generation American of Greek heritage.

Syracuse's African-American population in the late 19th and early 20th century remained small, generally no more than one percent. While new immigrants quickly moved into the expanding number of factory jobs, discrimination limited opportunities for blacks. The available jobs were mostly menial and low paying, oriented toward day labor or custodial or housekeeping activities.

But local African-Americans continued to make their way, looking for opportunities for advancement no matter how modest. Syracuse's first black letter carrier, and just the third in the United States, was Edward Wilson, who was hired in 1881. In 1897, Edward Robinson, a third-generation black Syracusan, sued the Mills Brothers Restaurant on West Washington Street for refusing him service in the main dining room. A jury agreed and awarded him $100. In 1903, his nephew, Charles Robinson, would be one of the first African-American graduates of Syracuse University's College of Engineering. A few African-Americans struggled to start small businesses catering to other blacks. Benjamin Garland opened the city's first African-American funeral home on East Fayette Street in 1936.

Churches were important to the social fabric of the black community. AME Zion was the first, established before the Civil War. Located on the near east side, it drew the African-American population to that neighborhood in the 1850s and 1860s. The next, Bethany Baptist, was formed in 1887 and built its first church in 1894 on East Washington. By 1920 both congregations were located within two blocks of each other, near Almond Street. The adjacent blocks housed most of the city's 1,260 blacks.

The Erie Canal lay north of this neighborhood. Beyond it was a north side populated first by Irish, then German and later Italian immigrants. These new groups arrived with limited resources. And they traditionally viewed African-Americans as potential rivals for employment. Plus, it was common for each wave of new immigrants, concerned about being relegated to the lowest class in American society, to feel above the African-American. So the black community expanded slowly south. By the early 1920s it occupied the quadrant southeast of downtown along with the Jewish population. It was sometimes called "Jew Town" but came to be known as the 15th Ward.

A Bustling Center

They might arrive from different neighborhoods, but whether of Slovak, African or Italian heritage, Syracusans in the early decades of the 20th century could find just about anything they desired downtown. It was the most diverse commercial center for nearly 100 miles in any direction. Specialty clothing stores sold everything from hats to shoes. All sorts of doctors and dentists occupied second and third floors. One could find billiard halls and bowling alleys. Shop windows displayed musical instruments, luggage, jewelry, stationary, bicycles, books, furniture, hardware and produce. There were dozens and dozens of storefronts with barbers, druggists, bakers, confectioners, tobacconists, dressmakers and tailors.

And while the courthouse might be architecturally impressive, the real public showplaces of this era were downtown's department stores. Here, the stunning display of America's commercial

The interior of Hunter's downtown department store in 1934. The 15-foot columns dated from its original construction in 1894 as McCarthy's dry goods establishment. The building remains today as an office complex at Salina and Fayette streets. *OHA Collection*

Syracuse, N.Y. New York Central R.R. Station.

The third passenger depot of the New York Central Railroad opened in 1895 at Franklin and West Fayette streets. It was replaced in 1936 and was soon demolished. A surface parking lot has remained there for over 65 years, although a surviving 19th-century stone railroad bridge borders it. *OHA Collection*

Crossroads in Time: An Illustrated History of Syracuse

prowess must have appeared to recent immigrants like so many sparkling treasures. Syracuse had E.W. Edwards, Dey Brothers, Witherill's, D. McCarthy & Son, Hunter-Tuppen and Chappell's, all boasting multiple floors of clothing and household merchandise. They drew both the elite of James and West Onondaga streets as well as the working masses.

Downtown in the 1920's also contained more than 30 hotels, a dozen local banks, two train stations and an interurban railway depot. A growing variety of theaters featured classic performances, vaudeville and the latest "picture" from Hollywood. And just about every organization, real estate firm, lawyer and business that needed office space had its desks and file cabinets on the upper stories of downtown buildings.

Syracuse's skyline began noticeably climbing in the 1890's. Previously, buildings were structurally supported by exterior masonry walls, limiting height. Most did not exceed five stories. The introduction of structural iron and steel in the late 1880s freed architects. The Snow Building on Warren Street rose to eight floors in 1888. Salina Street department stores took advantage of the technology. Dey Brothers opened a new six-story building in 1893 at Jefferson, complete with a test track on the top floor for bicycle purchases. McCarthy's followed in 1894 with eight stories at Fayette Street. It boasted that it was filled with the "products of three continents" and employed 700 people. In 1896 Onondaga Savings Bank built a 10-story tower. In 1897 the University Building hit 11 floors. All still stand.

Hotels caught up a bit later. Many had remained 19th-century leftovers, often small and lacking elaborate public spaces. The 1892 Yates Hotel, across from City Hall, was large but not inspiring. Construction of the Onondaga Hotel

Structurally, Syracuse's 1884 Post Office at Fayette and Warren streets (center) employed heavy masonry walls. The 1888 Snow Building (right) and 1894 McCarthy store (rear) used iron and steel members, which allowed greater height. *OHA Collection*

at Warren and Jefferson in 1910 changed that, becoming Syracuse's first truly grand hostelry at over 12 stories. But it was surpassed by the Hotel Syracuse in 1924, a 600-room giant that still reflects an era of downtown elegance and status.

Entertainment also evolved dramatically. The popularity of live vaudeville shows among America's burgeoning urban population led to the establishment of a national network of traveling acts. And by 1910, silent motion pictures were the new rage. Both national entrepreneurs and local businessmen responded with new venues. At first, movie theaters were primitive storefront nickelodeon operations, dwarfed by the live performance houses. By the 1920s that was all changing as America's young cinema industry increasingly became the entertainment choice of the masses.

The favored location for theaters was South Salina Street, adjacent to the highly trafficked department stores. The Empire opened with 1,500 seats for traveling musicals in 1911. In 1926 it was converted to movies. The Temple Theater was built as a vaudeville and silent movie house in 1914 by local capitalists William and Edward Cahill. In 1929 this ornate classical palace took the name of its new owners, Paramount

The Downtown Glamour of Movie and Hotel Palaces

Perhaps nothing so typified the style of downtown Syracuse from 1910 through 1950 as the presence of its grand hotels and movie palaces. Fortunately, one splendid example of each still survives, the Hotel Syracuse and the former Loew's State, now proudly renamed The Landmark Theater.

The Onondaga Hotel used this custom dinner plate, produced locally by Onondaga Pottery, now Syracuse China. It featured a Native American image to reflect the hotel's appellation. *OHA Collection*

This 1943 view shows the Strand after it became part of the Loew's chain. It opened in 1915 at Salina and Harrison streets as a 2,000-seat movie house. Designed by Thomas Lamb, the same architect of Syracuse's Landmark Theater, it was demolished in 1959 for a parking garage. *OHA Collection*

South Salina Street literally glowed at night in this era. An explosion of neon and cascades of bulbs spelled out the thoroughfare as Syracuse's entertainment and shopping destination. *OHA Collection*

The Onondaga Hotel was built in two phases: the original 11-story tower of 1910 was expanded in 1915 with a second tower. The latter housed the city's famous Roof Garden restaurant, which offered unparalleled views of the city while dining and dancing. *OHA Collection*

A 1934 view of the Onondaga Hotel's Tudor Lounge *OHA Collection*

Even during the Depression of the 1930s, the Onondaga Hotel serenaded guests with a quartet and vocalist. *OHA Collection*

Crossroads in Time: An Illustrated History of Syracuse

The Hotel Syracuse added its art deco **Rainbow** Lounge in 1937. The hotel remains but the colored lighting, mirrored **columns** and black **glass of** the famous bar have unfortunately been removed.
OHA Collection

The Hotel Syracuse suffered through financial difficulties during construction. But led by visionary Joseph Griffin and local investors like department store virtuoso Daniel Edwards, it successfully opened in 1924 as the city's largest and grandest hotel.
OHA Collection

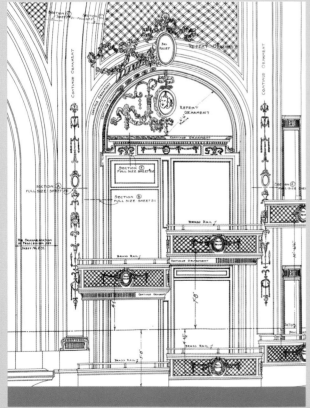

The Temple Theater was designed locally and only became part of the Paramount chain later. The original 1914 drawings of architects Asa Merrick and James Randall, including this detail of the private boxes, are now part of the holdings at the Onondaga Historical Association. *OHA Collection*

B.F. Keith's 1920 theater rivaled the nearby Loew's State for opulence and size. Its style was completely different, however, offering classical baroque elegance as opposed to the State's Hindu-Persian extravagance. Interestingly, Thomas Lamb was architect for both. Keith's was demolished in 1967. *OHA Collection*

Studios. Nearby, Benjamin Franklin Keith built a $2 million giant of 2,500 seats for his national vaudeville chain in 1920. And in 1928, the grandest of all, Loew's State opened, 3,000 seats amid the imagined splendor of a Hindu temple. Only the latter still exists. Downtown's retail, lodging and movie palace prominence held sway into the 1960s until eclipsed by its potent but less-inspiring suburban cousins.

Across the Lake

But what about a little outdoor amusement in 1910? Where could a young man take his best girl on a beautiful summer day? The answer sat "across the lake." Onondaga Lake, although associated with salt manufacturing and canal shipping, also was home to a sequence of waterfront resorts from the 1880s to 1930s. Although modest, they offered many seasons of pleasurable diversions.

The lake's northwest shore in the town of Geddes remained undeveloped after the Civil War; beyond the reach of industry and canals.

Although there were resort hotels at Oneida and Skaneateles lakes, Onondaga was much closer to Syracuse. Entrepreneurs began building resorts there, accessible by steamboats from the city. These attractions expanded greatly in the 1890s as faster and less-expensive electric railway lines arrived, bringing thousands of additional patrons.

Rockaway Beach, Pleasant Beach, Maple Bay, Long Branch and White City featured amusement rides, restaurants, bowling alleys, vaudeville performances, dancing pavilions, roller skating rinks, games of skill and plenty of locally brewed beer. Another spot, tagged the Iron Pier, opened in 1890 at the head of the lake. Five thousand visitors at a resort on a summer Sunday was typical.

This whimsical era, unfortunately, crashed headlong into some harsh realities. By 1920 the auto was increasingly popular, allowing greater mobility to distant, perhaps more attractive places. Some of the resorts, in fact, were developed by the railways as attractions. As the auto impacted their profits, so did their ability to

A 1908 view shows Onondaga Lake's most elaborate resort, White City. It operated for only about 10 years, closing in 1915. It was located between the State Fair and Onondaga Lake. *OHA Collection*

maintain these destinations. Onondaga Lake's industrial and municipal pollution was growing. Periodic spring flooding also hurt. Most resorts were already closed when the Depression arrived and finished the job. The last was Long Branch, located along the lake's outlet to the Seneca River.

Long Branch had been a favorite of church groups, veteran reunions, company picnics and family outings. The abandoned rides and pavilions were severely damaged in a 1948 fire and removed. Its land was incorporated into the county's Onondaga Lake Park. Long Branch's exquisite 1909 merry-go-round was spared and moved to another amusement park in Canandaigua, New York.

It returned to the lake in 1990. The ride was enshrined at the new Carousel Center mall, which opened a few hundred yards from the site of the long demolished Iron Pier.

Newspaper advertisements of July 1, 1904. *OHA Collection*

Musical entertainment by local bands was a staple of Onondaga Lake's resorts. This is the Long Branch orchestra about 1910. *OHA Collection*

The resort tradition carried on, in spirit, with the annual state fair. The fair had been held in rotating locations around the state for decades, but came to rest in Geddes in 1890, just a short distance from Onondaga Lake's west shore. In 1900, led by Governor Teddy Roosevelt, the state took over operation from the State Agricultural Society and a period of great expansion began.

So citizens continue to make a summer lakeside pilgrimage to enjoy amusement rides, musical entertainment and games of skill. Today, nearly 1 million visitors experience the exposition every August and September.

Mobility Forms the Modern City

The electric railway fostered the era of lakeside resorts. This efficient urban transit system also helped produce new residential districts along its lines that spread up to and beyond the traditional city limits. The increasing availability of autos aided this ability to live farther from smoky factories and congested streets. In 1916 *The Syracuse Herald* called these original suburbs "most conducive to health and happiness."

These new city developments drew affluent buyers who were ready to leave older neighborhoods to the new immigrants. By 1908 the first 17 houses were up in a tract laid out on the old Sedgwick Farm off James Street. Scotholm was a 1914 development along outer East Genesee. In 1919 the Strathmore tract opened to the southwest, just beyond Summit Avenue.

Their lots were larger than traditional city neighborhoods. Many could accommodate an

The court of the Kanoono Karnival around 1907: This annual celebration, run by clans of the "Mystique Krew," after the manner of a Mardi Gras, started in 1905 as a promotional activity for the State Fair. At the Karnival's height, it featured a major parade including one that literally floated down the Erie Canal.
OHA Collection

In 1910 visitors arrived at the State Fair by both auto and carriage. *OHA Collection*

"Motoring on Two Wheels"

By 1921 automobiles were a fact of life. Companies in many cities were producing thousands each month. People loved the mobility but already were challenged by traffic congestion, operating costs and parking shortages. Motorcycles existed but were considered too dangerous or awkward for the average American, especially a woman in a skirt or a well-dressed man.

A Syracuse company responded by developing what it dubbed a Nera Car. It was a two-wheeled motor scooter, designed especially for comfort. Riders sat on the vehicle, as in a chair, as opposed to straddling a motorcycle. Its low engine and center of gravity provided extra stability. Broad fenders and a covered drive mechanism offered cleanliness. It promised 85 miles to the gallon and the ability to ride to office, shop or golf course "in whatever clothes befit the occasion."

Businessmen from New Process Gear and other local firms owned the company that built the "car" in a small factory at Geddes and Fayette streets. Manufacturing rights were licensed and the Nera Car was also made in Great Britain. One owner was King Gillette, inventor of the disposable razor. Gillette advocated a utopian future with modern technology freeing cities from sprawl and pollution. The Nera Car fit his philosophy but that of relatively few others. Production lasted only a few years. Today, the cycles are a vestige of Syracuse's diverse industrial past.

The Nera Car or sometimes "Ner-A-Car" was marketed as a progressive vehicle for liberated young women in the 1920s who wished to be independent and mobile without the burden of maintaining a large auto. *OHA Collection*

A c. 1929 view shows the early development of the Bradford Hills subdivision along Meadowbrook Drive. An upscale tract, a promotional brochure labeled it an area where, "you will find neighbors of your own kind who are able to think in your terms on all matters of community interest."
OHA Collection

Syracusan Gustav Stickley advocated an entire design philosophy that extended well beyond his furniture business. He especially promoted a pure, "Craftsman" architecture. Local architect Ward Wellington Ward often produced accomplished buildings reflective of this style, such as this 1915 residence for Oak Street.
OHA Collection

automobile garage. Early-20th-century home styles abandoned the cluttered, vertical Victorian look. They copied colonial forms or sometimes echoed Mediterranean imagery. Others reflected new philosophies of a more natural, simpler lifestyle. The one-and-a-half-story bungalow seemed especially adapted to this style, and superb examples can be found throughout Syracuse. Some evoke the house designs promoted by local furniture maker Gustav Stickley, a national pioneer in establishing a new Post-Victorian design vocabulary that is much admired today. His first, trend-setting "Craftsman" interior of 1902 still exists in Syracuse, a community with a rich legacy of Arts & Crafts period artisans.

In contiguous towns, a few communities evolved that were linked to Syracuse by streetcar line and employment activity, such as Onondaga's Elmwood and Valley sections or Eastwood in

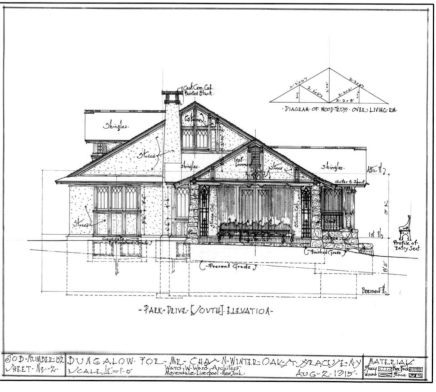

Chapter Three

The Eclectic Squire of Primrose Hill

The expansion of Syracuse through the 1920s engulfed some 19th-century estates along the outskirts. One was Primrose Hill, a picturesque gothic manor that sat on 19 acres south of downtown, about halfway to the Valley. It was built well before the Civil War but its most famous resident was the Reverend Samuel R. Calthrop, pastor of Syracuse's May Memorial Unitarian Church from 1868 until 1911. Primrose was his wife's maiden name.

Calthrop's expansive interests were legendary. A native of England, he excelled at sports. He coached crew at Yale, played and promoted tennis in Syracuse, and was a formidable chess, billiard and even boxing aficionado. He once won a chess

game in just 22 moves while playing blindfolded! In 1880 he prophetically espoused that society should provide more recreational opportunities for women.

Late one evening, the minister discovered a prowler had invaded his abode. Drawing on his pugilistic skills, the reverend floored the intruder with a single blow, where the police collected him when they arrived. Calthrop was also proficient in Latin and Greek, designed a visionary streamlined train in 1865, and actively used the telescopes he installed at his Primrose Hill observatory to become quite adept at astronomy. Old age finally caught up with the minister in 1917. His beloved estate was demolished in the 1920s and homes were developed there. Today, the east end of Calthrop Avenue points to the site of Primrose Hill, now buried under Interstate 81.

Reverend Calthrop at Primrose Hill. *OHA Collection*

Adapting a 19th century city to the auto has been a challenge for over 100 years. At first parking garages were often designed to blend in with the surrounding architecture. This 1926 example on Madison Street was demolished for the MONY office towers in 1964. *OHA Collection*

DeWitt. While there was some sentiment to remain separate, the city's professional fire and police departments, expansive school services and modern utilities beckoned. Elmwood was annexed in 1899. Eastwood joined in 1926 and the Valley followed in 1927. These additions augmented the city's population, which jumped to over 209,000 by 1930.

The auto brought even more change to Syracuse. Car registration in Onondaga County reached over 18,000 vehicles by 1920, mostly in the city. Businesses to sell, service and fuel autos sprang up everywhere. Downtown streets became choked, as cars dodged around electric railway cars or were stopped cold at the dozens of railroad grade crossings that laced the central district.

There was increased demand for paved roads. Space for parked cars became a real challenge. After the Erie Canal was filled in the 1920s, most of Clinton Square was turned into a parking lot. Curbs lined with parked autos became a permanent

image of downtown after a century of open streetscapes. Calls to improve downtown traffic flow would come to dominate city planning for the next 50 years.

But the motorized vehicle helped to revolutionize municipal services. Delivery trucks replaced horse-drawn wagons. Fire trucks were faster and more efficient than hitching up a four-legged team. Police took to patrol cars. And as internal combustion replaced horses, a nagging source of street filth disappeared.

Streets became cleaner, but Syracusans increasingly looked to the sky, as airplanes became a regular sight. Mayor Charles Hanna, a former World War I flyer, led the city to acquire its first municipal airfield in 1926. The Amboy Airport, in nearby Camillus, featured commercial flights, airmail service and the occasional but always festive visits of early flying celebrities like Charles Lindbergh, Amelia Earhart and Wiley Post.

Enduring the Depression

The 1920s had brought some bad news to the local economy. The last remnants of salt-making

shut down in 1926 and there had been some fall-out from the great experiment of Prohibition. Syracuse had a large population of dedicated beer drinkers who supported a dozen local breweries, most on the north side. Prohibition's arrival in 1919 hit local producers hard and only four breweries would survive: Haberle, Bartels, Moore & Quinn and Greenway.

Onondaga Lake Park was dedicated in 1933. Its re-creation of two historical sites reflected the mutual interests of its original advocate, Joseph Griffin, and the local public works administrator, Crandall Melvin, Sr. *OHA Collection*

But most industries were humming in the late 1920s, housing tracts were rising all over the city, municipal finances were stable, and three major new buildings had just been completed downtown: Loew's State Theater and office tower, the Hills Building and the tallest ever, the 22-story, art deco State Tower. Local residents looked to the future with confidence.

The stock market crash that ushered in the Great Depression on October 29, 1929, changed the playing field. Thousands lost their jobs. Home and commercial construction practically ceased. Some industries and businesses adapted, but several could not. Onondaga Pottery and others cut back hours or production lines and survived. Franklin Manufacturing, which made a famed but expensive car, had no lower-priced model to help it weather the contraction of its market. Franklin developed a relatively inexpensive Olympic model in 1932, but it was too late. The company that once was Syracuse's largest employer declared

bankruptcy in 1934. Between 1929 and 1933, it was estimated that Syracuse lost almost 50 percent of its industrial jobs, impacting 13,000 workers and their families.

Franklin Roosevelt was New York's governor until 1933. He initiated a public works program at the state level that served as a model for later federal efforts. An Emergency Work Bureau was created in Onondaga County under the administration of banker Crandall Melvin Sr. Supplied with state dollars, it undertook a series of reforestation and park building projects that gave birth to the county parks system.

In 1918 the state had opened its new Barge Canal, making the old Erie and Oswego canal routes through Syracuse obsolete. They had been quickly filled and turned into streets. But along the east side of Onondaga Lake, the Oswego decayed into a stagnant mess. Local businessman Joseph Griffin envisioned a landscaped parkway, with recreational grounds and historical museums celebrating the community's salt and colonial heritage. Melvin's troops were set loose. By 1933 Onondaga Lake Park, the Salt Museum and the re-created 17th-century mission of Sainte Marie were opened, all linked by an attractive parkway. This park is now one of Greater Syracuse's most treasured resources. And it provided precious jobs for the hundreds of previously unemployed men who built it.

One park worker reported that he had quit his Onondaga Pottery job when cut back to just two days a week. Helping construct Onondaga Lake Park, he made $8 per week. About half went to groceries for his family and another $2 for rent. He set aside $1 for installment payments left over from purchases made in better times. He and his wife had little left for clothes so wore hand me downs from others. Yet he was happy to have the work rather than be idle and "on the dole."

At the lake's Syracuse end, where empty yards of the once mighty salt industry lay, Griffin hoped to see a lakefront park for the city. But the city preferred economic development. The state had constructed a terminal for the Barge Canal there

The last New York Central passenger trains rumbled down Washington Street in 1936. They were relocated to a new elevated route, construction of which provided hundreds of jobs during the Depression. *Painting by L. F. Tantillo, commissioned by Key Bank N.A.*

and Syracuse officials hoped it would draw new industries to the site. It eventually did. A forest of metal storage tanks arose as transporting fuel oil and gasoline by barge became the major use for the terminal district. A scattering of other small businesses filled in between. It was not seen as a problem to open a municipal sewage treatment plant in this industrial area in 1925. In fact, it was considered great progress in treating a growing civic problem. Syracuse traded off direct public access to its lake shore a second time for the lure of economic progress.

Other work opportunities arose in the 1930s with a massive railroad track relocation, a $23.5 million public-private effort that elevated all of the dangerous grade crossings throughout the city by 1940. The job employed nearly 1,900 men for four years. It had been a controversial undertaking, in the planning stages since 1911, as politicians, railroad executives, planning consultants and citizens argued about the best solution. Some wanted the trains re-routed north of the city. But many residents and businessmen could not comprehend their downtown without major rail stations, so the tracks were elevated through the center city. One line is still used today for a local rail shuttle.

Area leaders took a lemon and made lemonade when the city foreclosed on the sprawling, empty Franklin factory. They virtually gave it away in 1937 as an incentive to lure a promising manufacturer from New Jersey. The arrival of Carrier air-conditioning brought 1,000 much-needed jobs almost overnight. In the 1940s Carrier moved from Geddes Street to modern facilities in DeWitt where it built an international headquarters.

But problems continued elsewhere. In 1929 Remington Rand employed 1,350 Syracusans making typewriters on Gifford Street. Efforts by the company to consolidate in 1936 and move local production out of town resulted in union action and a strike. It was marked by months of violence, near riots and bombings as the company opposed union efforts and resorted to strikebreakers. Eventually federal rulings sided with the union, but production never returned to normal. The plant was closed in 1939.

The city administration of Mayor Rollie Marvin was aggressive in seeking aid and provided other jobs by tapping into Roosevelt's national Works Progress Administration. WPA funding repaved city streets, removing obsolete streetcar rails as buses replaced the electric lines. Syracuse also used federal dollars to renovate schools and improve several parks including Burnet and Elmwood. The latter retains picturesque stonework of that era. Clinton Square's unsightly parking lot was replaced with grass, pine trees and a small fountain.

One of America's first public housing projects was undertaken in the depressed 15th Ward. Financed by the Federal Housing Administration, several blocks along McBride Street were leveled in 1938 and replaced with two- and three-story brick apartments known as Pioneer Homes. Due in part to efforts by the Dunbar Center, about 7 percent of the 730 initial resident families were African-American. Pioneer's units, many of which still exist, offered promise of improved housing conditions for those trapped in slum neighborhoods.

Additionally, through federal programs, library books were rebound, clothes sewn for the poor and housekeeping aides provided to needy homes. A new regional market was opened in 1938 on Park Street. But the major appropriations from Washington for the city went into sewer work including a $2.25 million installation at Ley Creek. At the height of WPA funding, there were almost 8,700 men and women employed throughout the county on agency-backed projects.

Entertainment also played a vital role in dealing with the hardships of the Depression. A triumph during the 1930s was the return of a professional baseball team to Syracuse. The legendary Stars had left for Rochester in 1928 when the city refused to build a new ballpark. But Depression-era mayor Rollie Marvin enticed an International League franchise to move from Jersey City with the construction of a new north side field in 1934. A public contest resulted in the club's name, Syracuse Chiefs. Later, Municipal Stadium was renamed after General Douglas MacArthur during the patriotic years of World War II. Beloved MacArthur Stadium was home to the franchise, now the SkyChiefs, until the tired facility was replaced by P&C Stadium in 1997.

Syracuse Songsters

Talented musicians and composers have long called Syracuse home. Harold Arlen, a prolific songwriter who won an Oscar in 1940 for "Over the Rainbow", vistited his family here often. His father, Samuel Arluck, was a cantor at Temple Adath Yeshuran. Another composer was Edward C. Babcock, better known as Jimmy Van Heusen, a native Syracusan who once lived on Roberts Avenue. Van Heusen penned the familiar "Swinging on a Star," introduced by Bing Crosby in the 1944 classic film, *Going My Way*. Others carry on the tradition today in a variety of folk, classical, pop, blues and jazz forms.

Some local composers have even been inspired by their own hometown. As early as 1852, Syracusan J. S. Jacobus published the "Onondaga Polka." Henry J. Lautz turned out the "Salt City March" in 1886. And in 1912, F. Davis created the sentimental lyrics for, "I'm Glad I'm Back in Syracuse," in which the homesick songster predicts that, upon his return, "Gee! Won't Salina Street look good to me."

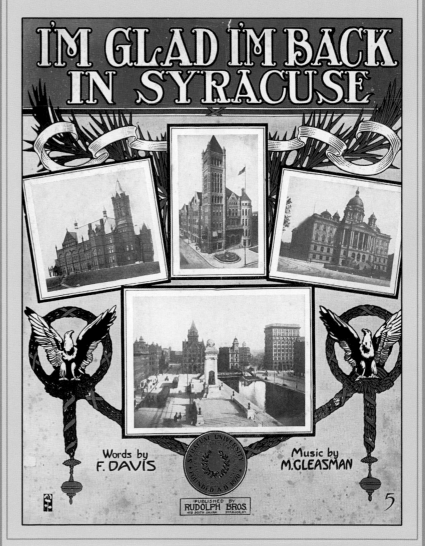

Fayetteville Free Library — Motto Sheet Music Collection

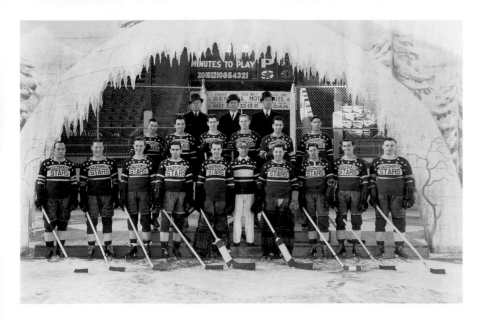

The AHL Syracuse Stars in December 1936. *OHA Collection*

(Below and right) Radios, like this typical 1930s model, linked Syracusans with the rest of the country. This 1941 promotional photo from WAGE was for the *Club Merry-Go-Round* radio show, which aired at 3 p.m. from its downtown studios in the Loew Building. *OHA Collection*

The Stars name had re-surfaced in 1930 when Syracuse organized its first professional hockey franchise. Playing in the State Fair Coliseum for the decade, the Stars skated well enough to snag the American Hockey League's first Calder Cup Championship in 1937. But the Depression found its way in. Dropping revenues led to the team folding in 1940.

Movie houses continued to shine bright on Salina Street and at dozens of neighborhood sites. The latter included the Palace on James Street, the Cameo along South Geddes, the Alcazar on Oakwood and the Avon at 443 Hawley. For a

mere quarter, movies and their ornate palaces transported Syracusans far from unemployment and bread lines. And if Hollywood provided escape for only one or two nights, there was radio the rest of the week.

Radio arrived in Onondaga County during the early 1920s. The roots of WSYR and WFBL start in 1922. WOLF became a third broadcaster in 1940 and WAGE (later WHEN) followed in 1941. During the 30s, shows such as "Death Valley Days," "Captain Henry's Show Boat," "Lowell Thomas," "Tom Mix," "Jack Armstrong," "Lum & Abner" and "Abe Lyman's Orchestra" helped Central New Yorkers temporarily overlook their hardships. Radio also brought President Roosevelt's comforting fireside chats.

On October 30, 1938, Syracuse listeners of WFBL truly forgot the economy when the Mercury Theater presented its famous contemporary dramatization of H.G. Wells' "War of the Worlds." Police and newspaper phone lines were jammed with hundreds of frantic calls looking for more information about the attack from Mars. One Howlett Hill resident grabbed his family and headed off for Canada by car, stopping for his mother in-law on the way. The next day brought calm as the realization set in that America had been subjected to the creative talents of Orson Welles. Syracusans scrambled for copies of the original science fiction work but there were none. Local bookstores didn't stock it and the library's only copy, an old one, had been lost for years. Orders were quickly placed.

The Home Front During Two World Wars

The panic produced by "War of the Worlds" was due, in part, to the tense international situation of the late 1930s. The Axis powers were on the march and fighting was already terrorizing the Far East. Full-scale world war started in

OVER THE TOP FOR YOU

Buy U.S. Gov't Bonds
THIRD LIBERTY LOAN

Come On!

buy more LIBERTY BONDS

1939 and America was dragged in by the 1941 attack on Pearl Harbor.

Like everyone, Central New Yorkers were stunned by the surprise atrocity. Patriotism and resolve quickly replaced shock. The economy had been slowly recovering throughout the late 1930s. Syracuse had suffered but also made surprising progress during the period. Now, however, there would be a role for everyone. And the city's manufacturing strength would soon swing into action.

For those over 30, it was all too familiar. World War I, had been over for barely two decades. Nearly 12,000 Onondaga County men had marched off to that horror. Syracuse industry had also responded in 1917. Local factories provided parts for army trucks and the Solvay Process Company produced explosives at its Split Rock quarry, just west of the city. A hellish explosion there on July 2, 1918, cost 50 workers their lives. Additionally, residents suffered through a serious coal shortage during the winter of 1917-18 and a deadly influenza pandemic the following fall that killed 908 people in Syracuse.

In May 1917 a huge training and military assembly camp was established on the state fairgrounds. Thousands of soldiers from around the country quartered there prior to reorganization and reassignment. Hundreds of area women knitted socks for the Red Cross to send overseas. Others pitched in at the local chapter's Canteen Service site, which hosted over 330,000 troops passing through Syracuse by truck and train. Volunteers distributed coffee, refreshments, cigarettes and

Patriotic posters could be seen around the Syracuse area during World War I. They were used to recruit soldiers and sailors, promote sales of government bonds and encourage donations to the Red Cross.
OHA Collection

Dora Hazard (fourth from left, first row) organized a unit of hospital volunteers who went to London in 1918. She was the widow of Frederick R. Hazard, head of the Solvay Process chemical firm, and had already established a sizable track record as a leader in social and educational innovations among Solvay workers.
OHA Collection

SCRAP RUBBER
3 RUBBERS Make 1 ARMY OVERSHOE

SCRAP HARVEST DRIVE Sept 21- Oct 5

GENERAL MOTORS TRUCK

(Above and center) Local scrap drives during World War II not only secured goods for recycling into needed war materials, they helped unify the community in a patriotic effort to support those serving in the armed forces.
OHA Collection

stamps. Still others joined ambulance companies or packaged bandages.

Syracuse men and women wound up in several different infantry, artillery, airborne, naval and hospital units. But World War I was the last war in which a military organization might also consist largely of citizens from one community. Company C of the 27th Division's 108th Infantry was such a group. It arrived in France in May 1918. By September Company C was in the thick of the fighting. Between September 29 and October 1, the 27th helped break the previously impregnable Hindenburg Line, and the sons of Syracuse were there. The local casualties were numerous, more than seen since the Civil War. Germany surrendered on November 11, but 318 men from Onondaga County never returned.

BOYS AND GIRLS
JOIN THE BIG
RUBBER
Treasure Hunt
OF ONONDAGA COUNTY
August 10 to August 24
PRIZES

People marched down Washington Street on July 4, 1919, in a huge victory parade past a colonnade of classical columns in Vanderbilt Square containing battle memorials. One of these original plaques is now in the collection of the Onondaga Historical Association.

In the 1940s home front efforts were even more extensive. Local factories expanded to fill a flood of defense contracts. There was a shortage of workers as an estimated 40,000 Onondaga County men volunteered or were drafted into military service. To help, thousands of women left house-keeping chores to take positions on area assembly lines. Children assisted by collecting metal and rubber for scrap drives and tended family victory gardens to ease demand on the food reserve. Bond drives became common to raise money. Air raids were practiced, emptying

Salina Street of people in the middle of the day and darkening the city in the evening. And there were ration books to mind for gasoline, tires, shoes, meat, butter and other staples in short supply.

Brown-Lipe-Chapin made machine guns, testing them on the roof of its west side plant. The Easy Washer Company built anti-aircraft gun mounts and bomb fuses. Onondaga Pottery developed an effective ceramic mine, invisible to metal detectors. Remington Rand reopened its closed typewriter factory and produced 45mm automatic pistols.

Scrap drives were a regular occurrence. Amazing volumes of tin cans, rubber, waste metal and rags were gathered. Most of it was junk, but nothing seemed exempt in making a supreme effort. A number of trophies from earlier wars were sacrificed. American Legion Post 41 contributed a six-ton World War I German cannon. Abandoned railway bridges were razed and donated. The Syracuse fire department gave up a prized 19th-century steam pumper. The 1870 cast iron fence around Fayette Park was even considered. Fortunately, it still graces downtown.

It was often a challenge to find certain goods. There was a line around the Doust camera store when 1,000 roles of film arrived one day in 1945. They were sold out in one hour. Nylon stockings were almost impossible to buy. The first to arrive in Syracuse after the war did not show up until December 1945, resulting in over 1,700 persons waiting outside the store to each grab a single pair.

But the sacrifices on oceans and battlefields thousands of miles from Central New York overshadowed all. A young generation, raised in the Depression, was called

in record numbers to continue its sacrifices and win freedom for millions. Over 1,000 county residents paid the ultimate price with their lives.

The victories over Germany and Japan in 1945 were also achieved by the application of America's economic muscle and effective new technologies. Like Americans everywhere, the young men and women of Syracuse and Onondaga County concluded World War II with the determination to make a safe and prosperous future for their families.

Onondaga County women went by the thousands to work in area factories during World War II. *OHA Collection*

The increasing numbers of women at the Easy Washer Company promoted the athletic opportunities for a female softball team. *OHA Collection*

The surrender of Japan on August 14, 1945, drew crowds of revelers to downtown Syracuse. One of the happiest places that day was the USO bureau near Columbus Circle. An entire generation would remember that moment for the rest of their lives. *OHA Collection*

CHAPTER *Four*

Meeting the Challenges of a Changing Nation

Central New Yorkers who fought World War II returned to face a changing social and economic landscape. The New Deal and the wartime economy had helped pull Syracuse from the depths of the Depression. But they also opened up industrial growth in southern and western states that would be future competitors.

During the 1950s and 60s, the Syracuse area expanded into new manufacturing fields, such as electronics, as old technologies were swept away. But as with many communities in the Northeast, the city's industrial might slowly and painfully waned. Yet in becoming leaner, it spawned a more diversified and resilient economy. The population became more diverse too. Southern African-Americans streamed north seeking economic opportunity and, although sometimes challenged with adversities, sought to make their own contributions to Syracuse.

The city, which had been growing continuously since its founding, watched new, idyllic suburbs draw residents away from its neighborhoods. Syracuse studied itself and ventured into urban renewal with hopes of reversing the trend. The formula had its successes, but often at a disturbing price. In the process, the city discovered that some of its aging 19th-century

(Previous page)
As the 20th century came to a close, Syracuse's focus increasingly shifted toward a rediscovery of its waterfront location at the head of Onondaga Lake.
Photo by John Dowling

(Below)
A display of television sets for sale in the early 1950s at Chappell's department store.
OHA Collection

structures could be a key to revival, along with a long-neglected lakefront. Syracuse also realized the value of having cultural strength and, most recently, its potential as a tourist destination.

As it confidently shapes a dynamic future, Syracuse seeks not to forget the value of knowing a distinctive past, one that bestows both identity and inspiration upon all its citizens.

Television:
A Symbol of the Postwar Years

As Central New Yorkers moved past the Depression and World War II, they looked to a brighter future, a revitalized economy and new technologies to enjoy. One recent invention would have a major impact on their lives — television. Early in 1948 America had only 16 stations. By 1950 it had climbed to 100. Programs rose in number and quality, and advertising revenue increased, fueling the growth.

The Meredith Company, an Iowa-based magazine publisher and radio station owner, decided in 1948 to expand into the new medium. It secured a license for the Syracuse market and rapidly set to work. A former factory on Syracuse's north side was acquired for studios. A young staff and crew were assembled. Renovations and equipment installation proceeded at a hectic pace. It was hoped that the signal would reach at least 10 miles to Cicero.

On December 1, 1948, local history was made at 8:32 p.m. when the estimated 40 or so sets in the Syracuse area received the city's first local TV broadcast on WHEN, channel 8. Some people watched at home, but many saw the two-hour local show on sets in downtown stores or area taverns.

WHEN was the third television station in the state, outside of New York City. For the next year, WHEN broadcast strictly local programs and film shorts. It was December 1949 before WHEN secured network connections from CBS.

A second station, WSYR, opened in 1950 on channel 3. Syracuse became the first city in upstate New York with two stations. WSYR already operated a local radio station; TV was a logical expansion. The new station, located in downtown's Kemper Building, affiliated with the NBC network. In 1958 WSYR opened its current facilities on James Street. When the radio and TV operations were separated in 1979, the TV half changed to WSTM.

WHEN-TV *Creates A New Children's Show and a Central New York Icon*

In 1953 WHEN-TV celebrated its fifth anniversary. Its audience had grown from about 100 sets to 400,000. General Manager Paul Adanti and Program Director Gordon Alderman assembled an advisory panel of teachers, parents, librarians and educators to consult on the development of a new program for children. TV was still in its infancy and there was concern about it simply entrancing children and not engaging them. The station's public affairs programmer, Jean Daugherty, was selected to develop a pilot.

Daugherty created a make-believe world of stories and plush toy animals, centered on a place known as the *Magic Toy Shop*. Following more than a year of fine-tuning, the program debuted on February 28, 1955. It would become one of the longest-running local children's television shows in the country.

Five main characters were the "residents" of the make-believe shop: Merrily, Eddie Flum Num, Mr. Trolley, Twinkle the clown and the Play Lady. For 27 years, their morning visits with children provided a setting for original stories, music and songs, local talent, children's films and educational visits to many places. Knowing these characters became part of what identifies a Central New Yorker.

Jean Daugherty, the creative soul and guiding light of the *Magic Toy Shop*, played a pioneering role for women in Central New York TV. She went on to produce and script countless special programs for WTVH, including a well-loved annual Christmas show. But the necessity to create a new character for the show, when hostess Merrily (Merrilyn Hubbard Herr) took maternity leave, forever bestowed upon her the devoted title as the "Play Lady" for generations of Central New Yorkers.

"Magic Toy Shop" cast and set, including creator Jean Daugherty at center in her role as the "Play Lady" *OHA Collection*

Television spread rapidly in the early 1950s. Production of "receivers" soared. Programs and advertising increasingly shaped the schedule of people's lives, the news they learned and the lifestyle they sought. Entertainers like Lucille Ball, Milton Berle, Sid Caesar, Arthur Godfrey and Howdy Doody became national figures.

Local programming also remained a staple. News, weather and sports, community education and talent contests were broadcast. With aspects unique to each community, these shows became a shared symbol of geographic identity for residents.

The federal government eventually approved a third channel for Syracuse and WNYS went on the air as channel 9 in 1962. The proximity of its signal to WHEN's channel 8 resulted in the latter's switch to 5. WNYS became the ABC network's first full affiliate in Syracuse. The station survived a devastating fire at its Shoppingtown studios in 1967 and rebuilt. It moved to its current Bridge Street headquarters in 1985. By then, its call letters had changed to WIXT.

Educational TV developed as a non-commercial format. It offered informative programming,

(Opposite page top) Channel 3's local variety TV show during the 1950s starred Jim DeLine and his "Gang." *OHA Collection*

including shows for instructional use in schools. Central New York's ETV station went on the air in December 1965 as channel 24, with a frequency in the UHF range. This created an early challenge since most TV sets, except the very latest, were not equipped to receive UHF. WCNY-TV today provides a wide range of cultural and educational offerings and is known for quality local programs along with those on the PBS system.

Local cable TV first arrived in Syracuse and Onondaga County during the 1970s. The expansion of cable TV broadcasting in the 1980s added even more local stations. WSYT, channel 68, came on the air in 1987 as part of the Fox network. WNYS, of the UPN network began in 1991, followed by WSPX in 1998.

After several buyouts and mergers in the industry, local cable service came to rest with Time Warner Cable in 1997. In early 2002 its local management decided to undertake an exciting multimillion-dollar renovation of Syracuse's

1936 landmark New York Central Railroad station. Train traffic had permanently left the terminal in 1962. Following several years of service as a bus station, the once handsome Art Deco facility sat empty and forlorn. The landmark is housing Time Warner Cable's 24-hour regional news channel.

A Changing Economic Portfolio

Television shows and stations were not the only impact the new medium had locally. In 1945 General Electric broke ground for a massive new 155-acre campus for research and production near Liverpool named Electronics Park. Soon thousands of employees were developing both sophisticated radar equipment and assembling TV sets for the burgeoning consumer market. Employment levels blossomed so rapidly, reaching 9,000 by 1950, that electronics promised to become Syracuse's new signature enterprise, replacing the fading typewriter industry.

Reception building at
GE's Electronics Park.
OHA Collection

A 1956 magazine ad of an ideal basement family room, complete with an essential TV set, reflects the suburban lifestyle that was marketed during the 1950s. Such efforts helped fuel the interest in moving out of the city to new developments surrounding Syracuse. *OHA Collection*

Meanwhile, Carrier expanded east to DeWitt. One mile south, Bristol Laboratories opened a new pharmaceutical plant. The landscape of manufacturing in Syracuse was changing. Industries that had survived the Depression were abandoning their inefficient, crowded 19th-century city factories for the suburbs. Expansive tracts outside the city provided more productive, one-level manufacturing. Products involved increasingly sophisticated electronic components or chemical compounds, requiring sophisticated research by highly trained specialists in state-of-the-art laboratories, rather than by machinists in greasy shops. GE's decision to build a world-class complex here was influenced by the proximity to Syracuse University.

The skyrocketing television market and equally burgeoning defense business of the Cold War era energized GE and it spread to 19 area locations by 1960. Employee levels passed 17,000 in the mid-1960s. This fueled a demand for housing, especially north of Syracuse, creating a suburban explosion of developments, like Bayberry, with associated school and retail expansion.

But eventually, an increasingly global economy beckoned with cheaper, offshore labor opportunities. GE's local TV set production was based on vacuum tube technology. But solid-state transistors were the future. In 1972, rather than engage in expensive retooling, TV set manufacturing was moved out of town. Picture tube production remained but GE sold off its consumer lines in the late 1980s and those jobs left town too. By the 1990s the work force had slipped to under 3,000. GE sold the entire local operation, limited mainly to sonar defense contracts, to Martin Marietta in 1992. When the new owner consolidated with Lockheed in 1995, the underutilized Electronics Park, once a world-leading facility, almost closed. But local leaders assembled a package of incentives that retained and expanded operations.

It was a story often repeated in Central New York and the Northeast over the last 50 years. Competition with Sunbelt or foreign sites drew production away. Promising firms were bought by out of town conglomerates. Advances in air transportation and telecommunications allowed managers to command production from far-flung locations. Even Syracuse's signature headquarters operation, the Carrier Corporation, was purchased by United Technologies of Connecticut in 1979. These trends have produced a large loss of local manufacturing jobs since 1950.

But the local economy has evolved in positive ways, as well. Sometimes acquisitions have

The Syracuse University campus, about 1903, is visible in the distance of this postcard view. The surrounding homes were mostly still private residences at this time. *OHA Collection*

strengthened and preserved area companies, by bringing new investment and more expert management. GE may be gone, but a number of the bright engineering minds it concentrated here stayed and developed new firms of their own. They may be smaller, but Onondaga County still boasts these and other companies using cutting edge technology to produce a variety of telecommunications, electronics and diagnostic medical equipment.

Higher Education Assumes a Prominent Role

Another major factor in the evolving postwar period was the increasing value of higher education to the local economy and identity. Syracuse University, chartered in 1870, held its first classes in rented downtown space in 1871. In 1873 it moved to a single building, still called the Hall of Languages, on a sparsely populated hill overlooking the city. The following year, it boasted 177 students.

The liberal arts college grew slowly at first, then its pace picked up in the early 20th century with aggressive expansion under James Roscoe Day, chancellor from 1894 to 1922. During his tenure student enrollment increased from 700 to nearly 6,000. Several classical-style buildings were added to the original row of Victorian structures to form a traditional campus quad. The university held a significant but modest presence in the community's life, but that began to change rapidly after World War II.

The GI bill brought more than 1 million veterans to America's colleges. Syracuse University admitted 9,706 in 1946–47, almost tripling its enrollment. While the school played catch-up to house them all, the influx began SU's growth into a major university. That maturity created new programs that benefited the local economic and cultural life of Syracuse while expanding the university's work force to nearly 5,000 today.

SU's Maxwell School is highly regarded in the field of social science and public administration. The Drama Department and its associated

Syracuse Stage facility produce plays of Broadway caliber. The campus' Lowe Art Gallery maintains a remarkable collection. Several high-tech research programs housed at the university also give the area advantages in computer intelligence, biomedicine and indoor environmental quality. Syracuse University's Newhouse School is a leader in training for the media industry.

Adjacent to SU is another local college, often overshadowed by its bigger brother. It was 1911 when the State University of New York's College of Environmental Science and Forestry began, a collaboration between chancellor Day and powerful local state senator Francis Hendricks. The school used SU's Lyman Hall until 1917 when its first building, Bray Hall, was completed. The school continues to maintain a special relationship with Syracuse University where Forestry students also take courses. The school enjoyed renewed interest with the environmental movement of the 1960s.

(Top)
Syracuse University opened its immense stadium in 1907, underwritten by a gift from John Archbold, Standard Oil executive and cohort of John D. Rockefeller. It was the largest concrete stadium in America when finished and a community landmark until replaced by the Carrier Dome in 1980.
OHA Collection

The 1930 construction of Marshall Hall expanded the New York State Forestry School campus. The governor at the time, Franklin D. Roosevelt, had a keen interest in the institution that reflected his own curiosity for land management issues.
OHA Collection

It has expanded into a national center for the study of environmental resource management, wood products engineering, paper science, landscape architecture and forest biology, with over 400 employees and 1,700 full-time students.

On a second hill, two miles east of SU, another campus was born in 1948. Administered by the Jesuit order, LeMoyne College fulfilled the long-term dream of Syracuse Bishop Walter A. Foery to establish a local Catholic college. Classes were first held downtown and in a former James Street mansion until the first building opened on what is known as LeMoyne Heights. The campus grew steadily over the next half century. LeMoyne established its own sporting traditions, with the dolphin as the college symbol. It has also achieved national recognition as a leading small liberal arts college with an enrollment of 2,900 during the 2004-2005 academic year.

In 1950 financial challenges led Syracuse University to transfer its medical college to the State University system. The medical school had beginnings in 1834 at Geneva, New York, affiliated with Hobart College, then moved and became part of SU in 1871. Its presence led to a concentration of hospitals near the campus including Good Shepherd in 1875, Crouse-Irving in 1912 and Memorial Hospital in 1929. In 1953 the federal government opened a 500-bed medical center nearby to service a large number of World War II veterans. Eventually, the state erected its own University Hospital in 1964. There is a continuing concentration and expansion of medical and associated facilities adjacent to the extensive SU campus, giving University Hill a skyline rivaling downtown Syracuse. They also make health care and medical research a vital segment of the local economy. Syracuse University and the Upstate Medical University are the county's top two employers, with a combined total of nearly 11,000 employees.

A local technical college began to take shape in 1961 as Onondaga County partnered with the state university system to organize a two-year "community college." Classes began in 1962. Its initial home was the former Smith typewriter factory on East Water Street, revitalized as a commercial space known as Midtown Plaza. But an increasingly bitter debate arose about the permanent location. It revolved around a common postwar issue. Should this new college be in a city or suburban location? Being a county decision, the debate raged in the local press, on street corners and in the halls of the courthouse for nearly five years.

Many Syracuse officials hoped a new college campus could aid downtown urban renewal efforts, perhaps adjacent to Clinton Square. This position was strongly backed by the *Syracuse Herald Journal,* which editorialized that a technical college did not require athletic fields, arts buildings or grassy quads. Onondaga Community College (OCC) administration and new County Executive John Mulroy leaned strongly toward a large suburban location, where acres of adequate parking could be accommodated. Also a rural campus would allow for additional facilities since many wanted the school to also offer the well-rounded beginnings of a liberal arts education.

Several sites were considered, including the state fairgrounds, near Electronics Park, at the

A Castle Over Onondaga's Vale

One of Syracuse's most distinctive residences was a mere two years old when an 1854 print featured it overlooking the young city. Cornelius T. Longstreet made his fortune in the clothing business. He selected a prominent hillside on which to build a spectacular home to showcase his status,

with dramatic views up and down the Onondaga Valley. Longstreet hired one of America's leading architects, James Renwick. Renwick, who is most remembered today as the designer of the 1847 Smithsonian Castle, created a similar-looking Gothic abode in Syracuse. But the Longstreets soon tired of the remote location and traded for the James Street home of Alonzo Yates.

The Yates family enjoyed their unique acquisition for many years but the grand estate eventually was taken over by an expanding Syracuse University in 1906. Last used to house the school of journalism, the remarkably intact structure was sold to New York State, which quickly demolished it in 1953 to expand its medical college. Only a portion of its stone fence remains along Irving Avenue. If standing today, the "Castle" would be one of America's most famous architectural landmarks.

Yates Castle in 1854 and again in 1953, *OHA Collection*

northwest corner of Onondaga Lake, on former railroad yards along Erie Boulevard West, and among the pastures of the Pompey hills. Finally, by 1966 it came down to an existing county-owned farm in the town of Onondaga or a downtown urban renewal site. A public referendum was considered but rejected. County and college officials finally pushed through the picturesque Onondaga site. Construction was underway by 1969.

OCC has been a successful component of local educational opportunities for over 40 years, offering both skilled technical training as well as launching college careers for many who continue elsewhere toward baccalaureate degrees.

New Suburbs Alter Traditional Patterns

The 1960s odyssey over where to build OCC reflected the era's shift of population growth from Syracuse to surrounding towns and the momentum of financial might from city to county. These trends continue today and form ongoing debates about the future.

This population movement was underway throughout the 1950s. New housing tracts were sprouting in towns to the north, east and west. South of Syracuse sat the Onondaga Territory, essentially a sovereign Native American nation. Also south stood a hilly landscape, dominated by dairy farms and corn fields, with geology and topography that challenged developers. The traditional transportation networks already spread east and west. And to the north lay flat farmland, reaching toward Oneida Lake, easily laid out into suburban housing patterns. Also north was Syracuse's new commercial airfield, a converted World War II-era B-24 and B-17 bomber base. It opened in the town of Salina as the Clarence

E. Hancock Airport in 1949, helping stimulate growth in that direction.

Suburbs meant escape from tightly packed, 19th-century street patterns, often lined with dingy factories, populated by an increasing number of minorities, and congested with more and more autos. Once postwar prosperity arrived, many returning veterans wanted to start new families and live the peaceful promise of the future that they had won. The new, neat suburbs seemed just the place.

Since Syracuse's last streetcar had run in 1941, the once all-important electric railway lines were gone, officially replaced by buses. The Eisenhower administration committed to

building a new system of superhighways, ostensibly a vital transportation strategy for national defense, but essentially linking the nation together by car. One proposed route, dubbed the Empire Stateway, ran north and south directly through Syracuse and was under construction by 1958. It became part of Interstate 81 and provided a convenient new commuter route.

The federal government also encouraged banks to provide generous mortgages in these new suburbs. Surrounding towns welcomed the increased tax revenue. It was more money than small family farms, descended from 19th-century settlement, were paying.

Early postwar housing tracts, like this 1952 Town of Geddes development, often featured small, quickly erected homes set in repetitive, unadorned vistas. Later on, suburban homes grew larger, predominately split levels and raised ranches, featuring popular family rooms and more agreeable landscaping.
OHA Collection

(Below) Highways carved up American cities in the postwar years and Syracuse was no exception. The connections of Interstate 81 with the Route 690 arterial in 1967 introduced an intimidating series of elevated roads to downtown's east side. They effectively segregated the University Hill complex from the center city.
OHA Collection

This new pattern was obvious in the 1960 census. Syracuse's population had peaked in 1950 at 220,583, with the rest of the county standing at just 121,136. By 1960 the city had begun to slip, falling to 216,000. But the population outside Syracuse climbed dramatically, reaching almost 207,000. Within one decade, the long-expanding city had stalled while the surrounding towns pulled almost even. By 1970 the evidence was unmistakable. Syracuse was down to 197,208 while the county beyond

Westvale Plaza, seen here in 1961, was developed after World War II at the western edge of the city. It was one of the community's first shopping plazas and still exists, although the Genesee Theater was demolished for an auto parts chain store. *OHA Collection*

it soared to nearly 275,000. There also was a general slowdown in overall growth in the region as jobs moved to the western and southern states. The 2000 census showed Syracuse had just 147,306 residents while the towns were home to over 311,000 inhabitants, a 32 to 68 percent split.

The impact in the towns varied. Some saw growth early in the 1950s and 60s, then a slow down. Camillus jumped 172 percent during the 1950s but actually lost population between 1980 and 2000, stabilizing at about 23,000. Fabius only went from 1,432 in 1950 to 1,974 in 2000, retaining its predominately hilly and agricultural look like much of Onondaga County's southern reaches. Salina, Clay, Cicero and Lysander to the north and Manlius to the east absorbed the majority of suburban expansion.

There were no corner stores at the end of suburban streets. Cars brought one to shopping plazas such as Northern Lights, Fairmount Fair and Shoppingtown, which all opened in the 1950s. Malls followed. Smaller retail plazas, giant chain stores and fast food outlets spread across the landscape, shifting locations and appearance in a never-ending strategy of finding the optimum location and style. Erie Boulevard through DeWitt, Route 11 toward North Syracuse and West Genesee Street into Camillus transformed into quintessential suburban retail strips in the

1960s and 1970s. Towns approving new housing tracts sought new roads and schools. The roads filled with new stores to pay more taxes for new schools and new sewers. And the new stores brought more traffic on to the new roads.

The movement continues with some tracts now boasting multi-gabled homes of more than 3,000 square feet, three bathrooms and costing $300,000 or more. But simple or elaborate, virtually all the housing built since World War II in Onondaga County has been auto dependent, spreading the same population out over a wider area.

This has left the city, with 70,000 fewer people than it once had, overloaded with abandoned houses and managing a declining tax base. That has impacted resources for schools, which, in turn, are a major factor in where people want to live. Altering that cycle, by attracting residents to stay in the city or return to it, remains a challenge.

The Struggles of Urban Renewal

"...urban renewal is for people — not just for government or private redevelopers. It can make the city more comfortable and bring people who have left for the suburbs back to it."

Syracuse Planning Commissioner Sanford Getreu, January 24, 1965

Of Lost and Unborn Landmarks

The proposed 22-story Primex Building, a combination downtown hotel and office tower, excited the community with its plans for a rooftop revolving restaurant and outdoor pool. Footings were installed during 1963 at the northwest corner of Warren and James Street. Then, construction halted. Financing disappeared when addition of another new downtown office building, MONY Plaza, was announced. The Primex footings were buried, where they remain today, beneath a surface parking lot.

The first phase of the Primex project had called for a supporting parking garage. That unique, oval structure did go up in 1963, prominently located at the southeast corner of James and Warren streets. The design, by King & King architects of Syracuse, reminded some of Frank Lloyd Wright's Guggenheim Museum in New York City, finished four years earlier. It was the only part of the Primex dream that was completed and, until its demolition in 1981, provided Syracuse with one of its most unusual architectural legacies.

Clinton Square's monumental courthouse opened in 1857. It was replaced in 1906 by the "new" courthouse on Columbus Circle but continued to serve government functions. Editorials in the early 1960s called for its preservation. Original urban renewal plans emphasized a need to save it. Dreams of re-use were promoted but legal landmark protections were not available at the time. One day, urban renewal plans changed. The limestone courthouse was pulled down in 1968. As a gesture toward public sentiment, the stones of its three-story tower were saved to be re-erected. Over 35 years later, they still lay in storage.

"The imposing limestone edifice certainly lends character to Clinton Square. Extensive plans for the development of the Square as the north downtown anchor are being prepared, and the courthouse should, if possible, be a part of that renovation."

From a Syracuse *Post-Standard* editorial, November 1964

The Third Onondaga County Courthouse and the Primex Parking Garage, *OHA Collection*

Syracuse began looking to reinvent itself following World War II. Older parts seemed neglected and frayed. The suburbs were a new competitor. By the 1960s the federal government was ready to pour large urban renewal dollars into cities. Syracuse city planners focused on two major areas around downtown. One was the civic heart, Clinton Square. Another was the near east side, between downtown and the university.

Clinton Square

Once replaced by the State Barge Canal, the outdated Erie had been filled in the 1920s with great celebration. The space was eagerly taken over by the auto. The canal's path became Erie Boulevard. Clinton Square served as a parking lot. Basic landscaping was completed in 1933, but accommodations for traffic remained paramount.

By 1960 Syracuse planners had long been calling for construction of a major east-west arterial through downtown to "relieve traffic congestion," usually a realigned version of Erie Boulevard. City leaders also wanted Clinton Square to shed the shabby look presented by some buildings. Planners responded with a variety of proposals throughout the 1960s and early 70s for the square. But always, the car reigned supreme.

Highway engineers found their arterial solution in 1962 by reusing the abandoned elevation of the New York Central, now Route 690. But the dream of a reborn Clinton Square persisted. The northeast corner was set aside for a combination hotel/office building. Eventually, the square's northern edge was targeted for a facility to house the daily newspapers. And the southern quadrant was earmarked for a new Edwards department store.

The reality became a mixed bag. Construction started on the hotel tower, known as the Primex, but it was never finished. The new home for the Syracuse Newspapers, now *The Post-Standard*, was dedicated in 1971 and it continues as an important anchor for Clinton Square. But the landmark 1857 courthouse was lost in the process.

In this 1965 urban renewal scheme for a future Clinton Square, streets were to be re-routed, buildings demolished, skyscrapers added and the public square shifted north. If completed, much of what became the adjacent Hanover Square Historic District would have been lost.
OHA Collection

The new Edwards retail store opened in late 1972 but fell victim to competition from national chains in suburban locations and closed in 1974. The building served a few years as the innovative Syracuse Mall, populated with a dynamic variety of local merchants and craftspeople, but was eventually converted to basic office space.

Through urban renewal, landmarks had been razed and some new buildings gained around Clinton Square. But there was a lack of civic vitality since the space was still divided by Erie Boulevard. Early proposals for relocating Erie Boulevard traffic once assumed demolition of every structure on adjacent Hanover Square's north side, including the 1867 Gridley and 1894 Gere buildings. By 1973, however, all the schemes for moving Erie Boulevard were proving too costly.

Hanover Square hosts a variety of summertime concerts in a setting considered by some to reflect the feel of an intimate European plaza.
Photo by John Dowling

The old 15th Ward originally supported a mix of ethnic groups. Over time it stayed a tightly knit community with an increasing concentration of blacks. Commercial streets like Harrison and Townsend provided neighborhood shops and services.
OHA Collection

Growing interest in preserving the remaining historic structures, especially in Hanover Square, began to surface. The Gere and Gridley, acquired by urban renewal for demolition, were restored in the mid 1970s. All of Hanover Square was designated an historic district in 1976, a remarkable reversal of fate from 10 years earlier.

In 1975 and 1978, Mayor Lee Alexander tried to resurrect the dream of unifying Clinton Square. His proposed traffic relocation, although calling for no demolition, directed excessive flow into nearby Hanover Square, which generated opposition. Rerouting was dropped and a simple landscaping of both squares undertaken in 1980.

A series of major festivals in Clinton Square during the 1990s revived the hope for a unified, major park. With city planners agreeing to respect adjacent Hanover Square, a plan was approved to simply close Clinton Square's one block of Erie Boulevard. Traffic was adjusted in minor ways and a large public space created, complete with a canal-like reflecting pool that forms a popular outdoor skating rink in winter.

The new Clinton Square opened in September 2001 to great acclaim. The grand Soldiers and Sailors Monument, originally dedicated in 1910, was completely restored and rededicated as the city's civic centerpiece. At the same time, a project to convert a number of small 19th-century Hanover Square landmarks into innovative residential housing began. Over a long and sometimes volatile journey, a major municipal square was reborn and a concentration of nearby historic structures rediscovered. The combination of revitalized Clinton and Hanover squares offers much promise for renewed vitality at downtown's north end.

Near East Side

This urban renewal proposal was more ambitious and controversial. The district between State Street and Syracuse University was to be reborn as a government complex, cultural center and high-rise residential neighborhood. All that stood in the way were the overcrowded "slums" of the 15th Ward. Much of the housing was seriously substandard. It would be a blessing, planners felt,

The junior ushers at Bethany Baptist Church, located at 608 East Washington Street, around 1950.
Beauchamp Branch, Onondaga County Public Library Documentary Heritage Program

Herman Edge, seen here at center in 1965, helped integrate Syracuse's police force when he became a rookie in 1957. He eventually became the first African-American to hold a sergeant and deputy chief post. Dennis Duval was appointed Syracuse's first black police chief in 2001 by Mayor Matthew Driscoll. *OHA Collection*

to eliminate them. In 1960 the 15th Ward also was home to almost the entire African-American population of Syracuse. African-American churches like Bethany Baptist, Hopps Memorial Methodist and AME Zion, plus distinctive black nightclubs and barbershops, helped create a unique cultural vitality. The Dunbar Center on McBride Street offered recreational opportunities. The urban renewal plan included relocating the residents to expected better housing. African-Americans, long suffering from the economic disadvantages and discrimination that pushed them into the district, hoped it would improve integration.

Before World War II, Syracuse's small African-American population had been nearly invisible to many residents and mostly restricted to menial service jobs. Many of Syracuse's factories simply did not hire blacks. Working for the New York Central as a "redcap" baggage handler or porter was considered prime employment. There was practically no black middle class.

But like many northern cities, Syracuse's black population soared after World War II. Relocation from the South began when some northern factories needed workers during the war. Others moved to seek work as laborers harvesting crops. These better-paying jobs continued to beckon in the 1950s. The 15th Ward was virtually the only place African-Americans were allowed to

live. In 1950 almost 4,000 blacks, eight of every nine in Syracuse, lived there. By 1960 the African-American population was up to 11,210, a 144-percent rise. But black citizens made up just a little over 5 percent of city residents; they lacked political clout. The city council did not see an African-American member until 1970 when Robert Warr was appointed. Warr also had been the first black elected to the Board of Education in 1966.

The centerpiece of the east side urban renewal plan was to be "Community Plaza," combining four city blocks and closing portions of State and Jefferson streets to create one super block. Townsend Street was even shifted east to create more room. A new city hall, public safety building and jail were to be concentrated on the north half. A complex combining museums of history, art and science with a concert hall would form the southern section. A multicultural restaurant pavilion would bridge the two areas. Pedestrian malls built along the closed streets would link all the components. Some high-rise housing was to be added to the east.

The city's 1945 Post-War Plan had called for an expansion of cultural facilities. One of its goals, creating a civic auditorium, was married to the desire for a World War veterans' monument and the resulting Onondaga War Memorial opened in 1951. Satisfactory for sports or conventions, it proved inadequate as a concert hall. In 1953 a new Planning Commission report spelled out an ambitious dream for a true "Cultural Center." A large monetary bequest in 1941 from Helen Everson to build a new art museum stimulated the process, which ultimately led to the 1960s urban renewal plan.

The demolition and relocation of residents began in earnest during the early 1960s. Aiding the process was the decision to run the city portion of Interstate 81 through the urban renewal zone. Over

27 blocks in the 15th **Ward** were targeted, impacting 75 percent of the local black population. But it soon became apparent that most of the remaining city was unwilling to accept blacks so much of this population was relocated into other run-down, older neighborhoods south and east of the 15th Ward. Some settled into the nearby Pioneer Homes public housing. Others moved a few blocks south to Central Village, a low-income project opened in 1963. As some whites saw an influx of minorities into their neighborhoods, they joined the exodus to the suburbs, increasing de facto segregation. The Syracuse school district struggled to find ways to provide racial balance.

A City Hall by Any Other Name, or Architect

One image of a grand municipal center for Syracuse surfaced in 1930, before the full impact of the Depression was felt. Local architect Fred O'Connor suggested a classical setting along Montgomery Street, around the existing 1906 courthouse. At 20 stories, a proposed new city hall would have dwarfed the courthouse. But it reflected the lingering optimism of the 1920s that cities like Syracuse would continue to expand in size and population.

"Syracuse's. . . size, importance and future, is such as to justify the statement that it should have a [municipal] Center, of such distinction as to mark it as one of the progressive cities of the United States."

Syracuse Chamber of Commerce Report, 1930

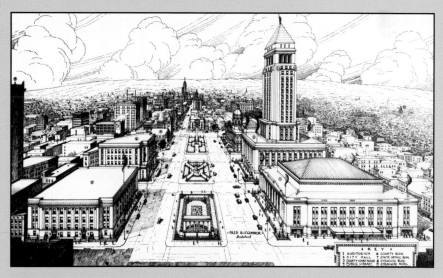

A newer vision for city hall surfaced again in 1964 as part of the Community Plaza urban renewal plan. Seeking to create a signature look for Syracuse, the city sought out Paul Rudolph, one of America's most prominent architects. His $5 million, terraced vision shocked many locals as an unrealistic and inefficient fantasy. Disappointed city officials shelved the controversial plan. Syracuse kept its Victorian city hall and the Plaza site served as an open parking lot for over 30 years, until utilized for construction of the new municipal Justice Center jail which opened in 1995.

"...a handsome, modern building — a City Hall of which all can be proud."

-New York State Senator John H. Hughes, August 30, 1964

" ...that horrible multi-tiered, high stepped design ....atrocious architectural nightmare produced... by Paul Rudolph... would not only be an eyesore esthetically, but it would also be inefficient to maintain."

Syracuse *Post-Standard* editorial, January 29, 1969

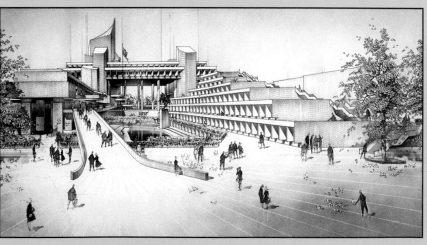

1930 plan (above) and proposed 1964 city hall. *OHA Collection*

This mid-1960s image of the planned Everson Museum of Art, as envisioned by architect I.M. Pei, is a perspective from the proposed cultural section of the Community Plaza. Pei went on to build an international career but the 1968 Everson, his first museum project, remains a favorite.
OHA Collection

Another urban renewal vision was of high-rise apartments and domed botanical gardens for downtown's west side, near an Onondaga Creek lagoon. Massive demolition would have eliminated every single structure now forming the Armory Square Historic District, one of downtown's bright spots.
OHA Collection

This corresponded to a time of growing civil rights activism, both nationally and in Syracuse. Locally, a chapter of CORE (Congress on Racial Equality) held protests at urban renewal demolition sites in 1963 and assailed city hall for not offering better solutions. CORE and others also challenged local corporate hiring policies during 1965 and helped in opening new employment opportunities for minorities. Both efforts involved sit-ins and arrests. There was some protest rioting that occurred in 1967 along East Genesee Street but

it was minor. And after Dr. King's assassination in 1968, local black leaders acted quickly to keep reactions peaceful. It took brave leadership to push Syracuse's political, religious and business establishments toward needed reforms in this era while avoiding the violent disturbances that plagued other cities. This effectiveness was demonstrated by both white and black citizens, such as Monsignor Charles Brady of the Catholic Interracial Council, Reverend Emory Proctor of People's AME Zion Church, Dennis Dowdell of the Urban League and Reverend Walter Welsh, rector of Grace Episcopal Church.

While some older African-Americans regret the loss of the 15th Ward's cohesiveness and identity, it was a time when there was little experience with programs aimed at renovating older homes. The 15th Ward clearance, termed "urban removal" by residents, seemed a difficult but unavoidable passage toward improving living conditions.

Ultimately, demolishing the old buildings of the Ward proved easier than marshaling all the forces to build the replacement Community Plaza. The suburbs were the new destination for business and people. It became an ongoing struggle to find the economic energy to realize all the grand visions.

Planners hoped for completion of the Community Plaza by 1980. The Public Safety Building and jail, adjacent North Parking Garage, Everson Museum of Art and reflecting pool were in place by 1968. Some mixed-income apartments were built along Townsend Street. But a continuing decline in city population made it hard to justify an expensive new city hall. Private underwriting for a new concert hall and other museums did not materialize. Hopes for a restaurant pavilion and movie theater fell victim to downtown's shrinking retail activity. And no one seemed to like the idea of closing streets. Perhaps leveled too soon, much of the cleared land was simply converted to surface parking lots. Some parcels continue that way, 40-years later, still awaiting development.

Local Government Changes its Stripes

As the 1960s brought population, urban renewal and civil rights challenges to Syracuse, Onondaga County faced its own modern struggle. Formed in 1794, county government functioned with an outdated system lacking any effective executive branch. The Board of Supervisors, with representation from 19 city wards and as many county towns, fulfilled both legislative and administrative functions. Yet the community had new needs beyond the ability of towns and the shrinking tax base of Syracuse to meet. Onondaga County

Reorganization of county government in 1962, in combination with executive John Mulroy's homespun but visionary style, turned it into a major force for community development. *Mulroy Family*

In the early 1970s, the county tackled the languishing proposal to build a performing arts center. The Mulroy Civic Center, a multi-use facility combining government offices with three theaters, opened in 1975. Musical Director Christopher Keene is seen touring the construction site of the future home of the Syracuse Symphony. *OHA Collection*

131

voters finally adopted a critical new charter in 1961 and got their first county executive, John Mulroy.

Mulroy liked to quip that his goal was to drag the county into the 20th century. Under his guidance, Onondaga County built a community college campus, developed a massive project to bring a water supply from Lake Ontario, then revitalized and diversified its county parks.

Although not a metropolitan government, the county relieved the city of responsibilities that it could no longer handle financially. In 1975 it took over MacArthur stadium, upgraded it

A souvenir pennant for the last season at MacArthur Stadium
OHA Collection

and then completely replaced it with P&C Stadium in 1997. In 1975 the county also created a new library system, acquiring operation of former city libraries and managing shared functions with town libraries. And in 1979 county parks assumed

Thomas J. Corcoran was elected Syracuse mayor in 1949. He and his wife, Virginia, had 10 children, eight of which are seen here. A south side high school is now named after him.
OHA Collection

responsibility for the city's decaying Burnet Park Zoo. After a $12 million refurbishing, it reopened in 1986 to rave reviews and during the 1990s developed an impressive program in breeding elephants. More recent expansions have kept the Rosamond Gifford Zoo at Burnet Park a place of local pride.

Both John Mulroy and Nick Pirro, who succeeded him as county executive in 1988, carried the Republican party banner. Except in 1978-1980, that party has also controlled the county legislature. At one time, the Republican party dominated all local politics. It consolidated control over both the city and county by the early 20th century, even drawing support from immigrant groups. From 1902 until 1970, Republicans controlled the mayor's office for all but eight years. John Walrath in the 1920s and Thomas Corcoran in the 1950s were the only Democratic exceptions. Each was elected through the combination of having popular personalities and running when there was weariness with the status quo.

The election of Democrat Lee Alexander as mayor in 1969 marked the shift of urban politics in Syracuse, as elsewhere. His ethnic origin was Greek, not the traditional German, Irish or WASP background of his predecessors. Democratic ranks rose in the city as the concentration of poor and minority accepted that party as its own. For the next 30 years, Democrats were generally victorious. The exception was the 1993-2001 terms of Republican Roy Bernardi, who first gained office after a primary split among Democrats.

The result is a strong Republican base in surrounding town and county governments, needing to work with an equally entrenched Democratic presence in the city. Despite political differences and an often-regrettable unfamiliarity between generations of suburban dwellers and city residents, a

successful future for Syracuse and Onondaga County requires that both work together to prosper.

That cooperative spirit often shines through most when Central New York's notoriously changeable weather is at its darkest. Syracuse enjoys four full seasons, each boasting its own special beauties. But it cannot deny its record as one of America's snowiest cities. There have been many awesome storms, but none brought the community to its knees quite like the Blizzard of January 1966. For three days, the region was pounded with heavy snows and winds, setting up immense drifts. There were unfortunate deaths from exposure and snow removal accidents, and it took the community a week to return to normal.

A similar catastrophe occurred on an unusually warm Labor Day in 1998. Late in the evening, a powerful cold front thundered down on the city from the northwest bringing winds with tornado intensity. Two vendors at the New York State Fair were killed by falling debris and a swath of destruction swept across the city and county, felling hundreds of trees and leaving thousands without power for days. The historic landscape of Oakwood Cemetery was devastated and many parks and streets will take decades to fully recover. But if anything, the sense of community was strengthened as young and old, rich and poor, city dweller and suburbanite, all worked together to help clean up and recover.

Athletic Identity

In addition to being united in the face of hostile weather, area communities recognize that many of the prime institutions that create the culture and soul of Onondaga County sit within Syracuse. One measure of how the city identifies the surrounding community is reflected in the names of major sports entities. And the last half of the 20th century saw a rise in the visibility of local athletics.

The long tradition of professional baseball resides in today's Syracuse SkyChiefs of the International League, the current franchise dating from 1961. The team earned the league championship Governor's Cup in 1969. In 1970 it won both the International League pennant, its first, and the subsequent playoffs. The cup returned to Syracuse in 1976 and the pennant in 1989.

Another storied tradition resided here from 1946 to 1963 when Syracuse was home to a National Basketball Association franchise, the Syracuse Nationals, fondly remembered as the Nats. It was an era when a fan could chat with players while they sat around the restaurant at owner Danny Biasone's bowling alley in Eastwood; a time before multimillion-dollar superstars, lucrative TV contracts and plush private boxes.

The Nats originally played at the State Fair Coliseum and sometimes in the downtown National Guard armory, but after 1951, home court stayed at the War Memorial. The community developed a fierce pride in the Nats. The Memorial took on a reputation as one of the most boisterous venues in the league.

The team improved throughout the early 1950s, especially with the play of future NBA Hall of Fame inductee Dolph Schayes. The NBA

A sampling of the Syracuse area's rich sports heritage is displayed in this montage. These items are from the collections of the Greater Syracuse Sports Hall of Fame, private individuals and the Onondaga Historical Association.
Photo by Hal Silverman

in those days was not the national phenomenon it became later in the century. Much of the nation didn't follow the contests. The best players in the world then, athletes such as Bill Russell and Bob Cousy, tangled on the War Memorial floor with Nats hoopsters Paul Seymour, Johnny Kerr and native-son Larry Costello. Earl Lloyd joined the Nats in 1952, just two years after becoming the first African-American to play in the NBA.

The 1954-55 Nats outing would be magic. The Syracuse team battled with league rivals like the New York Knicks, Boston Celtics and Minneapolis Lakers. The Nats could shoot but were best known for tenacious defense and a scrappy style. Some of the latter was surely a reflection of Nats coach Al Cervi, a tough, uncompromising leader.

The Nats finished the season on top of the Eastern Division with 43 wins against 29 losses. The Western crown went to the Fort Wayne Pistons with a matching record. Each team moved through the playoffs and faced down in the championship series. It went the full seven games, with the final held at the War Memorial in Syracuse on April 10, 1955, Easter Sunday. Fort Wayne came out fast and built an early lead. The Nats fought back, tying the score at 91 with a minute left; then earning a foul shot with just 12 seconds on the clock. But the Nats player stepping to the line was George King. King was a good ball handler but regarded as the team's worst foul shooter.

In a moment forever etched in Syracuse sports history, 7,000 fans held their breath, Coach Cervi said a prayer and King let loose a one-handed hope. To most everyone's amazement, including King's, it went in. The Pistons tried to hurry the ball back down court. Paul Seymour harassed their ball handler. In trouble, the Fort

A West Side High School Helps Save the NBA

As the 1950s arrived, the pace of the average NBA game had slowed to a level where fan interest was dropping. Superior teams could build up a lead and then let the time run down with stall tactics. Games lost their exciting edge. Sometimes only three shots would be taken in the entire fourth quarter. Syracuse Nats owner Danny Biasone, a self-made Italian immigrant who arrived through Ellis Island as a 9 year-old in 1919, had an idea. He envisioned a time limit on possession. A large sideline clock would count down the time remaining before a shot had to be made. Twenty-four seconds seemed about right.

Biasone lobbied league owners for years to try it. Finally, in desperation, they agreed. Biasone set up a demonstration game in Syracuse on August 10, 1954. It was the off-season, but a few Nats players stayed in town. Some other local hoopsters were recruited. The site was the gym in Blodgett Vocational High School, a hulking 1918 landmark on Oswego Street. The clock forced the game to speed up and was adopted. It saved the NBA from oblivion and helped the Nats secure the NBA championship the following year. But ultimately, it cost the Salt City its franchise. The 24-second clock created a dynamic contest, spreading interest in the game and ultimately dictating that only larger cities could support the necessary fan base.

The Nats left in 1963 but the history survives. The pioneering clock resides in a memorial exhibit to Biasone at LeMoyne College, and Blodgett still stands.

Blodgett Vocational c.1918. *OHA Collection*

Wayne player turned for position. He never saw King, who had left his man open and gambled on a steal. It worked. King took the ball and dribbled the last seconds away. The horn sounded and Syracuse owned a NBA championship, 92-91. The town savored the glory.

But the NBA was changing. As it grew up, especially with the dominant play of Wilt Chamberlain drawing attention, smaller cities like Syracuse could not support the changing economics. The Nats continued here until 1963, often competitive, but never again gaining the lofty championship. The franchise was sold for $500,000 to Philadelphia and became the 76ers.

Local boxing also enjoyed a national spotlight in the 1950s. Carmen Basilio, of nearby Canastota, fought his way to the welterweight crown in 1955 by defeating Tony DeMarco before 9,000 fans in the War Memorial. In 1957 he moved up a class and took on Sugar Ray Robinson for the middleweight title in New York City. His upset victory was seen as one of Central New York's greatest sports highlights.

Keeping track of professional hockey in Syracuse after World War II is a challenge. Teams and minor leagues seemed to change every decade. The 1967 to 1976 era of a particularly hard-hitting team known as the Syracuse Blazers is fondly remembered by many, including an Eastern Hockey League championship in its final year. The arrival of the American Hockey League Syracuse Crunch in 1994 stabilized the game's presence in town and continued the War Memorial's rich athletic heritage. Its 2001-2002 division crown and 2004 run for the championship Calder Cup captivated Central New York.

SU's robust students had long competed in many venues and helped expose local residents to crew racing, golf, ice hockey and other activities early in the 20th century. Before college

basketball was closely followed, SU won a national championship in 1918 and then again in 1926, the latter behind the legendary play of Vic Hanson. But the decades following World War II contained many notable moments for Syracuse University sports. The national collegiate rowing regattas were held annually on Onondaga Lake from 1952 to 1992 with Syracuse championships in 1978 and 1980.

Of course, football was the collegiate giant. SU's Archbold Stadium witnessed some mighty gridiron battles, including rivalries with Cornell and Penn State. The home team reached national prominence in 1959 when it went 11-0 and then on to SU's only national football championship by

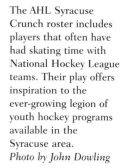

The AHL Syracuse Crunch roster includes players that often have had skating time with National Hockey League teams. Their play offers inspiration to the ever-growing legion of youth hockey programs available in the Syracuse area.
Photo by John Dowling

Syracuse University's talented backfield during its 1959 championship season included (left to right) halfbacks Gerhard Schwedes and Ernie Davis, quarterback Dave Sarette and fullback Art Baker.
OHA Collection

defeating Texas in the Cotton Bowl. Ernie Davis, the first African-American to win the Heisman Trophy, powered the backfield in the legendary #44 tradition of Jim Brown, Syracuse's most famous football alumnus.

Crumbling Archbold was replaced in 1980 by the Carrier Dome, the first domed stadium on a college campus. It too sheltered some impressive squads, especially in 1987 and 1992 with respective post-season appearances at the Sugar Bowl and Fiesta Bowl. The former ended in a disappointing tie with Auburn, but SU conquered Colorado in

Bethaida (Bea) Gonzalez was elected president of the Syracuse Common Council in 2001.
Photo by Glenn Holloway

the latter, a finish considered second only to the stature of the Cotton Bowl win.

By the late 1970s, although the Nats were long gone, Syracuse University basketball again provided the community with national visibility. The SU Orangemen squad under coach Jim Boeheim has had consistently winning runs, reaching the NCAA national championship game in 1987, 1996 and 2003. The agonizing loss by one point in '87 was finally redeemed by the 2003 victory, placing Syracuse on the long-sought pinnacle of college basketball.

But perhaps no SU sports tradition has been as impressive as its recent record in lacrosse. Fielding this ancient Native American game in the heart of what is traditional Iroquois territory makes for historic and, perhaps, spiritual inspiration. National championships were garnered nine times between 1983 and 2004 during 22 consecutive NCAA Final Four appearances. Playing brothers Gary and Paul Gait electrified fans during the 1980s as did Mike Powell in 2003–04. And Roy Simmons Jr. added to the coaching legacy begun by his dad in 1932.

New Voices Add Dimension and Vitality to the Chorus

Of course, lacrosse also remains an honored tradition on the nearby Onondaga Nation. But the Native American presence in Central New York is not limited to its own territory. There is a growing urban population, a little over 1 percent of Syracuse's residents, concentrated on the west side. They are just one constituency creating new ethnic shades in a diverse community tapestry.

Earlier waves of immigration were predominately European. Recent trends have increased the presence of other races. Syracuse's African-American population reached 23,597 in 1970 and 33,170 by 1990. The 2000 census shows that the trend continues. Blacks represented about 25 percent of Syracuse's population at the end of the 20th century.

But there also has been an increase in the Asian population. It rose by nearly 40 percent during the 1990s and now accounts for about 3 percent of city residents. Hispanic numbers increased too, up 55 percent in the county and nearly two-thirds in the city since 1990. Syracuse had 7,768 residents of Latino background in 2000, mostly of Puerto Rican ancestry. Middle Eastern representation expanded, as well. Recent arrivals have begun small businesses, like earlier immigrant groups, and shown a desire to make their own contributions to Syracuse. In 2001 Syracusans voted Bea Gonzalez to the president's post of the Common Council, the first Latino elected to citywide office. New churches, mosques and temples have arrived on the landscape. Associated clubs and social organizations sometimes offer wonderful opportunities for citizens to experience new cultural festivals and traditions.

The census also reflects minorities progressing into new areas of the city and suburbs. The black population in DeWitt grew 32 pecent during the 1990s. Clay added 369 black residents. The suburbs continue beckoning, especially to those drawn by schools that are more prosperous than their urban counterparts. City schools struggle with the challenges of having many students from impoverished homes, but continue to develop an array of innovative programs with hundreds of successful graduates each year.

White flight to the suburbs has meant that parts of Syracuse continue to reflect disproportionate concentrations of minorities. But there are also a growing number of neighborhoods managing a more integrated mix than existed 40 years ago. African-Americans and other minorities offer Syracuse and other U.S. cities a more diverse cultural mix. This reflects an ever more international awareness in American life. And it also mirrors the reality of America as a nation formed from many traditions.

Syracuse boasts numerous music, ethnic and art festivals throughout the summer. All offer an exciting opportunity to experience the community's diverse cultural spirit.
Photo by John Dowling

EPILOGUE

Seeking a 21st-Century Definition for Syracuse

While recognizing that diversity brings depth and energy to the city, there remains serious concern about Syracuse's population decline. The city has lost 73,000 residents since 1950. In 1950 there were only a couple of dozen places in America larger than Syracuse. By 2000 it found itself in 145th place. And the overall population of the county is not growing. Some experts attribute it to the general economic setback that occurred throughout the 1990s in upstate New York. Many people simply left the area in search of better job opportunities.

Yet Syracuse still serves as the major hub, cultural center and source of community identity for Central New York and its suburbs. Although challenged by a population slump and sometimes less-than-robust economy, Syracuse is making the transition to its new circumstances with much less physical distress than many places. It now has a remarkably diverse business base, less dependent on heavy manufacturing, which can better weather the inevitable cycles of the economy. It boasts a diverse cultural life, inexpensive housing, major educational institutions and a strong entrepreneurial spirit.

Mansion Memories

Most 19th-century American cities had residential avenues where conspicuous wealth was showcased. Syracuse spawned three: West Genesee, West Onondaga and James Street. One hundred years ago they were lined with the prestigious homes of local industrialists, judges, bankers and politicians. Many featured bold architecture that would cost millions of dollars to replicate today. Their occupants, the community's power brokers, often lived lavishly; with a few demonstrating eccentric, intriguing or impassioned behavior worthy of any television soap opera.

Changes in lifestyles and economic fortunes, in combination with suburban growth, made these American castles obsolete by the end of World War II. Most cities lost some portion of this glorious architectural heritage but none more so than Syracuse. West Genesee went first, its estates leveled as their acreage was converted by the 1930s to automobile dealerships and other commercial

Only a couple of these homes photographed along the 700 block of West Onondaga in 1894 remain today. One was razed as recently as February 2002. *OHA Collection*

uses. The architecture of James, the grandest, died its slow death during the 1950s and 60s. Actually seeking to avoid the fate of West Genesee, the city encouraged a higher level of commercial development along lower James, primarily office and apartment buildings. But the results were generally ordinary. A street that once captivated Syracusans inspires little fondness among current citizens. Outer residential sections of James, developed in the early 20th century, have fortunately been protected through local historic preservation legislation.

Despite the obvious lessons of James and West Genesee, the 19th-century remains of West Onondaga continue to suffer from neglect and lack of vision. Many homes have deteriorated beyond repair within just the last few years despite dozens of examples in other cities that have reclaimed their boulevards of architectural dreams. But some opportunities remain, both on West Onondaga and along countless Syracuse streets of more modest means, where inviting historic residences still stand.

A typical scene along James Street in 1890. This is now the site of the Skyline Apartments building. *OHA Collection*

These two examples of late-19th-century mansions once stood at the northeast corner of Leavenworth and West Genesee. By 1924 they were already surrounded by three automobile dealerships. *OHA Collection*

This 1840s Greek Revival was built as the home of Elias Leavenworth, second mayor of Syracuse. In 1950, it was one of the first James Street homes threatened. Despite great community concern, no organized effort was made to save it. Its loss set the tone for the next 40 years.

OHA Collection

The family of local department store owner Daniel M. Edwards resided in this James Street residence until the end of World War II. It was later used by LeMoyne College before being demolished by developers. *OHA Collection*

The interiors of James Street's mansions reflected the ostentatious lifestyle of another era. Fortunately, the Barnes-Hiscock home survives today as the Corinthian Club, where this dining room serves as a member lounge. *OHA Collection*

This stunning Georgian Revival residence of State Senator Hendrick S. Holden was removed in the 1960s and replaced with a motel. Local historian Jasena Foley managed to document many James Street structures with color photography prior to their loss. *OHA Collection*

And there is recognition that modest size is not necessarily a bad thing. Many fast-growing communities elsewhere have watched their quality of life deteriorate into a morass of congested highways, two-hour commutes, an endless monotony of sprawl and an ever-escalating cost of living. Without such pressure, Syracuse and Onondaga County have an opportunity to better manage growth. Unchecked, it can only create a huge surplus of housing in the city and older suburbs, driving down their value and appeal. With intelligent planning, smaller cities like Syracuse can foster and maintain a dynamic urban vitality.

In seeking to revitalize older urban areas, many cities have opted for measures to augment quality of life factors, increasing investment in education, parks, cultural facilities and neighborhood planning. More than a few have also responded with historic preservation.

Historic preservationists recognize that older cities like Syracuse have a preponderance of homes and buildings that were built before 1930. Preservation advocates seek to consider the unique qualities of these structures as assets rather than liabilities and to place a system of incentives, guidelines and planning philosophies into place that can create historic districts with an appeal that the suburbs cannot match. While many find the suburbs to their liking, back-to-the-city movements in other localities show that there is a market for older housing, which, properly nurtured, can help revitalize cities.

Syracuse passed a municipal historic preservation ordinance in 1975, partially in response to the massive demolition of older landmarks in the 1950s and 60s. Although many buildings have been protected with designation since then, the percentage is smaller than in comparable cities. Syracuse is

implementing a number of housing rehabilitation and replacement strategies to maintain attractive neighborhoods. A comprehensive preservation plan promises to be given a higher profile in Syracuse's future strategic planning efforts.

While residential Syracuse considers the possibilities of historic preservation as a tool for revitalization, downtown Syracuse has witnessed ample success with the rehabilitation of several older structures. Much was lost during the urban renewal years of the 1960s. But eventually Syracuse's first official historic district, Hanover Square, was listed in 1976. In conjunction with the 2001 reconfiguration of adjacent Clinton Square, it is showing signs of continued renewal.

One amazing preservation feat was the 1977-78 rescue of downtown's last grand movie palace, Loew's State. Through the leadership of a cross-section of citizens, the financial support of hundreds of average Central New Yorkers and a timely state grant, this 2,800-seat national treasure was purchased by a non-profit organization to save it from demolition. Today, re-christened as the Landmark Theater, this Hindu-Persian fantasy hosts a variety of events, from weddings to concerts.

The revitalized Armory Square National Register Historic District has been a bright spot for downtown retail, dining and housing during the 1980s and 1990s. But this wasn't always so. Up through the early 1970s, most of Armory Square was scheduled for urban renewal clearance. Then-visionary capitalists saw potential in the 19th-century warehouses and old railroad hotels. The 1992 conversion of the district's empty centerpiece, a national guard armory, into the outstanding Milton J. Rubenstein Museum of Science & Technology was a further catalyst for renewal and dynamic mixed use.

The locally based Pyramid Companies' 1990 transformation of a lakeside industrial wasteland into the retail giant Carousel Center mall stimulated a complete re evaluation of the city's Onondaga Lake waterfront. A massive effort to

reclaim water quality, following decades of industrial and municipal pollution, is well underway. The former Barge Canal terminal was transformed into the nucleus for an attractive harbor front. And nearby, developers have remade a former industrial district of early 20th century brick factories into the pleasant, mixed use Franklin Square neighborhood. Plans call for linking these areas to Armory Square along the Onondaga "Creekwalk." Rediscovery of this long neglected, historic waterway offers further chances for urban revitalization. And the promised transformation of Carousel Center into an expanded entertainment and retail center called Destiny USA holds great potential, especially if it relates creatively to the adjacent harbor and historic North Side areas.

Downtown, which lost the last of its major retail stores in 1992, has been seeking a new formula for

Armory Square's historic facades have inspired the creation of sympathetic new in-fill construction, such as 1994's multi-use Center Armory Building, at left.
Photo by John Dowling

The landmark Plymouth Congregational Church housed an active abolitionist membership at the time of the Civil War. Today, it serves as an intriguing backdrop during the annual Columbus Circle Arts & Crafts Festival.
Photo by John Dowling

success. One critical piece is the county's modern convention center, which opened the same year. And Armory Square has proven the appeal of mixed use historic structures. There is a growing commitment to developing more downtown housing. A final element may be the creation of a special cultural spine centered along Montgomery Street and through Columbus Circle.

This "Cultural Corridor" would encompass the historic 1850 canal weighlock, redeveloped in 1962 as the Erie Canal Museum; a completed Onondaga Historical Association Museum and Research Center complex; and an expanded Everson Museum of Art, a stunning contemporary architectural masterpiece. In addition to these major museums, this cultural spine would include the performing arts Civic Center, home to the superb Syracuse Symphony Orchestra and outstanding Syracuse Opera, the county's convention complex and a litany of historic architecture along the way. Further capital development of some of these key facilities, incentives for artists and galleries, selected new housing, a new hotel in the renovated Mizpah Tower, creative

building lighting, additional restaurants and streetscape identity have the potential to create a vibrant downtown centerpiece of activity closely linked with Clinton and Hanover Squares along East Genesee and with nearby Armory Square along Jefferson Street. And everywhere one looks in this zone are the buildings and sites that reflect the dramatic history of this city and its people. Syracuse University Chancellor Nancy Cantor recognizes these attributes. SU is working closely with the community to link these downtown assets to the University along a dynamic "Connective Corridor" transportation system.

If the Destiny project truly increases Syracuse's tourism potential, a critical mass of engaging historic and cultural attractions in downtown might be the most effective way to draw out these visitors into the city. Once there, they can help stimulate further renewal and community vitality, perhaps helping create a new economic paradigm for Syracuse's future.

Of course, a city's future is more than structures. It is nothing without a dedicated population committed to working together to provide good education, economic opportunity and an appealing quality of life for all. Syracuse and Onondaga County have the institutions, organizations, leaders and will to continue working toward this goal. The area's history is one of struggle, change, adversity, success, tragedy and triumph. But always, there have been citizens willing to step forward and make a difference. Syracuse moves into the 21st century with renewed optimism and a growing appreciation for the inspiration and lessons drawn from its past.

The collections of the Onondaga Historical Association are among the largest and most diverse history museum holdings in upstate New York. The continuing development of its facilities is a key for expanding the appeal of downtown's cultural assets.
Photo by Richard Kampas

Like these youthful step dancers parading past the 1906 county courthouse, the next generation to lead Syracuse will profit by balancing an appreciation for the past with an excitement for the future. *Photo by John Dowling*

PARTNERS IN SYRACUSE

Building a Greater Syracuse

Hardy Construction Services 148
ABC Refrigeration & Air Conditioning Inc. 152

Manufacturing & Distribution

Carrier Corporation 154
Syracuse China Company 156
Jaquith Industries, Inc. 158
Bristol-Myers Squibb Company 160
Cathedral Candle.........................161
Harrison Industrial Supply...................................162
Stickley, Audi & Company 163

Marketplace

Comfort Inn & Suites 164
Pastabilities 165

Networks

Department of Aviation, City of Syracuse 166
National Grid/Niagara Mohawk.................................170
The Post-Standard 171

Professional Services

Costello, Cooney & Fearon, PLLC 172
Dal Pos Architects, LLC.....................................174
JCM Architectural Associates 176
King & King, Architects LLP 178

Quality of Life

Onondaga Historical Association 179
Syracuse Home Association 184
Hal Silverman Studio...186
Le Moyne College 187
New York State Fair 188
Syracuse Convention & Visitors Bureau 189
The State University of New York
Upstate Medical University 190
Visiting Nurse Association of Central New York 191

Technology

CXtec 192
InfiMed Inc. 196
Lockheed Martin
Maritime Systems & Sensors 198

HARDY CONSTRUCTION SERVICES

Building Trust and Growing a Company

Equal parts versatility and optimism, a healthy work ethic, a ton of integrity and a dash of entrepreneurial daring. These are the ingredients in the special recipe that founder David J. Hardy used to build his award-wining, growth-oriented business, Hardy Construction Services.

Since its founding in 1979, Hardy Construction Services has experienced unprecedented growth from its headquarters in Central New York, opening a satellite office in Frederick, Maryland and obtaining licenses to operate in 22 states. In fiscal 2001, Hardy earned over $32 million in annual sales and licensing fees, a significant increase over previous years.

A mainstay on the "Syracuse 100" list of the area's fastest-growing and most productive companies since 1990, Hardy Construction has certainly come a long way from its humble beginnings as a one-man operation. " I didn't have a crew. I

didn't go to the bank and borrow a bunch of money. I didn't even have a business plan. It was strictly a pay-as-you-go operation," Hardy recalls.

With only a pickup truck and a wheelbarrow—but an excess of faith, ambition, and confidence—David Hardy launched Hardy Construction with just one employee on the payroll, himself. The Camillus native and Bradley University graduate was finally realizing his dream after several years as a construction foreman.

Operationally, Hardy Construction Services lives by a different credo than most local construction companies. While many contractors concen-

Craftsman House is a stunning 5,500-square-foot restaurant in Fayetteville that features intricate cultured stone work, extensive oak veneers, Stickley furnishings and more.

The SportsCenter 481 Indoor Recreation Center, located in Dewitt, New York, is a 75,000-square-foot Butler pre-engineered building with a mammoth 200-foot clear span.

trate exclusively on local jobs, Hardy's business strategy has been to develop not only a local, but also a regional and national client base.

Employee development and retention remain a top priority of Hardy. "We train our people in Total Quality Management, continuous improvement, OSHA and safety issues," Hardy explains. "Another key is attitude. We look for a positive attitude in all employees. If you have the right attitude, we can train you to do the work."

Following the building boom of the 1980s, the construction market slowed considerably in Central New York during the early 1990s. That is when Hardy began looking beyond the state's borders to keep his workers employed. The gamble paid off, with projects in the southeast keeping his team busy through the long Syracuse winters.

As the construction industry's recession continued through the 1990s, Hardy responded by creating a sales department devoted to marketing his company to "hospitality groups"—hotels and restaurants—which continued to thrive despite the struggling economy. This amended recipe for survival has more than paid off, with hotel and restaurant work accounting for a significant percentage of Hardy's total revenue. "Our national accounts have been good to us," Hardy explains.

Over the years, Hardy Construction Services has grown to include over 100 full-time employees. And their client list has grown to include accounts with large national chains such as the Bob Evans, Wendy's Burger King, Perkins, Chili's and Cracker Barrel restaurants, along with NAPA Auto Parts and Barnes & Noble bookstores. Local clients include General Electric, Bristol-Myers Squibb, Stickley & Audi furniture, Oneida Ltd., Lockheed Martin, MacKenzie-Childs and many others.

These and other loyal customers return again and again to the one company they trust for design consultation, design-build and construction management services, site selection and acquisition services, build-lease financing, approval and permit process consultation, and overall construction value. Hardy Construction also performs industrial maintenance and remodeling of manufacturing facilities, where strength, durability, speed and efficiency are critical.

Today, Hardy Construction Services excels in all phases of building projects, while focusing on what David Hardy calls the four fundamental areas of construction: quality, price, schedule and safety. Hardy firmly believes all four must be prominent in order for a project to succeed. Completing the job on time and on budget, handling quality issues in a professional manner and keeping the job site safe are integral parts of every Hardy project.

A full-service, multi-market, commercial general contractor, Hardy Construction has built everything from churches to shopping centers, schools to medical facilities, as well as warehouses, manufacturing plants, industrial complexes, hotels, restaurants and more. And the company stands behind each and every job it performs, offering extended warranties far beyond the one-year standard.

The following is just a sampling of Hardy's latest success stories:

In 2000, Hardy signed on to develop the $3 million SportCenter 481—a 75,000 square foot facility set on 26 acres—which opened in the summer of 2001. Hardy overcame many obstacles to create a state-of-the-art complex for its client. The facility boasts both indoor and outdoor playing fields, sophisticated lighting, video equipment and more.

Hardy Construction also spearheaded the $2.4 million expansion and renovation of the Raymour & Flanigan Plaza in DeWitt, which includes a uniquely designed Barnes & Noble Booksellers store. The 25,000-square foot structural steel addition to the existing plaza accommodated the build-out of the Barnes & Noble store. The 27,000 square foot interior renovation retrofitted the existing plaza space to accommodate the new furni-

The 174th Fighter Wing Cold Storage Facility at Hancock Field houses this busy branch of the Air National Guard's F-16s.

ture store as well as several other retail operations. During this project, the existing Raymour & Flanigan remained opened for business.

When Craftsman House Restaurant in Fayetteville commissioned Hardy to construct a high profile, heavily-detailed project in the middle of a brutal Syracuse winter, the company gladly welcomed the challenge. The result was an absolutely stunning 5,500-squre foot restaurant featuring exterior stone work fabrication as well as extensive interior finishes of oak veneers, molding and trim highlighting the beautiful Stickley furnishings.

Located on the grounds of Hancock International Airport, just north of Syracuse, a 37,000-square foot Butler Building acts as a cold storage facility for the Air National Guard's 174th Fighter Wing. These Gulf War veterans needed a simple, safe structure that could accommodate their fleet of F-16 fighter jets. And once again, Hardy delivered on budget and met all specifications. Featuring a leak-proof standing seam roof, this Butler facility was the ideal solution for this client's unique needs.

Other satisfied Hardy Construction clients include dozens of national and regional dining establishments, several hotels and motels along the East Coast, big-name retail stores such as Blockbuster video, Ross Department Stores, Rite Aid and Eckerd Drugs, as well as countless commercial and industrial customers across the country.

The success stories go on and on. And in 2000, David Hardy was recognized for his accomplishments by being named the "Entrepreneur of the Year" in the construction and real estate category by Ernst & Young. The winning criteria included an "enthusiasm and passion in growing their companies, ability to take reasoned risks, ability to creatively seize new opportunities and the ability to give generously to the community." Sounds very much like David Hardy's special recipe for success over the last 25 years.

The Barnes & Noble Booksellers store, located on Erie Boulevard in Dewitt, New York, was completed despite some adverse weather conditions: namely a typical CNY winter.

151

ABC REFRIGERATION &
AIR CONDITIONING INC.

The Syracuse business of ABC Refrigeration & Air Conditioning Inc. is an excellent example of the axiom: if you do good work, word gets around. Based on its reputation, ABC has grown from a $200,000 three-person operation in 1969

to a company that boasts over $8 million in annual revenues.

Now with about 100 employees, ABC serves the refrigeration and air conditioning needs of major commercial and industrial clients located across New York State and beyond, according to owner and president, Carmen Ligoci.

Ligoci was hired by the company in 1969 after he had served four years in the Navy and worked for another refrigeration company. He purchased ABC in 1976 and gradually hired others to assist in his growing enterprise, personally selecting and training his service people.

The company has never relied on advertising, gaining new work primarily by word-of-mouth. Under Ligoci's leadership, ABC progressed from selling walk-in coolers using a two-horsepower unit to installing state-of-the-art, computer-controlled parallel compressor rack systems for contracts that include a 50,000-square-foot supermarket, a 200,000-square-foot supercenter and refrigerated warehouses.

Today, ABC maintains over 200 commercial, industrial and institutional clients, including

supermarket and department store chains such as P&C, Tops, Wal-Mart, Peter's, BJ's, Price Chopper, and Aldi. With the amount of clientele that ABC has obtained, service branches were established in the areas of Albany, Schenectady, Oneonta, Ogdensburg, Watertown, Binghamton, Olean and Ithaca. All of its over 50 technicians are certified, and the company backs up its work with a 100-percent guarantee.

ABC customizes each of its projects to include design, production and installation of refrigeration and air conditioning equipment to meet clients' particular needs. The company also has its own construction foreman and crew to see that large and complicated projects requiring more than installation and service can be successfully accomplished from start to finish. One example is an 11,520-square-foot building in Watertown, New York, that ABC built from the ground up. It involved erecting steel grid beam supports for cooler panels as well as carpentry work. The finished product was a state-of-the-art freestanding freezer and food distribution center with loading docks.

A freestanding freezer in the making: network of steel beam supports for cooler panels constructed by ABC Refrigeration and Air Conditioning Inc.

The company's crews will work simultaneously on various supermarket projects. A typical installation takes eight to 10 weeks to complete and usually includes walk-in coolers, display cases, food fixtures and food preservation units, all constructed and installed in such a way as to satisfy customer requirements.

ABC's diverse clientele has included the U.S. Army at Fort Drum, where it installed equipment for a 30,000-square-foot commissary, and the U.S. Coast Guard, for which it set up air conditioning units on boats. In addition, ABC specializes in ultra-low-temperature refrigeration. Customers such as the American Red Cross, hospitals, Syracuse University and Cornell University require low temperatures to suspend blood, tissue and organisms for research. Cascade systems, with several computer-controlled compressors in series, are used. Ultra-low-temperature refrigeration is an area of expertise that continues to see considerable growth for the company.

Because of its range of clientele, ABC technicians have the advantage of being exposed to nearly every type of manufacturer's equipment in the field. A strong advocate for continuous training of his employees, Ligoci holds once-a-week job meetings plus a weekly in-house training session he himself teaches. Each service person first learns from the ground up to build and install, then to service each component. Eventually Ligoci steers his production people into areas in which they excel to increase their expertise.

The foundation of the business is service. ABC technicians will update programs, service parts and perform federally mandated annual inspections for their clients as well. The company keeps service crews in Albany as well as in the southern tier and northern region to cover the scope of its New York clientele. It also services a number of customer locations throughout the northeast and Florida. Each technician is equipped with state-of-the-art tools and information. To ensure prompt response time, they all wear pagers. The 52 vans or trucks in the ABC fleet all come equipped with cellular phones as well as two-way radios.

ABC constructed its current business location on Factory Avenue in 1982 and recently renovated and expanded it to include more office and warehouse space to meet its growing needs. In addition to its over 50 technicians, the company has a sales, office and management staff of 14 who keep the hiring, contractual and billing aspects of the business running efficiently.

ABC Refrigeration and Air Conditioning is a corporate member of the national Refrigeration

Refrigerated units ABC installed at a 208,000-square-foot Wal-Mart Supercenter in York, Pennsylvania

The completed project — an 11,520-square-foot freezer and food distribution center in Watertown, New York

A typical parallel compressor rack system that ABC sets up to control frozen food cases and walk-in coolers at supermarkets

Service Engineers Society (RSES). A long-term member in RSES, Ligoci is past president of the Central New York Chapter. He actively mentors his employees to participate in its events and continuing education programs.

Under Ligoci's guidance, ABC has established a well-trained and experienced work force that is always ready to serve its long-term and new clients. Ligoci has charged his company with this ongoing mission: to provide its customers with the highest standards of service, quality and value while ensuring employees a safe, honest and open workplace with continuous employment.

CARRIER CORPORATION

In 1937 native son Willis Haviland Carrier returned to New York, bringing his company to Syracuse to occupy a long-unused 31-acre parcel on Geddes Street, the site of the former Franklin automobile plant. Though no one knew it at the time, a dynamic new era had

begun. By the century's end, Carrier's development of air conditioning was to appear high on the lists of America's greatest inventions, and Carrier Corporation was to become one of the region's largest employers.

Born in the western New York town of Angola in 1876, Cornell University graduate Willis Carrier devised the world's first practical air conditioning units. Today air conditioning is often taken for granted, but it began as a technique to improve manufactured products and processes.

In the summer of 1902 Carrier designed and installed the first scientific air conditioning system at a printing company in Brooklyn. As temperature and humidity changed, the dimensions of the paper changed. Printers were having trouble

Since relocating to Syracuse in 1937, Carrier Corporation has grown into a global corporation with more than 42,000 employees, doing business in 171 countries.

getting their red, yellow, blue and black impressions to line up and form full-color images. Carrier stabilized the temperature and moisture in the air so the paper stayed the same size throughout the day.

Similar problems were occurring in textile mills on dry days as static electricity caused cotton fibers to misbehave. When threads got fuzzy, they broke and fabric couldn't be woven evenly. So Carrier had to figure out a way to add tons of moisture to the air. He solved the problem in 1906, believing the extra humidity would "condition" the fibers. It did. That year, U.S. Patent No. 808897 was issued to Carrier for "Apparatus For Treating Air."

By 1914 the Charles Gates mansion in Minneapolis had become Carrier's first application of air conditioning in a residence. A new industry was growing. Six young engineers banded together with Willis Carrier, staking their fortunes and futures, and started Carrier Engineering Corporation, incorporated in New York on June 26, 1915. They were Irvine Lyle, Edward Murphy, Logan Lewis, Ernest Lyle, Alfred Stacey Jr. and Edmund Heckel.

In 1922 Carrier developed the centrifugal chiller, the device that allowed the cooling of people as well as industrial processes, and would eventually change the face of urban architecture and open up whole areas of the world for development. A key feature was the use of a refrigerant fluid that was much safer than the ammonia common at the time. It made the cooling of large public places practical for the first time.

Theatergoers benefited first. The centrifugal chiller brought comfort to the Rivoli Theater in New York's Times Square in 1925. "Air Conditioned Comfort" drew large audiences. Meanwhile in Hollywood, air conditioned studios could keep doors and windows closed, eliminating outside noise while keeping actors cool despite the heat of the klieg lights and the local climate.

Department stores were next. Macy's New York installed a centrifugal chiller air conditioning system in 1929 and used it as a drawing card for patrons who wanted to shop in comfort. The air conditioning industry was beginning to change commerce, and it would soon change the face of urban architecture, freeing business from the limits imposed by summer heat and humidity.

Large buildings no longer required center courtyards and open windows for cross-ventilation during heat waves. These central refrigeration and air distribution systems made large, permanently enclosed work spaces cool enough to be productive. With windows that opened no longer a necessity, architects could design high-rise glass-walled structures in direct sunlight that could still be kept comfortable inside. The results are evident in skylines worldwide.

Like many manufacturers, Carrier Corporation converted its production during World War II. The Syracuse plant manufactured systems that were used in the vital production of synthetic rubber and in high-octane gasoline. Carrier chillers were removed from department stores (including Macy's) for installation in war production plants. (They all got their chillers back after the war.) Carrier air conditioning and refrigeration equipment was required for warships and cargo vessels, for munitions plants and for factories specializing in the production of such essential war material as bombsights and other precision instruments. Carrier made thousands of refrigeration units for walk-in coolers used by the Navy to keep perishables. Special portable coolers were made to permit the servicing of airplanes in hot climates. Carrier also turned out airplane engine mounts, sight hoods for

guns, tank adapters and other military items.

Perhaps the greatest of all of Carrier's contributions to the war effort was something Willis Carrier called his own greatest engineering achievement. This was a system designed for the National Advisory Committee for Aeronautics and installed in its wind tunnel to simulate freezing high-altitude conditions for the testing of prototype planes. In 1950 Dr. Carrier said, "Once, I accomplished the impossible ... and because of its success, high officials in the Air Force told me that World War II was shortened by many months."

After the war, Carrier Corporation's expansion to the 506-acre Thompson Road campus, in the Syracuse suburb of DeWitt, opened an era of unprecedented growth.

In 1955 William J. Levitt, then America's leading home builder, predicted that air conditioning would soon become a basic feature of American homes. Levitt was right, but it took a while. By 1965 10 percent of American homes were air conditioned. Today, more than 80 percent of American homes are air conditioned and in some portions of the South, 95 percent of homes have comfort cooling.

Since becoming a unit of United Technologies Corporation in 1979, Carrier has proudly continued its founder's tradition of firsts. In 1993 Carrier cooled the famed Sistine Chapel. When Carrier announced a worldwide CFC phase-out that same year, it came 10 years in advance of requirements in some markets. In the mid-1990s Carrier introduced the world's first non-ozone-depleting, chlorine-free centrifugal chiller and residential central air conditioner. Keeping up with the changing times, in 1999 Carrier became the first HVAC manufacturer to offer window/room air conditioners over the Internet. In the 21st century, Carrier introduced a Web-enabled, programmable thermostat. Dr. Carrier's inventive spirit lives on, in Syracuse and around the world.

SYRACUSE CHINA COMPANY

Recognized worldwide for its trademark of excellence, the Syracuse China Company maintains its premier standing in food service china production. Its shining reputation is rooted in over 150 years of product craftsmanship that is Syracuse homegrown. In 1995 Syracuse

China became a unit of Libbey Inc., another prominent and well-established company that manufactures glass and flatware. This formed a strategic alliance enabling Syracuse China to further expand into tableware markets around the world.

Syracuse China's main clientele is the food service/restaurant industry, in addition to a small percentage of retail and industrial clients. It not only is a top supplier of china products in the United States, it exports to over 20 countries. Offering a wide array of high-quality tableware, the company displays over 80 china patterns in its product catalog and introduces more than 100 new products yearly. Syracuse China also stands ready to fill customized orders — its designers create over 2,000 original design motifs each year to meet restaurants' special needs.

Manufacturing operations take place at the modernized Court Street plant in Syracuse. A 4,000-square-foot outlet store, also at this location, showcases a number of Syracuse China's popular designs along with some Libbey glass products, both for discount sale to the public. Also at this site is housed a complete archive of the pottery's hundreds of original designs since its origin.

An elegant banquet setting is attained with Syracuse China's award-winning white tableware along with lovely glass and flatware by parent company Libbey Inc.

The history of Syracuse China can be traced to a family pottery business established in 1841 by W.H. Farrar in the small community of Geddes, just west of Syracuse. In 1857 he sold his business and relocated near the Erie Canal in Syracuse to produce mold-formed Rockingham ware items that included bean pots, mixing bowls and figurines. The potter eventually introduced "white ware" table items, for which the company became well known. Farrar's successor added partners, forming the Empire Company, which in 1871 was reorganized as Onondaga Pottery Company. Its stockholders capitalized the company for $50,000 and expanded its lines to produce white table and toilet earthenware.

While located far from the centers of clay and coal mining and ceramic manufacturing found in New Jersey and Ohio, Onondaga Pottery was able to easily arrange for needed materials by transport on the Erie Canal and the railroads.

The tableware had remained mostly undecorated until 1886 when the company established an in-house decorating department. In 1896 the company was the first to install an in-house lithographic shop to print its decals. After years of research, general manager James Pass produced America's first truly vitreous clay body in 1886; publicly introduced as the *Imperial Geddo* line in 1891. It won a national Medal of Honor in 1893 at the Columbian World Exposition in Chicago. Starting in 1895, this superior ware was identified on the company's products as "Syracuse China."

With the introduction of its chip-resistant Round Edge shape in 1896, Onondaga Pottery became the national leader in the fast-growing hotel ware market where heavier, more durable products were needed. To demonstrate the superiority of the Syracuse China hotel ware,

company salesmen began leaving samples for the hotels to test. Over 2,500 samples were given away, and in 1902 a large backlog of orders resulted.

The company's finely decorated translucent china for home use also became a national bestseller. Made of the same durable Syracuse China body as hotel ware, it was jiggered into thinner, stylish shapes. Entering a new age of marketing and advanced technology, the company perfected its underglaze decal process and began national advertising campaigns in women's magazines. In 1921 the company built a new hotel ware factory in Syracuse on Court Street — the first linear, one-floor plant in the American china industry.

The company grew more diverse in its product lines and ventures. It was in the 1930s that the company's chief art designer created the art deco Econo-Rim shape, still in production, which ideally suited railway cars and diners where table space was at a premium. For decades it manufactured 70 percent of the nation's railroad china. During World War II, the company contributed to the war effort by making ceramic components for anti-tank land mines. From 1954 to 1959 an Electronics Division produced printed circuit ceramic components for radio and television. The company also began a Canadian china manufacturing subsidiary in 1959, expanding its business with a Made-in-Canada stamp for some 35 years.

It was in 1966 that the Onondaga Pottery Company changed its name to Syracuse China Company, taking advantage of the name of its long-famous product.

Marking its 100th anniversary in 1971, the company underwent a major transition, restructuring from a family-owned operation to a public stock company with the Syracuse China name. In 1978 shareholders voted to merge with Canadian

(Far left)
The Syracuse China stamp denotes such translucent white, beautiful table settings.

One example of an exquisite plate design by Syracuse China, many of which are created exclusively for restaurant clientele.

Pacific Investments, Ltd., a multibillion-dollar corporation with successful worldwide investments including hotels and food services. Retaining its own corporate identity and management team, Syracuse China entered a new era stronger than ever when, in the 1980s, it purchased Mayer China Company and Shenango Pottery. Efficiency improvements in the Court Street plant allowed the company to close the old Mayer and Shenango plants and move its production there as well.

When Canadian Pacific experienced an economic recession in 1989, Syracuse China was acquired by Susquehanna-Pfaltzgraff Company. This company eventually decided to return to its retail roots, and in 1995 Libbey Inc. of Toledo, Ohio, purchased Syracuse China to complement its strong presence in the food service industry. Together they offer two of the oldest and most respected brands in their categories, helping to solidify their markets in the United States and overseas.

Syracuse China's dedicated work force consists of over 320 hourly paid members of the Glass, Molders, Pottery, Plastics and Allied Workers International Union, as well as 80 salaried people. Employees are known for their community involvement, participating annually in the Corporate Challenge Road Race and fund drives for various charitable agencies.

JAQUITH INDUSTRIES, INC.

Jaquith Industries' stationary runway approach lighting masts not only show pilots the way to a safe landing, they safely get out of the way if the plane dips below the glide path. This versatility — a common engineering thread in the company's products — has made Jaquith the world leader in airport lighting supports.

High-flying Jaquith Industries began modestly as the Chemical Toilet Corporation, founded by C.L. Carpenter and Willard Jaquith in 1919 to manufacture and sell commodes and chemical toilets. It was the emerging age of inside "water closets," and the company's products were designed to ease this revolutionary convenience into living areas by making it as people-friendly as possible. The toilets were sold both commercially and to the military, beginning a customer profile that remains to this day. Military contracts account for about 15 percent of Jaquith's business. The company logically expanded the product line in 1921 to include septic tanks, quickly becoming that industry's leader. Leadership, both in management vision and specific industry focus, has been part of Jaquith Industries' corporate culture from the start.

The company's versatility and core competency — custom fabrication — made it possible to leap from underground septic tanks to airport lighting supports. The first products in this line, introduced in 1960, were light bases actually built into the runway. Not surprising, they were custom steel fabricated, as are the majority of Jaquith's products, from the molds that allow concrete to be poured to form median barriers on Interstates or sidewalks along Main Street to anchors that moor canoes or 150-foot yachts.

"We can manufacture almost any steel or aluminum product a customer wants in our state-of-the-art manufacturing and fabricating facilities," says D. Scott Jaquith, president. Donald S. Jaquith, Scott's father, formed modern Jaquith Industries in 1977 when he acquired and renamed Vega Industries' Syracuse operations — an outgrowth of the original family business. The expanding company had adopted the name Vega Industries in 1955 to reflect the diverse product lines, which

included the successful and patented Heatilator heat-circulating fireplaces.

Scott Jaquith maintains the management continuity in the family-owned business. It's contagious. William D. Schai holds the same position — vice president of sales — that his father did before retiring. The company is proud that there are other second- and third-generation workers in various departments. These familiar faces are also on familiar ground. Still on the same site, the original plant, built in 1926, now has four connecting factory buildings and an adjoining building for office operations. The company enjoys continued growth.

Corporate vision has been as constant as the company's employment continuity. Proactive management decisions that anticipated the Federal Aviation Administration's changing airport requirements are directly responsible for Jaquith Industries' global reputation. First, the company secured worldwide rights to a frangible (breakaway) Swedish-designed aluminum lighting approach mast and was production-ready when the FAA mandated this safety improvement.

Jaquith worked with the FAA in developing new safety standards, which led to the company's introduction of high-performing fiberglass lighting supports when FAA stipulations called for this safety upgrade. Jaquith's engineering ability to adapt to a changing marketplace has made the company the world's leading supplier of frangible fiberglass masts.

The challenges established by FAA guidelines, however, made even visionary Jaquith engineers blink. The lighting supports must be able to stand strong in the face of a 100-mile-per-hour wind, yet break away at the instant of impact from an off-course small plane making a 75-mile-an-hour approach. Jumbo jets, descending at 150 miles-an-hour, aren't much of a complication to the engineering-intensive task after that.

The industry word "frangible" does not simply translate to breakaway. It means the pole has the inertia-defying ability to accelerate to the speed of the plane as it breaks away, so the impact is unimpeding. This equipment is so high-tech that often the masts are sheared without the pilot's knowledge, sometimes only discovered through airport maintenance checks. All lighting masts and other extended navigational supports in the designated safe "clear zone" surrounding runways must meet these exacting requirements.

Jaquith Industries supplies frangible airport equipment to all 290 domestic airports serviced by commercial airlines. The equipment is growing in use — but not mandated until 2006 — internationally. Company engineers have basked in the sun dealing with the unique installation factors in the Azores, bundled up against hurricane-force winds siting masts at Shemya AFB, Alaska, and had to turn in their passports while helping install light supports at Warsaw (Poland) International Airport. The company also provided lighting supports for various landing sites for NASA's space shuttle program.

The company's long-range strategy for the airport lighting business is two-fold. Securing the international commercial market is one. The other, perhaps even more ambitious in scope, is working with the FAA to upgrade the airfield safety requirements and find ways to fund the improvements at the shoestring-run airfields that service non-commercial general aviation. There are 7,000 of these unregulated airports dotting the U.S. countryside.

Jaquith's product versatility is spotlighted by its lighting supports because at times, they can be showing a pilot the path to a touchdown on a cement runway that the company's BMF Metal Forms division helped build. Since 1961, Jaquith has engineered BMF metal forms that fashion concrete sidewalks, curbs and gutters, roads, highway median barriers, bridge parapets and slabs, and airport runways. The forms, which have industrial, residential and commercial applications, have helped build housing in Mexico, aprons for in-ground pools in California and setting fixtures for Atlanta's subway system.

In the early 1960s an employee backed up a Chevrolet station wagon to the loading dock and the company's first industrial washer/extractor laundry machine was delivered. Those 100-pound capacity machines went the way of that Chevy wagon. Now, trucks are needed to transport the company's 900-pound capacity washer/extractors. They are just one of the many products made by the custom fabricating division.

Because the company designs its own tools, dies, jigs and fixtures, Jaquith's in-house machine shop offers customers a facility unlimited in its ability, regardless of the exacting requirements, specification and end-use. Marine anchors, for years the immovable product line in Jaquith's custom operations, are still available, but the product line is being re-evaluated to bring it into 21st-century use.

The marketplace has changed dramatically since 1919 when the Jaquith family began its rise from outhouse to industry penthouse. The company's past success has been based on its vision to anticipate, its versatility to adapt and its engineering ability to develop successful new products. The company also considers these the foundation for the future.

Jaquith Industries, which supplies the world with an array of custom fabricated products, is the international leader in airport lighting supports. *Photo by Graphics Depot/Image Express*

BRISTOL-MYERS SQUIBB COMPANY

A critical miracle drug and a vital wartime mission marked the local beginnings of this world leader in pharmaceuticals, launching over a half-century of historical achievements in the discovery, development and distribution of life-saving medications.

World War II was raging and the company known in 1943 as Bristol-Laboratories had just received Washington's approval to manufacture the miracle drug, penicillin. The Allied invasion of Europe was coming; planners knew the dangers. The mission was to make as much penicillin as quickly as possible. The company purchased Cheplin Biological Labs on Taylor Street in Syracuse. There, the company produced its first commercial batch of penicillin in 1944. Within three months, Bristol-Myers and the country's other newly established penicillin manufacturers had produced enough of the antibiotic to treat all of the Allied soldiers wounded during the D-Day invasion of Normandy.

By 1945 the company was expanding to a new site on Thompson Road in East Syracuse, enlarging operations for civilian production and searching for new antibiotics. Dramatic breakthroughs soon followed, including the discovery of a new process to manufacture tetracycline and of methods to form synthetic varieties of penicillin. Each new discovery saved numerous lives and helped establish the company at the forefront of the pharmaceutical industry.

In 1989 E.R. Squibb Corporation joined Bristol-Myers Company, creating — at that time — one of the largest pharmaceutical companies in the world.

In its over 60 years, the Thompson Road campus has grown to encompass over 750 employees in 70 buildings on 90 acres. The company has invested over $70 million in safety and environmental improvements and was awarded the 1996 New York State Governor's Award for

The quest for pharmaceutical wonders is ongoing at Bristol-Myers Squibb's Biotechnology Development Facility in East Syracuse.

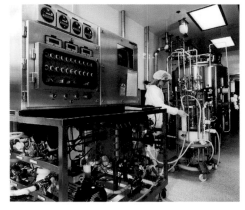

Pollution Prevention. Always known as a developer of new medicines, Bristol-Myers Squibb Syracuse became known in 2001 as the corporation's Center of Excellence for Biotechnology. Its employees are developing new compounds, manufacturing new biologics for use in clinical trials and hoping eventually to supply the worldwide market with these new medicines.

All along the way, Bristol-Myers Squibb has continued to believe in keeping close ties with the Syracuse and Onondaga County community. In addition to major corporate and employee contributions to the United Way, the company's highly visible community activities include support of a wide range of cultural, human service, health care and civic organizations. Its educational sponsorships, academic scholarships and special programs benefit individuals, local school districts and institutions of higher learning. The Bristol Omnitheater at the Museum of Science and Technology is a tangible philanthropic example — a place where thousands are exposed to the exciting world of science.

Bristol-Myers Squibb's local presence in Syracuse has meant notable milestones in the relentless pursuit of more effective solutions for the world's ills. From the early attempts to synthesize penicillin to the more recent development of anti-cancer drugs like TAXOL® (paclitaxel), the wonders worked by the company's dedicated employees have impacted health care worldwide. It's a mission all can be proud of, from a world leader with a local point of view.

CATHEDRAL CANDLE

Operating out of the same location for over 100 years, Cathedral Candle is the premier manufacturer of liturgical candles in North America. One of Cathedral's founders, Jacob Steigerwald, came to the United States in the latter part of the 19th century to apply his

extensive knowledge of candle making to the then-burgeoning American market. At the time, North American churches of all denominations were shrugging off the cold attitudes of religious reformism and were once again integrating decoration and adornment into their churches, fueling a tremendous growth in the specialty candle market. The early church candle industry literally "grew up" in Syracuse due to its concentration of those workers skilled in old-world craftsmanship and their desire to innovate and improve, and Steigerwald came to Syracuse to ply his trade for one of the largest manufacturers at that time. In 1897 Cathedral Candle was created, a company that for four generations of Steigerwalds has carried on his tradition of quality, innovation and service.

The manufacturing process itself is still housed in the brick factory on the north side of Syracuse where Cathedral first set up shop. Workers still continue the art form Steigerwald perfected by dipping and re-dipping beeswax candles by hand. Interestingly juxtaposed with traditional methods are some of the world's most advanced extrusion and compression machines. Extremely sophisticated and fully automated, they produce candles of varied dimensions, wick and all, from pulverized wax. The artistry continues three stories above the manufacturing floor where wax-working artists painstakingly decorate candles used for special occasions with sheets of 24-karat gold leaf and other materials.

Service is an age-old quality as well at Cathedral. By understanding that local dealers know their markets well and by not selling directly to churches, Cathedral has been able to build a large and very loyal customer base. Some dealers have been doing business with them for over a hundred years, and stories abound regarding Cathedral's legendary customer service.

Cathedral carries the tradition of quality and service over into its involvement with the local community as well. While manufacturing and service industries have gradually shifted to the suburbs, the company has stood its ground and still operates out of the same north side neighborhood where it was founded. This locale gives it access to a talented and loyal group of workers,

High technology and tradition — fourth generation (left to right) John Hogan, Mark Steigerwald, Louis Steigerwald III next to their high-production candlemaking line.

many of whom live within walking distance and of whom management is justifiably proud.

Jacob Steigerwald would be proud to see the company he started achieve domestic market leadership with the values he founded it upon: quality, innovation and service. As the 21st century dawns, Cathedral looks forward to serving the world market with those values as well.

HARRISON INDUSTRIAL SUPPLY

Founded in 1974 by Clarence "Harry" Harrison, Harrison Industrial Supply, Inc. is a leading distributor and service provider to industry. Headquartered in Syracuse, New York, Harrison also operates a facility in Rochester, New York. The operation

began at a desk in the bedroom of the home in historic Split Rock. Harry established a reputation of delivering the products customers ordered, along with providing good sound advice on how to properly apply the tooling in their application. Today Harrison distributes over two-hundred product lines to hundreds of customers in New York and Pennsylvania. International sales include Canada, China and Russia. Along with brand name products like Guhring, Mitsubishi, Norton, and Stanley Vidmar, Harrison offers a broad list of value-added services including, vendor managed inventory systems, automation equipment, tool resharpening, center repairs, and special cutting tools. Harrison's mission is to provide the best level of service to our customers in the industry. President Theodore Harrison and office manager James Nitsch look to make continuous improvements to meet the ever changing requirements and objectives of our customers. Theodore Harrison is quoted, "Our people are our strength; we have good caring experienced personel. Our focus is on providing value-added service with quality products. That is the foundation my father built, and this is the direction of our company into the future."

The East Syracuse headquarters of Harrison Industrial Supply, established in 1996.

The Rochester area facility for Harrison Industrial Supply, opened in 1997.

STICKLEY, AUDI & COMPANY

When your business is designing and producing the finest-quality furniture, which will be lovingly passed from generation to generation of proud owners, it helps to be family-owned. There's no corporate red tape — just family tuned passionately to the family business, its dreams

and traditions. That's how it's always been at Stickley.

The first family of Stickley was the Stickley brothers. Furniture making was in their blood. In 1900 Leopold left the Craftsman Shops in Eastwood, New York, when he and brother John George purchased a factory in nearby Fayetteville. They incorporated as L. & J.G. Stickley Furniture four years later. Leopold had worked at the Craftsman Shops with brother Gustav, a major proponent of the Arts and Crafts movement, which traced its roots back to John Ruskin's England. The movement favored a new aesthetic, stressing function and unadorned beauty over the ornate excesses of the Victorian age. The Stickleys believed in straightforward, honest craftsmanship in a shop where men could take pride in their creations.

When Gustav introduced the Mission Oak line in 1900 as "Simple furniture built along mission lines," it set the standard in fine American woodwork for the furniture industry. L. & J.G. Stickley also produced fine mission style pieces. In time, the mission style lost its popularity, but these early pieces became much coveted by museums and collectors. Experts over the years have recognized Stickley craftsmanship and acclaimed these creations for their purity of form. In 1922 Leopold Stickley announced "A line of period designs in popular finishes," taking inspiration from the houses of England, New England and Pennsylvania. Keeping the English influence in mind, Stickley inaugurated his Cherry Valley adaptations of American colonial designs. The company prospered and its reputation grew.

However, by the 1970s the brothers had died, and Leopold's widow, Louise, was struggling to keep the tradition going. Enter the second family of Stickley, the Audis.

Furniture is in Alfred Audi's blood; he was raised in the business. His father, E.J. Audi, was the country's largest retailer of Stickley furniture, located in New York City. Aminy, Alfred's wife, shares his enthusiasm for beauty and quality. Together, the Audis pulled Stickley back from the brink, purchasing it from Louise in 1974.

With faith and vision, the Audis went to work. They expanded the plant in 1981. They introduced the Traditional 18th Century line in the mid-80s and moved operations to a brand-new facility, Stickley Drive, Manlius. The Audi children began entering the family business. In what a noted editor called "The revival of the fittest," they reissued the Mission Collection in 1989. Each piece is made from solid quartersawn white oak or solid cherry; each is signed and dated by a proud craftsman. This was followed by Stickley's 21st Century, Directoire and Metropolitan Collections, and in 2000, by the Williamsburg Reserve Collection, in an exclusive agreement with the Colonial Williamsburg Foundation.

The families of Stickley have always seen furniture as something special to pass on, as something timeless, with integrity. They share that vision with their employees and customers. That's how it's always been.

Alfred and Aminy Audi.

COMFORT INN & SUITES
SYRACUSE AIRPORT

Conveniently located at the intersection of Interstates 81 and 90 (New York State Thruway), the Comfort Inn and Suites of Syracuse Airport features easy and quick access to the business, educational and entertainment locales of Upstate New York.

Hancock International Airport, the Walsh Regional Transportation Center (train/bus), the New York State Fairgrounds and Syracuse University are all within a 15-minute drive from the Inn's front door. And when one considers that one of the Northeast's premier shopping destinations—Carousel Center—is literally "down the street," it becomes obvious the Comfort Inn & Suites location is second to none in the Syracuse area.

Superior location, however, is only one of the many advantages that a guest enjoys at the hotel. Owned and managed by the largest hotel ownership group operating in the Syracuse market.— Tramz Hotels, Inc.—the Comfort Inn & Suites manages to serve both business and leisure travelers with ease.

The Comfort Inn & Suites caters not only to the business needs of today's traveler, but to their recreational desires as well. The hotel offers a full-scale fitness center and provides access to the largest indoor pool of any property in Central New York. In keeping with the Tramz marketing strategy of balancing business and leisure use of the property, the Comfort Inn & Suites has effectively used the fitness center and pool as assets for tapping into the weekend leisure market. The pool itself becomes a feature attraction on the

weekend when the hotel turns from a business to a weekend leisure destination. The Comfort Inn & Suites relationship with the community, however, extends well beyond its position as a weekend recreational destination. It also offers prime banquet facilities that can be used for catering wedding receptions, bridal showers and family reunions.

The Comfort Inn & Suites features:
- 156 Rooms & Suites
- Complimentary Deluxe Hot Breakfast
- Indoor Pool & Whirlpool
- Fitness Center
- Cocktail Bar
- Business Center
- Meeting/Banquet Facilities to up to 350
- "Guest Privileges" Room Upgrades Available
- A 100% Guarantee

Some of the area and regional attractions are:
- Carousel Center Shopping Mall – 3 miles
- Hancock International Airport – 4 miles
- Convention Center at Oncenter – 5 miles
- Onondaga Historical Museum – 5 miles
- Everson Museum of Art – 5 miles
- Historic Landmark Theater – 5 miles
- The Carrier Dome – 6 miles
- Syracuse University – 6 miles
- New York State Fairgrounds – 8 miles
- Turning Stone Casino – 30 miles east
- Waterloo Premium Outlets – 40 miles west

The management and staff at the Comfort Inn & Suites look forward to the opportunity of serving both local and visiting guests with a high standard of professionalism and true hospitality.

The Comfort Inn & Suites offers its guests access to the largest pool in Central New York.

PASTABILITIES

Pastabilities became a downtown Syracuse restaurant mainstay in 1982 at a time when restaurants in the city's business district were disappearing almost as quickly as the 30,000 downtown workers were leaving each night for their commute to the suburbs. The owners used

their noodles to help stem that tide by creating a niche eatery that immediately appealed to the busy lunch crowd and soon became a popular beginning for people meeting in the city for a night on the town.

Karyn Korteling, proprietress, credits Pastabilities' success to an unwavering commitment to serve food made from scratch. Homemade pasta, sauces, soups, salads and desserts highlight a versatile menu that includes a variety of breads baked fresh throughout the day in the restaurant's bakery.

While food is the most important part of a Pastabilities visit, it is not the only element that sets this restaurant apart. Pastabilities was a labor of love for Korteling and co-owner Patrick Heagerty, and it showed right away as a large and loyal clientele was quickly built. The partners' commitment and customer-oriented ethic fostered a congenial atmosphere that continually draws new diners and constantly lures repeat ones. Providing this alluring dining experience at a price that feels as good as the food tastes headlined the owners' plan from the start.

The plan was jolted in 1995 when Heagerty died unexpectedly from illness. The bond that had developed between the partners, restaurant and the public, however, was strong enough for Korteling to continue the tradition. "It was difficult at first," she says, "but Pat's sense of commitment made it a little easier for me."

Pastabilities' dinner menu is peppered with special entrees along with pasta staples for the less adventurous. Pasta with red or white sauce, meatballs, sausage and fettuccine Alfredo are there if a diner passes on items like sweet potato ravioli, grilled sesame-soy tuna with portabello, cremini and button mushrooms or sautéed chicken with roasted cherry tomatoes and basil. The two-page evening menu — also homemade — contains a wide selection of meat, vegetarian and pasta dishes. Korteling says a visit to Pastabilities isn't complete without trying her special spicy hot tomato oil.

Pastabilities has evolved from a one-room lunch spot into a three-dining-room establishment with a full-service bar and seasonal outdoor dining in its quaint piazza. True to its modest roots, however, a handwritten lunch menu hangs behind the open preparation area, and the interior's early-1900s natural brick walls have been restored for unassumingly charming dining.

Pastabilities moved to its current location in 1985, becoming the restaurant centerpiece in the redevelopment of a promising section of Syracuse. Armory Square — Syracuse's answer to New York City's SOHO district — is now downtown's fashionable social hub, in part because of Pastabilities' popularity.

Armory Square may be trendy but that's not a word Korteling uses for her restaurant. She says her menu purposely stays away from trends while continually being updated to reflect changing tastes. Pastabilities, she says, will always be a restaurant experience designed to comfortably challenge a diner's adventurous appetite while also providing pasta dishes mom would make at home.

Karyn Korteling blends tradition and innovation at Pastabilities.

DEPARTMENT OF AVIATION, CITY OF SYRACUSE

The 20th century saw the fledgling aviation industry grow from its humble beginnings of one- and two-seater propeller-driven aircraft to the familiar commercial, cargo and military jets of the present. Visitors to Syracuse Hancock International Airport can catch a glimpse

of that remarkable history and get a feel for aviation then and now. Owned by the City of Syracuse and operated by the Department of Aviation, the Airport has entered the 21st century as a vital community activity center. As such, it remains faithful to its colorful past, yet is always looking for ways to improve. Its people are continually striving for safer, more reliable air travel and seeking to both educate and engage. Today, the Airport is not only a good neighbor; it has also emerged as a powerful economic force essential to the fiscal well being of Central New York.

At the *Discover the Airport* Exhibit in the Main Terminal, visitors can sit in the cockpit of a Boeing 727, listen to Federal Aviation Administration Air Traffic Control Tower communications, learn everything they always wanted to know about luggage tags and see that a black box is actually orange (they can look inside one too). Visitors can choose from a variety of selections on the video wall, view other interesting displays, and review historical information and photos dating back to the early days of aviation when barnstormers and celebrities such as Amelia Earhart visited Syracuse.

In 1926 the City purchased Hinsdale Farm in Amboy Center, Camillus, for its first airport. The famed Transatlantic solo hero Charles Lindbergh brought his airplane, the *Spirit of St. Louis*, to Amboy Airport in 1927. Later, he attended a reception at Syracuse University's Archbold Stadium, thrilling thousands of cheering fans. The first airmail arrived on May 1, 1928. By the 1930s spectators were flocking to Amboy's grass runways to see the likes of humorist Will Rogers, radio personality Lowell Thomas or a famous World War I Flying Ace. The excitement and the mystique of aviation were growing rapidly in the public consciousness.

By the advent of World War II the Amboy Airport was becoming too small. Moreover, several local flying instructors were pressed into military duty, and Amboy became a flight-training center. In December 1941, just after the Pearl Harbor attack, the Army Air Corps authorized the construction of a Syracuse airbase on a 3,500-acre parcel north of the city. Several working farms were displaced by the construction. In 1942 three 5,500-foot runways were built over existing asparagus beds at a cost to the Army of over $16 million (asparagus can still be picked there in the spring).

In the summer of 1942, 1,200 men arrived at the base. Construction at the Mattydale Bomber Base was completed in 1943. The first airmen to train there became known as "the Boys from Syracuse." They assembled, tested and flew B-17 and B-24 aircraft on bombing missions to the European Theater. They also used the base as a staging and storage area, repairing and re-outfitting aircraft as needed for the war effort. The military base was formally deactivated in 1946.

On September 17, 1949, the property, by then leased by the City, was reopened as the Clarence E. Hancock Airport, named for the U.S. Congressman who served Syracuse and Onondaga County. The gala festivities, attended by over 25,000, included a night airshow. The first commercial aircraft to depart from Hancock was a Colonial Airlines flight piloted by Capt. Arthur Hinkley on September 19, 1949, bound for Pennsylvania, Baltimore and Washington, D.C., before returning to Syracuse. The original terminal was a renovated Army Air Corps machine shop just off Malden Road in Mattydale.

In 1962 a new terminal building opened in the center of the airfield to provide easy access from the planned Interstate 81. By 1970 over 2 million people a year were using the Airport. Later that year, Hancock earned international status as a port of entry for foreign travelers and a new name, Syracuse Hancock International Airport.

During the Gulf War, members of the New York Air National Guard 174th Fighter Wing, the contemporary "Boys from Syracuse," departed from Hancock and served the nation like their predecessors, flying hundreds of critical missions over Iraq in Operation Desert Storm. The 174th was one of only two Air National Guard units activated in that Middle East conflict.

In 1992 the Department of Aviation voluntarily initiated the Residential Sound Insulation Program (RSIP) to provide relief to area residents who were impacted by aircraft noise. The Federal Aviation Administration (FAA) funded the majority of the program, which was also funded by New York State and the City of Syracuse. Since the program's inception, over 1,000 local homes have received sound insulation treatment. This

cutting-edge program, one of the first of its kind in the nation, has been the model for subsequent programs around the country, including those in Cleveland and San Diego. The RSIP was completed at the end of 2001.

The expansion and renovation of the Main Terminal was completed in 1996. All through the renovation, the Airport remained open. The number of passenger gates was expanded from 15 to 23. By 1999, the FAA's new control tower, the $7 million Air Traffic Control Tower and TRACON (Terminal Radar Approach Control) facility, was completed. This facility was only the second in the country to be equipped with the Standard Terminal Automation Replacement System (STARS) using state-of-the-art technologies, including user-friendly color monitors and electronic alarms.

The Office of the Commissioner, Department of Aviation, has reported these vital statistics: the Airport site encompasses 2,000 acres of land in

Onondaga County, about 6 miles northeast of the city of Syracuse, giving Hancock more available land to expand than any other upstate airport. Its 325,000-square-foot main passenger terminal makes it the largest building maintained by the City. Hancock's cargo terminal is itself 100,000 square feet. There is a 9,000-foot primary runway and a 7,500-foot crosswinds runway. Proposed expansion of the primary runway will provide greater safety during marginal weather conditions by allowing more braking and acceleration distance. It will also allow larger aircraft to take off with a full load capacity. The Airport maintains 8 miles of fence line and 100 lane miles of pavement. There are more than 3,000 airfield lights. There are parking spaces for over 4,000 vehicles. Nationally, Hancock Airport ranks 85th by number of passengers, though the city of Syracuse ranks 145th by population. Half of North America's population lives within a 750-mile radius of the Airport.

Other notable improvements at Hancock include installation of the Deicing Fluid Collection and Treatment System (deicing system); the Flight Information and Display System (FIDS); and the launching of the Airport's own Web site. The deicing system enables the Airport to comply with the Clean Water Act and includes three aircraft deicing pads, two pump stations, a flow-routing structure (segregates dilute and concentrated deicing fluid flows), three 2.15-million-gallon aerobic treatment lagoons and two 62,000-gallon steel storage tanks. This project preserves and enhances the safety of the national air transportation system while protecting the local environment. Funded entirely by the Department of Aviation, the FIDS is a real-time updateable state-of-the-art video / computer system that was installed for the benefit of the more than 2 million passengers who use the Airport annually. Visitors to the Web site can find accessible information at their fingertips about the Airport, the airlines, ground transportation and Airport services, as well as Syracuse and Central New York.

Besides the popular *Discover the Airport* Exhibit, education and entertainment at Hancock take several distinct forms. The Airport Tour Program conducts several tours a year. These tours can be tailored to fit the age and interest level of the participants, who range in age from pre-kindergarten to senior citizen groups. Scheduled tours can be on foot or by bus. These might include informative stops at the Main Terminal and Ramp, the FAA Air Traffic Control Tower, the Aircraft Rescue and Fire Fighting Facility, the Airfield Maintenance Facility, the Airport Division of the Syracuse Police Department, the Cargo Terminal and the General Aviation Ramp.

Aviation Explorer Post #636 is the first chartered post of the Aviation/ Aerospace Education Foundation, Inc. and the Department of Aviation. Staff members volunteer to provide programs and activities that inspire and educate youth aged 14-19 about the many rewarding and challenging career opportunities in aviation. Members of the Post become involved in behind-the-scenes activities at the Airport. Youth who want to learn more about aviation and the military

Aerial photo of Syracuse Hancock International Airport, Syracuse, New York, c. 1999 can enroll in the Civil Air Patrol Syracuse Umoja Composite Squadron, New York #407. Members of the Civil Air Patrol progress through a program of aerospace education, leadership training and physical fitness.

Since 1997 Syracuse Hancock International Airport has hosted the Syracuse International Airshow, bringing to the community such world-renowned attractions as the U.S. Air Force Thunderbirds, three-time U.S. Aerobatic Champion Patty Wagstaff, the U.S. Navy Flight Demonstration Squadron Blue Angels and the Northern Lights Aerobatic Team. Besides phenomenal aerial entertainment, each Airshow has featured a vast array of displays, allowing the public to get up close to an F-16 Fighting Falcon, a C-5 Galaxy and an F-117 Nighthawk Stealth Fighter. Proceeds from the Airshow help to fund the Aviation Explorer Post #636; the Civil Air Patrol Syracuse Umoja Composite Squadron, New York #407; the Aviation/Aerospace Education Foundation, Inc; and four annual scholarships for students who are entering or enrolling in aviation-related curricula at qualified schools.

However it is measured, the impact of Syracuse Hancock International Airport is a benefit to the economy of Syracuse and Onondaga County. More than 2,000 people are employed at the Airport, which has an annual payroll exceeding $75 million. Airport tenants generate over $162 million in annual output. Economic studies have shown that nearly half of the enplanements at the Airport are visitors to Syracuse and Central New York. If the average visitor stays for 3 days, the survey figures indicate a nearly $200 million contribution to the local economy annually, principally in the areas of lodging, dining, local transportation, shopping and entertainment. Airport tenants add another $95 million annually for the region, with some 1,700-plus jobs and $44 million in annual payroll, making the Airport a formidable and powerful economic engine.

Syracuse Hancock International Airport has become an economic development hub and an

intermodal (air/truck) transportation center served by eight major airlines and several regional carriers. Its home, the seven-county area of Central New York, houses a population of more than 1.3 million.

Syracuse Hancock International Airport is well on its way to realizing the Department of Aviation's vision as a world-class airport and international gateway. True to its history, it has continued to accommodate general aviation, commercial and military operations, while becoming a community activity center, promoting aviation education and world-class aviation entertainment. The Airport meets its commitment to safety and reliability every day. For example, despite its reputation for snowfall, during calendar year 2005, Syracuse Hancock International Airport was closed less than 2 hours due to weather. This statistic is a mighty tribute to the facility's 18 major pieces of equipment; its advanced snow/ice mitigation system, which includes strategically placed electronic ground sensors; and its skilled, experienced personnel.

In summary, as the aviation industry enters its second century, Syracuse Hancock International Airport is a good neighbor, a vital economic force and a peerless community resource.

Visitors learn about the history of the Airport at the *Discover the Airport* Exhibit.

NATIONAL GRID/ NIAGARA MOHAWK

The tapestry that was Niagara Mohawk and now National Grid, an Upstate utility whose service crisscrosses 24,000 square miles of New York and provides electricity and gas to more than 1.5 million people, began with a stream in the frontier outpost of Oswego in 1823.

When the Oswego Canal Company, Niagara Mohawk's earliest predecessor company, dug a ditch creating a waterway to harness the power of the Oswego River, it opened a history channel that would help electrify a waiting world along the way.

Niagara Mohawk's growth pinpoints much of New York state's early economic progress and civic development. More than 90 power companies and their surrounding population and industrial pockets dotted the state's countryside in 1896 when electricity generated in Niagara Falls flickered lights in Buffalo, 26 miles away. The modern power generation and distribution business began that instant. The successful and efficient bulk transmission of electrical power over distance — a triumph for alternating current proponents — by the Niagara Falls Power Company, another predecessor, revolutionized worldwide industrial growth and dramatically transformed the state's power generation landscape. Those 90 pioneering water and gas generating companies eventually merged, forming the foundation of Niagara Mohawk. Hundreds more would join, each contributing tradition and strength to the evolving company.

National Grid's headquarters in Syracuse.

One history-altering impact of that first transmission was the freedom to locate industry anywhere wires could be strung. As usage grew, the demand for reliability required an integrated business model to improve service in these sprouting industrial centers. Smaller generating entities combined for economy and efficiency throughout Upstate, eventually consolidating into the Buffalo Niagara and Eastern Power

Corporation in the west, Northeastern Power Corporation in central New York and the Mohawk Hudson Power Corporation in the east. In 1929 these groups formed the Niagara Hudson Power Corporation, then the world's largest electrical utility system. Niagara Mohawk Power Corporation was established when the company restructured in 1950.

As Niagara Mohawk emerged, company commitment to the extended family grew with management emphasis on solid association and community involvement throughout the service area. That community conscience was woven with environment-sensitive principles into the company's fabric as far back as the 1850s during early development in Niagara Falls.

The modest beginning of Niagara Mohawk's community and environmental concerns grew through the company's evolution from water currents to electrical transmissions. The company is involved with quality-of-life issues in every community it serves, from what's in the ground to what's in the air and everything in between. Besides a tradition of employee volunteerism, National Grid financially supports the company's community commitment with grants to nonprofit organizations dedicated to the environment, conservation, regional development, and social and cultural advancement.

Niagara Mohawk, now a vital part of National Grid, an international networks business based in the U.K., is a blending of the pioneer spirit of its predecessors and a culture of insight and innovation resulting in a responsible energy provider and industry leader. It is a history stream that continues as the company meets the challenges of its third century.

THE POST-STANDARD

The Post-Standard has been the primary source of news, information and advertising in Central New York for the better part of two centuries. In the 21st century it enters another dynamic era of publishing with its $40 million pressroom expansion, completed in August 2001.

The Post-Standard building stands as an impressive focal point of Syracuse's newly renovated and vibrant Clinton Square.

The Post-Standard has realized great progress in the news gathering business since its origins in 1829 with publication of the *Onondaga Standard*. In 1939 Samuel I. Newhouse purchased and combined the *Standard* with the *Syracuse Post*. In 1944 *The Herald*, the *Syracuse Journal* and the *Sunday American* joined the Newhouse family. With the nationwide trend in morning readership, the evening *Herald Journal* gave way to *The Post-Standard* in 2001.

Today, *The Post-Standard* is the largest news gathering organization in Central New York. It employs more than 500 people at its modern plant in the heart of downtown Syracuse. It runs a busy Metro Desk and hosts regional bureaus in Cayuga, Madison and Oswego counties, as well as suburban bureaus in Camillus, Cicero and Manlius. The company also maintains offices in Albany and Washington, D.C., to provide strong state and national news coverage. Several wire services also contribute national and international news.

The high caliber of its journalists and other staff members has resulted in many local, state and national honors. *The Post-Standard* was one of three finalists for the 1992 Pulitzer Prize for a series on deadly prisons. The daily newspaper circulates to 305,000 readers, while *The Post-Standard on Sunday* reaches 379,000 readers. In addition, the company has two active Web sites offering daily news and features.

A vital part of the community it serves, *The Post-Standard* actively supports many community causes and area institutions. It contributes over $370,000 annually in donations and sponsorships supporting the S.I. Newhouse School of Public Communications of Syracuse University, the Syracuse Symphony, the Syracuse Opera, the Everson Museum, the Milton J. Rubenstein Museum of Science and Technology, and Literacy Volunteers, to name a few. The company also sponsors the annual Old Newsboys Drive that helps to buy toys and food for the needy.

Taking an active role in city renewal efforts, *The Post-Standard* chose to expand its downtown facility in 2001. It purchased a new offset lithographic press, one of only three of its type in the country, which allows for expanded color use virtually anywhere in the paper as well as faster, finer reproduction. The press is showcased for public viewing in the new north wing addition.

With its award-winning staff, strong ties to the community and cutting-edge publishing technology, *The Post-Standard* looks forward to providing world-class local news for many generations to come.

A view of *The Post-Standard* press hall addition.
Dennis Nett/ The Post-Standard

COSTELLO, COONEY & FEARON, PLLC

Costello, Cooney & Fearon, LLP has played a prominent role in providing expert and diverse legal services to Syracuse and the wider community for more than 100 years.

Headquartered in downtown Syracuse, the practice was first established in 1896 by David F. Costello, a distinguished attorney and community leader. Costello was soon joined by other eminent attorneys who comprised the original group of partners: J. Henry Walters, Charles E. Cooney Sr. and Oliver D. Burden. By 1918 George R. Fearon became a partner succeeding Walters, and the firm assumed its present name.

The firm boasts a legacy of distinguished, active involvement in civic and community affairs by its members. Burden became U.S. Attorney for the Northern District of New York, while Walters became a New York State assemblyman and senator. Walters was also instrumental in creating legislation to fund the opening of the State University of New York College of Environmental Science and Forestry in Syracuse and served on its board of directors. He eventually left the firm to serve as chief counsel to the RKO Theater Group in New York City. Charles Cooney Sr. was an incorporator of Crouse Irving Hospital in Syracuse and for many years was president of the E.W. Edwards & Sons chain of department stores. Fearon also served a term in the state assembly and was then elected to the state senate in 1920, serving for 16 years, including a tenure as majority leader. Fearon later became president of the Onondaga County Bar Association, which honored him as its Distinguished Lawyer of the Year in 1970. Continuing the great tradition of Sen. Fearon, Vincent A. O'Neil, who has practiced with the firm for almost 50 years, was named Onondaga County's Distinguished Lawyer of the Year in 1998.

Costello, Cooney & Fearon continues its legacy of impeccable law practice and civic leadership with its current team of attorneys — all holding distinguished credentials and active in their communities. The firm's attorneys include former members of the Syracuse City Council and Onondaga County Legislature as well as two current town court justices, one of whom also serves as the Onondaga County public administrator. Members of the firm also serve as board members for civic and charitable organizations, including the American Red Cross, Catholic Charities, the Westhill School District, the Central New York Regional Transportation Authority, the Multiple Sclerosis Society, the West African Eye Foundation Inc., the Brady Faith Center Inc. and the Vietnam Veterans' Leadership Program.

While steeped in tradition, the firm succeeds by practicing law in a progressive and creative manner. Able to handle virtually any legal matter, the firm's attorneys deal in major practice areas that include litigation, labor and employment, health care, municipal, business/corporate, environmental, estate planning, banking/commercial

All photos by Klineberg Inc. Commercial Photography

and real estate. Its diversified clientele includes major corporations, a host of small businesses, insurance companies, banks and other financial institutions, municipalities and a variety of organizations in the health care field, including a number of area hospitals. Along with institutional clients, the firm handles all types of civil litigation as well as individuals seeking personalized, dependable legal services.

While the firm's founders practiced law at the turn of the 20th century in an era of limited governmental regulation and oversight, the firm's current attorneys practice in a complex and highly regulated marketplace. The firm's members have answered the challenges of the 21st century leading seminars on a variety of legal issues and by entering into the arena and engaging in some of the day's most complicated legal issues, including forming the area's first Health Maintenance Organization as well as the area's first hospice care organization; creating a laboratory alliance in a joint venture among three of the area's major hospitals; and litigating

complex and novel legal issues involving the energy industry.

By broadening its practice areas to meet client needs, Costello, Cooney and Fearon has realized a high rate of growth in recent years, with the firm having more attorneys now than at any time in its history. In 1999 the firm opened a second office in Albany, enabling it to provide efficient service to clients across upstate New York.

The firm operates under a philosophy of professionalism, efficiency, cost consciousness and personalized client service. Its over 25 attorneys, along with a staff of paralegals and administrative personnel, effectively serve the firm's spectrum of clients. The moderate size of the firm allows its members to have daily contact

with each other and work closely together. The firm also embraces modern management techniques that encourage all the lawyers to contribute to the operation of the firm, take part in business decisions and gain experience in diversified areas. Each lawyer concentrates in more than one legal area and can draw from many areas of expertise to provide excellent service to clients. With a resourceful, innovative legal staff and a supportive working environment, its team of attorneys can deliver the highest-quality services in the most economical manner possible.

Costello, Cooney and Fearon looks forward to continuing its tradition and promise of superior, customized legal services to a broad array of clientele in Syracuse and beyond.

DAL POS ARCHITECTS, LLC.

Dal Pos Architects, LLC., has drawn the lines that connect the changing profile of American retail shopping from the neighborhood strip malls of the 1970s to the regional megamalls of the 21st century.

The company's history begins with Alfred H. Dal Pos, who formed the architectural business in 1971 in Skaneateles, 20 miles from Syracuse. Work at the five-member firm was diversified from inception, with a mix of residential, small-office and retail buildings. The company's retail focus, which would become the Dal Pos hallmark, evolved as work expanded from the strip mall market. The multifaceted company established solid retail credentials, and suitors came knocking as its regional reputation grew. The retail and commercial niche now represents 90 percent of the company's overall business.

During these years, Dal Pos built a business relationship with The Pyramid Cos., a Syracuse-based developer. The two collaborated on a number of projects, one being Central New York's shopping jewel, the 1.5-million-square-foot Carousel Center.

In 1985 Dal Pos Architect, P.C. moved to The Clinton Exchange, an award-winning building it restored in downtown Syracuse. From its new headquarters, the firm provides a full array of professional services to a growing and diverse client list that concentrates projects primarily throughout the northeast, with signature buildings from Maine to Florida. These include regional shopping malls, free-standing retail facilities, restaurants, hotels, office buildings, governmental and public facilities, theaters and condominiums. The firm's five principals formed Dal Pos Architects, LLC. in 2000 after Alfred Dal Pos retired, continuing the uninterrupted Dal Pos tradition of excellence.

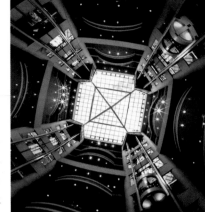

There are four observation elevators in Carousel Center's glittering seven-story glass atrium. *Photo by Photomedia*

Versatility and flexibility have been part of Dal Pos' corporate culture from the beginning. They have allowed the company to make its quantum leaps in architectural technology from drafting boards to computer-generated imaging and to stay ahead of the constant challenges posed by a whimsical shopping public and changing retail patterns.

"Shopping methods and approaches are always in flux, but some changes driving the design of up-to-date consumer-inviting centers during the last 10 years have been dramatic," says Edward W. Benjamin, partner.

Carousel Center is a case in point. When it was completed in 1990, the mall reflected the retail picture at that time. The major tenants were high-end. The architectural finishes were glitzy and high-tech. The seven-story glass atrium, with four interior observation elevators leading to the glittering skylight, attracted and wowed shoppers from the region, neighboring states and Canada. But, almost before Carousel's window washers finished their first maintenance, Dal Pos was making a 180-degree professional adjustment preparing the model of Palisades Center in West Nyack, New York. When Palisades Center opened in 1998, it reflected shopping and marketing shifts with a distinct industrial approach and character.

Dal Pos research enables the company to plan proactively. Carousel Center's floor plan, for example, has an inherent flexibility, facilitating location redesigning for changing tenants' requirements, a key in keeping the mall current. Dal Pos also incorporates utilitarian aspects in designing mall exteriors so the shell will age well.

Public demand continually alters mall designs, which now must provide for the entire shopping spectrum, from major discounters to top-of-the-line image retailers. "People go into these malls today expecting to find anything they want and the stores reflect that," Benjamin says.

One of the things people want more of has nothing to do with the core business of a shopping mall. Entertainment facilities have escalated from filling-time conveniences to important spending-time magnets.

"There is a different dynamic at work with entertainment components than a decade ago when we designed the carousel area off the food court at Carousel Center," Benjamin says. "Instead of peaceful merry-go-rounds, malls have become multiride action playlands." Carousel Center's experience was invaluable when Dal Pos incorporated a 60-foot diameter Ferris wheel and a small roller coaster into Palisades Center. Bigger and better amusement attractions are becoming a necessary draw in regional malls because of an emerging family trend turning shopping into a daylong affair, Benjamin says.

The flexibility patterns of Dal Pos' retail experience helped generate the amusement facility expertise. Carousel Center's carousel blueprint fell into place, but the company had the foresight to understand the evolving amusement climate. Dal Pos is now involved in a number of intricate entertainment facilities, including an aquarium, casino, restaurants and a number of large theater complexes.

Dal Pos' shopper-stopping regional malls — led by Carousel Center and Palisades Center — are just one area of architectural excellence that has made a name for the company. Two Syracuse historic restoration and adapted re-use projects, The Clinton Exchange and Bridgewater Place, received coveted American Institute of Architects awards. The Clinton Exchange restored the 70-year old abandoned U.S. Post Office and Federal Building into a vibrant professional complex. Bridgewater Place rehabilitated a 75-year-old decayed downtown industrial dinosaur into an urban showpiece at the entrance to the city.

Dal Pos' corporate work, including the Kodak Office Building in Rochester and the interior of Corning's technology-crisp Decker Engineering Building in Corning, New York, has been the source of referral business because of their award-winning features. Hotels and conference centers, department and retail stores, office interiors and parking structures, casual and formal restaurants, and a montage of projects, from the Stratton, Vermont Ski Lodge to the Skaneateles Country Club round out the company's diverse expertise.

The future could not be any closer for Dal Pos. Carousel Center, now scheduled for massive expansion, continues the redevelopment of Onondaga Lake's south shore and Syracuse's Inner Harbor initiatives. This new regional entertainment center will feature state-of-the-art interactive pavilions, restaurants, theaters and retail stores. Part of the overall expansion will include model research facilities for the study of sustainable design and more energy-efficient building systems.

Whether the project is to restore a dilapidated city eyesore into a stop on a sightseeing tour, combine the aesthetic and practical sides of business in a Fortune 500 company building or design a retail shopping jewel, versatility has been the Dal Pos trademark. Dal Pos Architects, LLC., simply calls it creative problem solving.

The Kodak Office Building in Rochester reflects Dal Pos' architectural versatility. ©1989 David Lamb Photography

JCM ARCHITECTURAL ASSOCIATES

From the unique date of its founding on the bicentennial Fourth of July, 1976, JCM Architectural Associates has flourished for more than a quarter century by providing its clients with creative, cost-effective design solutions and by taking on the toughest challenges.

From the outset, the firm's approach to project management has also been somewhat unique, as well as consistently successful. The JCM philosophy calls for hands-on principal participation with a strong accent on client service throughout each project.

The firm provides complete architectural design services and interior planning for commercial, municipal and residential buildings, with demonstrated expertise in restoration, rehabilitation, renovation, adaptive reuse as well as new construction. JCM offers all services, from schematic designs through working drawings and construction phasing, along with cost estimating that realistically reflects current construction techniques and economic conditions.

Dey's Centennial Plaza, Syracuse.

JCM's dramatic restorations have been recognized both locally and nationally and have won numerous awards. In the beginning, the firm's focus was on restoration work, starting in the Hawley Green Historic District of Syracuse with the restoration and adaptive reuse of four houses in the 300 block, conversions from single-family homes to offices and other commercial space. By 1982 the firm had completed the restoration of the Greenway Place Apartments, one of the city's first apartment complexes, which were originally built for the employees of the Greenway Brewery, Syracuse's first brewery.

During the 80s JCM completed Bishop's House Estates on James Street, converting the historic Bishop's residence to market-rate condominiums. Moving beyond Syracuse, the firm completed the first "open plan" office space design

for the Department of Social Services, Oswego County, New York. This became the prototype for social service office configurations throughout the state. In Pulaski, New York, the firm completed an historic restoration and a sympathetic addition to the circa 1826 Federal-style courthouse.

In the 90s JCM's focus expanded not only beyond Syracuse and Central New York, but also to encompass both state and national clients in a variety of exciting assignments and new venues. Educational clients such as Syracuse University, Le Moyne College and the State University of New York presented challenging renovation projects involving advanced technologies, distance learning and wireless classrooms.

With the spectacular Syracuse area Landmark Theatre project, JCM completed the restoration of one of Syracuse's urban treasures. The 1928 theatre, designed by Thomas W. Lamb as a Hindu-Moorish fantasy palace, was the talk of the town. By the 1990s the building's deterioration was severe enough to warrant hiring JCM to restore the Grand Lobby, Promenade, Musician's Loft, and Salina Street and Jefferson Street Lobbies, as well as to oversee the restoration and conservation of the magnificent Indo-Persian canvas mural. JCM addressed many other infrastructure issues including the lighting of exit ways, code improvements, Americans with Disabilities Act (ADA) compliance, heating, ventilating, air conditioning, electrical upgrades and seating modifications. The restored Landmark stands today as a symbol of the "golden age" of the theater industry.

JCM Architectural Associates received the Design Award for Recognition of Merit from the American Institute of Architects Justice Center Design Competition for its work on the Oswego County Public Safety Center, Oswego, New York. This 200,000-square-foot complex includes a 120-bed correctional facility, the sheriff's and probation departments and the family and county courts, as well as the 911 Operations Center and District Attorney's Office. The $23.9 million facility, designed as a classic civic building, began as a correctional facility and Sheriff's Department project, but evolved into a multiuse center during planning and as a result of the New York State Court Facilities Act. The correctional facility is at the rear of the building, not visible from Route 481. It is a full-service detention facility with "podular" inmate housing in all security levels from minimum to maximum.

JCM has worked with Sears, Roebuck & Co. since 1996 and has completed modernizing renovations and new additions to 56 stores in 10 East Coast states from Maryland to Maine. The modernization process has included implementing the latest interior and exterior national design standards, Americans with Disabilities Act (ADA) compliance, hazardous materials abatement and installation of life safety systems. Working with Sears sales personnel and contractors, JCM has prepared construction phasing schedules in order to maintain store operations and sales goals throughout the duration of the construction processes. JCM Architectural Associates received Sears, Roebuck & Co.'s Excellence in Design Award in 1998, 1999, 2000 and 2001.

For its adaptive reuse work on Dey's Centennial Plaza, Syracuse, JCM Architectural Associates received the American Institute of Architects Central New York Chapter Excellence in Design Award. Five buildings were built for the Dey Brothers Department Stores circa 1890-1915. The main 210,000-square-foot structure, designed by renowned architect Archimedes Russell, is a Second Renaissance Revival-style six-story structure. The Dey's Centennial Plaza demonstrates a level of architectural detailing and articulation that is a prime example of Syracuse's rich heritage of historic building. Removal of the 1969 amorphous marble façade unveiled the building's original splendor, creating a major impact on its surroundings and adding impetus to the continuing downtown revitalization process.

Syracuse-area Landmark Theatre, interior.

In recent years the firm has added new dimensions: golf course clubhouse construction and renovation of the courses themselves. JCM has completed the new 10,000-square-foot Seneca Falls Golf Course Clubhouse in Seneca Falls, New York. In addition, the firm has been involved in designing several new 18-hole courses throughout Central New York, including two in Onondaga County and one in Oswego County. Clubhouse renovations by JCM have been completed at the Oswego Country Club, the Tuscarora Golf Club and the famed Bellevue Country Club.

Since 1976 JCM founder Joseph C. Maryak's vision has been a hands-on practice. He and his partner, Daniel J. Manning, participate from the initial client phone call and apply strong customer service and unique problem-solving abilities to the toughest challenges. JCM's contributing staff helps solve those problems and meet those challenges. Mr. Maryak's founding vision has become reality.

KING & KING, ARCHITECTS LLP

As the oldest architectural firm in continuous practice in New York State and the fourth-oldest in the United States, King & King, Architects LLP has a long and distinguished history. Founded by the legendary Archimedes Russell in 1868 and joined

20 years later by Melvin King, the firm's signature structures tell a history of architecture in Upstate New York. From the gothic-like spires of Crouse College to the modern style of the Greater Syracuse Chamber of Commerce, the creative designs of King & King can be seen throughout the city of Syracuse and across the wide and varied geography of Upstate New York.

Through that history, the firm has built long-standing relationships with partners in both the public and private sectors. Working for various educational, health care, laboratory and corporate clients, the firm specializes in designing highly technical spaces.

The new Center for Forensic Sciences, as well as the expansions at Madison-Oneida BOCES, Marquardt Switches, Inc. and the Jewish Home of Central New York are all testimony to King & King's creative vision.

Always looking for innovative ways to serve its clients, King & King formed its interior design group

in 2000 to provide a more comprehensive scope of design services. Over the past decade, technology and sustainable design have transformed the way the firm provides its services, but its people remain the foundation of its success. The firm has invested heavily in its staff in both technical and soft skill development, knowing that as a service industry, its people are truly its most important asset.

Commitment to Syracuse and the Upstate community is very important at the firm. Its dedication garnered it a Central New York Volunteer of the Year Award as well as Business Partner of the Year by Partners for Education & Business.

The firm's success is embedded in its core values of: integrity, teamwork, innovation and relationships. These enduring values have made King & King a success for the past century and will continue to ensure its success into this new century as well.

The firm is currently led by David A. Johnson, James R. King, Peter G. King and Kirk W. Narburgh.

Russell A. King, AIA, and Robert Finch, counsel to President Nixon, 1972.

(Left to right) Greater Syracuse Chamber of Commerce, Modern, 1991; The Syracuse Lighting Company, Art Deco, 1932; Onondadga County Office Building, Bauhaus, 1955; John B. Crouse Memorial College for Women, Romanesque Revival, 1889.

ONONDAGA HISTORICAL ASSOCIATION

One of the OHA Museum's newest permanent exhibits is *Freedom Bound*, a dramatic exploration of the Underground Railroad in the Syracuse area. Along with several displays, it features a sound and light presentation that re-creates the actual flight of four fugitive slaves from Virginia to Syracuse in 1855. The quality of the exhibit led to the OHA Museum being listed as an official site to visit on the National Park Service's *Network to Freedom* system and to serve as a Regional Interpretive Center for New York State's *Underground Railroad Heritage Trail*.

ONONDAGA HISTORICAL ASSOCIATION

For well over a century, Onondaga Historical Association (OHA) has been known as the place where the memories of the greater Syracuse community can be found. Whether within an historic volume, on a rare map or perhaps within one of the thousands of poignant

photographic images in the OHA collection, the enduring legacy of this region has always been present. Today, while one of the nation's largest regional collections of historical treasures still awaits visitors, the focus of OHA has evolved to better meet the changing needs of an evolving community.

From its original mission of "collecting and preserving historical, genealogical... material, and

The amazing story of the success and doom of the famous Franklin automobile company and the rarest Franklin in the world await visitors at the Onondaga Historical Association Museum in Downtown Syracuse.
Onondaga Historical Association

(Bottom right) Creative genius in ceramics, the famous "Syracuse China," another among the dozens of fascinating stories to be explored at OHA.
Onondaga Historical Association

(Above right/below) OHA family programs, where students dive into projects that make history fun.

research library; the OHA Museum, the community's largest history museum; and community-based cooperative programming and exhibits. Using these resources, OHA plays an increasingly pivotal role in an exciting, widening and relevant communitywide "heritage conversation."

Whether celebrating the rich cultural or industrial heritage such as Syracuse China, the legacy of heroic human experience such as the Underground Railroad and struggle for Abolition, or providing wholesome vacation camps for children, OHA is the source of year-round heritage programming, live performance and exhibits for the entire family.

A future architect explains her designs at an OHA Summer Camp for Kids.

(Below)
OHA brings the dramatic stories of local history to the entire community.

(Bottom)
School children are amazed by abolilitionist-era carvings at the OHA Museum.

mementos... relics and facts," OHA now strives to provide intriguing programs, school curriculum support and exhibits that highlight the diverse heritage of the community. These goals are obtained by combining the diligence and dedication of OHA, "the community archivist," with the emergent pursuit of OHA, "the community educator." Using its renowned collection of documents and artifacts from its dynamic local history, in partnership with local school districts, cultural and community organizations, OHA works to foster an appreciation for individual and shared history in this community. From multimedia musical collaborations with the Syracuse Symphony Orchestra to theatrical performances at the Southwest Community Center, OHA is bringing the saga of local history to all Central New Yorkers.

OHA offers the unique combined resources of the OHA Research Center, the community's largest historical

The archival collections of the Onondaga Historical Association are ranked among the most diverse in New York State. One example is the extensive records of the stained glass studio of Syracuse's Henry Keck. They include this original watercolor design for a window installed in the New York State Capitol.
OHA Collection

A little known part of Syracuse's past is that the city's former automobile manufacturer, the H. H. Franklin Manufacturing Company, once produced a line of commercial vehicles including a police patrol wagon for the City of Auburn and a omnibus for Syracuse's Onondaga Hotel. Both are documented in an original 1911 catalog contained in OHA's large collection of material on the Franklin firm.
OHA Collection

SYRACUSE HOME ASSOCIATION

A Not-For-Profit Health and Transitional Care Campus

When a group of public-spirited women, led by Mary Maltbie and Clara Hibbard, banded together in Syracuse in 1851 to seek out families in need, these gentle humanitarians were known as "The Ladies Relief of the Poor and Needy, and Home Association."

These exceptional women extended helping hands to the community, and their courageous efforts and acts of kindness predated modern social services. Today, the organization they founded, the Syracuse Home Association, remains deeply committed to caregiving, though perhaps in a more rural setting than the founders might have imagined.

The early mission of Syracuse Home Association was the delivery of basic assistance to women and children in the rapidly growing city of Syracuse. Many of these unfortunate children were victims of domestic violence, left with a sick mother in terrible circumstances or abandoned. The ladies of Syracuse Home Association would intervene, providing shelter. By 1860 they had started an industrial school, where women and children could be instructed in age-appropriate programs such as sewing and general domestic skills, preparing them to go out on their own as wage earners. The Home also provided a safe haven to impoverished widows, some of whom had lost their husbands during the Civil War.

From the archives: "The Ladies Relief of the Poor and Needy, and Home Association."

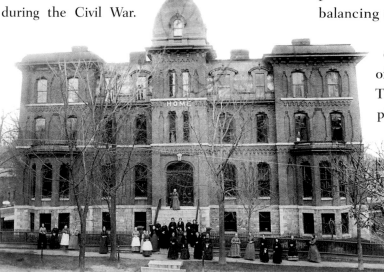

Syracuse Home operated in several locations until 1870 when Moses DeWitt Burnet donated property where Townsend Street crosses Hawley Avenue. There, the Home found a home of its own for well over 100 years. As the public welfare system gradually evolved, the caregiving scope of the Home changed as well. In 1895 the Home's mission was revised to caring exclusively for elderly women.

In 1978 Syracuse Home Association moved to its current location in the village of Baldwinsville. Originally built as an 80-bed health-related facility, it has grown into a retirement community consisting of Syracuse Home, a 120-bed skilled residential healthcare facility with a respite care program, and McHarrie Towne, an independent retirement neighborhood.

The mission of Syracuse Home Association is to provide an environment for the delivery of services designed to promote and expand quality care to aging persons, allowing them to lead full and dignified lives. These services are provided in a variety of comfortable, supportive settings by professional staff experienced in the delicate balancing of technical expertise and loving care.

The Home's health care services are organized and delivered through a plan of care individualized for each resident. The combined efforts of the attending physician and nursing staff, with other disciplines such as rehabilitation therapies, dietetics, social services and activities help ensure that each resident receives the quality of care for comfortable living with dignity and security. The staff, many of whom live in the Baldwinsville community, are caring people familiar with and committed to the residents. Some residents might be former neighbors or teachers they've known all or most of their lives.

The rehabilitation services staff is skilled in both restorative and maintenance therapies. Physical therapists work with residents, helping them to regain skills they might have lost, helping them maintain optimum physical freedom. Residents admitted for short-term stays are returned to their homes as a result of the excellent restorative rehabilitation program. Rehabilitative therapies offered include speech pathology and audiology, help with hearing deficiencies and occupational therapy.

The staff of Syracuse Home are always available to attend to residents' special needs and assist residents and their families with all types of counseling, planning and referrals.

Residents enjoy pleasant dining and socializing in the Home's dining rooms. The dietary staff is accomplished in preparing meals and menus that meet special needs.

Syracuse Home provides respite care, a program designed to give caregivers a planned, intermittent break from the responsibility of caring for a relative or friend. The staff understands the tremendous commitment involved in caring for a loved one at home. By placing a loved one in temporary respite care at Syracuse Home from one to six weeks, caregivers can be afforded a break from the daily responsibilities of home health care.

In 1984 the board of directors agreed to establish Syracuse Home Association Foundation, Inc. as a vehicle to receive, hold and administer gifts and bequests and to support programs and services for older adults. Careful and prudent investing of gifts allows for income from these investments to be used to benefit the residents of Syracuse Home and to enhance their quality of life. Gifts to the Foundation's endowment enrich the lives of residents, each gift helps provide continuing opportunities for living with dignity. There are numerous giving options. Gifts to the endowment may be unrestricted or commemorative, or designated to donor-directed or named funds.

The emphasis is on caregiving.

McHarrie Towne, Inc., an affiliate of Syracuse Home Association, is an independent retirement community where individuals and couples who have reached the age of 62 can live independently in a secured environment. McHarrie Towne, located on the Syracuse Home Association campus, was established in 1995 and offers single-level homes designed for independent, maintenance-free living. Each home contains an attached garage with automatic door opener, a large bathroom, a walk-in closet, a full pantry, a covered entry porch and choices of one or two bedrooms, or optional study, all in more than 1,200 square feet of living space. Residency includes a 24-hour emergency call system, interior and exterior home maintenance, lawn care, snow and trash removal, and many other amenities. All homes are handicapped accessible and adaptable. If the need should arise, McHarrie Towne residents are eligible for priority access to Syracuse Home on a bed-available basis.

Many residents of Syracuse Home and McHarrie Towne enjoy the peace and serenity of nature observation. The Home is located atop Sorrell Hill, a fly-over for migrating birds and with enough woods for deer and other gentle neighbors. Tucked among the trees, residents can find privacy in the gazebo. They can visit with family and friends indoors, or in an outdoor setting framed by carefully tended gardens and flowering trees. These beautiful settings demonstrate how far the art of caregiving has come these last 150 years.

HAL SILVERMAN STUDIO

Syracuse and the photography of Hal Silverman go together in the minds of hundreds of large and small corporations, graphic designers and advertising agencies. Hal's work appears in magazines, annual reports, brochures, product catalogs and on product packaging

throughout the United States, Europe, Asia and Latin America — wherever clients need an expertly crafted image to represent their product or services.

Whether in his 3,000-square-foot studio or on location, he is fully equipped for traditional or digital imaging. Hal and his associates have gained the confidence of customers worldwide by approaching each job as a one-of-a-kind challenge.

Any photographer has the power to capture time, but very few have the consistent ability to make that time count for their customers. Hal Silverman Studio has been doing it for years. No wonder so many roads lead to Syracuse and Hal Silverman.

LE MOYNE COLLEGE

Learning and Service: Our Shared Jesuit Mission

When Le Moyne College opened in 1946 as the first Jesuit college in Central New York, it embraced the order's 450-year-old tradition of educating the whole person by offering a comprehensive academic program designed to foster intellectual excellence and a commitment to service.

Sixty years later, that mission continues to thrive, as Le Moyne has evolved into a nationally acclaimed college of liberal arts and sciences whose graduates not only excel in the professions but also distinguish themselves in service to others.

The second-youngest of the 28 Jesuit colleges and universities in the United States and the first to admit women, Le Moyne is named after the 17th-century French Jesuit missionary Simon Le Moyne, who worked among the Onondagas. Sitting on a hilltop off Salt Springs Road in Syracuse, Le Moyne has grown from an initial enrollment of 450 to more than 3,000 students today. Approximately 2,300 of those students are undergraduates, and another 800 are pursuing graduate degrees. The college that once primarily served Central New York now draws students from dozens of states and a variety of foreign countries.

Academically, Le Moyne offers more than 700 courses leading to bachelor of arts or bachelor of science degrees in 29 different majors. Academics and student life are closely integrated, and in order to foster individualized attention to its students, Le Moyne maintains a student-to-faculty ratio of 14:1. Class size averages 22 students.

In addition to its undergraduate program, Le Moyne offers an innovative physician assistant program designed to prepare students to enter one of the fastest-growing medical careers in the country. In the 1990s the college added popular graduate programs leading to a master's in business administration or a master's in education.

As part of its MBA program, Le Moyne is home to the Michael D. Madden Institute for Business Education, which sponsors speakers, conferences and public programs on business issues and promotes relationships between the college and the business community.

As the college's enrollment has grown, its facilities also have expanded to fully meet the academic and social needs of an increasingly diverse campus community. Among the additions is the state-of-the-art W. Carroll Coyne Center for the Performing Arts, which houses the college's acclaimed theater arts program and rehearsal space for music and dance arts.

In keeping with the Jesuit tradition of service to others, Le Moyne offers students a variety of volunteer opportunities in both local and world communities. Coordinated through the Office of Service Learning students work with local service agencies and schools, while the college's Alternative Break program deploys student volunteers throughout the United States and beyond.

Entering its second half-century, Le Moyne continues to expand its vision as it strives to meet the academic needs of students in a rapidly changing world. Yet true to the Jesuit spirit of its founders, it remains committed to the mission of integrating learning and service in preparing students for life.

The clock tower of Grewen Hall is a landmark both on campus and on Syracuse's far east side.

NEW YORK STATE FAIR

In 1841 almost 15,000 people walked, rode horses and traveled by buggy or carriage to the village of Syracuse to attend the first state fair in the United States. They came from all across the state to see the prized farm animals and agricultural bounty their friends

and neighbors wanted to show off. The dusty trails billowed the start of something **big**.

There were only 26 states in the young republic back then, Missouri nosing out Arkansas for the westernmost. It would be 67 years before Henry Ford's Model-T would revolutionize transportation and eventually turn those trails into New York's Interstate crossroads. The state-sponsored budget for that first two-day fair was $8,000.

New York's fair didn't have a permanent home until 1890 when an enterprising Syracuse group dangled a choice piece of land on popular Onondaga Lake in front of the State Agricultural Society. The offer stipulated, however, the land was available if it served as the permanent site for the fair. The original 125-acre pasture has tripled in size, and the entire complex — now known as the Empire Expo Center — is valued at $115 million. It cost the community leaders $30,000.

While the State Fair, Expo Center's largest single event, is rooted in agriculture, the Syracuse group's offer was also motivated by economic potential. The 15,000 people who trekked to the first fair set the pace for the continually record-breaking attendance figure, surpassing the coveted 1 million mark in 2001. The entire Empire Expo

Center schedule attracts more than 2 million people annually and pumps more than $100 million into the local economy.

The State Fair's worth wasn't always obvious. Early in the 1970s, rising costs, dropping attendance and grumbling threatened its existence. But new corporate initiatives dedicated to overall customer satisfaction combined with the site's expansion into a multidimensional center to turn the fair into a self-sufficient, profit-generating event and the Empire Expo Center into a yearlong business and entertainment venue. Except for capital improvement funds, state subsidy for the fair ended in fiscal 1991 when revenues equaled the operating budget of $8,552,683.

The Empire Expo Center is also a major source of employment. Besides the hundreds of ongoing jobs created for regional contractors by expansion and constant facility upgrades, the fair provides 15,000 people part-time jobs each summer. Additionally, there are 75 full-time and 200 part-time employees that staff the center and its yearly activities.

Both former Fair chief Peter Cappuccilli, Jr. and current director Barbara Yunis point out that with unwavering support from Governor Pataki, his administration, the Fair's staff and corporate sponsors like McLane Northeast, annual Expo Center revenues have increased from $8.5 to $16 million during the last ten years

While economic impact is an essential element of its history, the New York State Fair is about dairy cows, not cash cows. It's about cotton candy and sticky kids and entertainment, education and amusement in August. Each year an agriculture-focused and people-friendly event provides a grass-roots snapshot of a growing New York.

Agriculture is New York's largest industry.

SYRACUSE CONVENTION & VISITORS BUREAU

Syracuse: An Absolutely Wonderful Place to Visit

There's a certain feeling of excitement that comes to mind when someone mentions Syracuse and Onondaga County. Whatever mood they're in, they can look forward to something wonderful, and perhaps the largest reason for all the excitement is the incredible variety

of recreational, entertainment, cultural and sporting opportunities that await.

Thanks to successful regional festivals like the New York State Rhythm & Blues Festival, the M&T Syracuse JazzFest and The Great New York State Fair, to name a few, Syracuse has become one of the major festival and special-event locations in the Northeast. The sounds of the Syracuse Symphony fill the air when the orchestra and its ensembles perform downtown in the magnificent Mulroy Civic Center at Oncenter, as well as in various parks throughout Central New York. And right alongside the variety of arts and special events is a sense of rejuvenation and enthusiasm, as continuing development and growth implement an incredible sense of pride.

Syracusans love their hometown sports teams with loyal ferocity. Nowhere is this more apparent than inside the massive Carrier Dome, home to Syracuse University's beloved football, basketball and lacrosse teams. Alliance Bank Stadium houses the Syracuse SkyChiefs, the AAA affiliate of Major League Baseball's Toronto Blue Jays. And minor league hockey's Syracuse Crunch (affiliate of the NHL's Columbus Blue Jackets) calls downtown's restored War Memorial Arena home.

The War Memorial is part of a larger series of facilities known as the Oncenter Complex, with the Mulroy Civic Center and the Convention Center completing the package. The surrounding area is thriving with businesses, restaurants, attractions and museums, including the Everson Museum of Art, designed by renowned architect I.M. Pei, and the Museum of Science and Technology (MOST), a hands-on science center that features an IMAX theater.

The MOST is actually located within historic Armory Square, the most diverse, boisterous

and exciting area of downtown Syracuse with over 50 dining, shopping, music and specialty establishments.

Natives of Syracuse are especially proud of their beautiful four seasons and abundance of outdoor activities. The area offers some of the best skiing in the country, with a number of downhill slopes and cross-country courses located just a short drive from the city. Golfers will be amazed at the variety of courses for every skill level, and those who want to enjoy nature at its finest can visit Beaver Lake Nature Center or experience the wonders of the animal kingdom at the Rosamond Gifford Zoo at Burnet Park. The great outdoors awaits!

One of the area's major attractions is the Carousel Center. Plans to transform the Carousel Center into DestiNY USA will make it the largest retail and entertainment complex in North America.

With a rich history, and continuing progression and development ahead, it's no surprise that Syracuse and Onondaga County are growing by leaps and bounds.

THE STATE UNIVERSITY OF NEW YORK
UPSTATE MEDICAL UNIVERSITY

The State University of New York Upstate Medical University is one of the country's key academic medical institutions. It is built around a medical school and a teaching hospital, along with colleges of nursing, health professions and graduate studies. Its research scientists,

many of whom also work as physicians, include experts in the areas of motor control, neural coding, pain perception, heart attacks and arrhythmias, colon and pediatric cancers, olfaction, enzyme structure and function, gene regulation and human retroviruses.

Upstate Medical University's mission is four-fold: improving the health of the communities it serves through education, biomedical research, advanced health care and community service. With the 350-bed University Hospital, Upstate is an internationally regarded source of medical expertise.

Acquired in 1950 from Syracuse University, Upstate traces its roots to the Geneva Medical College (now Hobart and William Smith Colleges) in 1834. Elizabeth Blackwell, the first woman in the country to earn a medical degree, was an 1849 graduate.

Upstate's physician-scientists are among the leaders in the fight against cancer by offering the newest tests and treatments, educating cancer specialists, conducting cancer research and participating in clinical cancer trials. These clinical trials, for which patients volunteer, help determine if promising new treatments are safe and effective, and give patients access to the newest medications and procedures.

The cardiovascular group studies cell communication within the heart, specifically as it relates to irregular heartbeats such as ventricular fibrillation. Other notable research includes the effects on drugs of heart attack patients, blood vessel activity in children with high cholesterol, development of a relatively

non-invasive method to measure stiffness of arteries as well as anti-blood clotting drugs.

The $50 million Institute for Human Performance, opened in 2000, serves as a multidisciplinary incubator for research aimed at extending human performance and dissolving the limitations of disease, disability and aging.

Upstate has a long tradition of investigation in systems neuroscience. Current research focuses on developmental neurobiology and central nervous system regeneration, and other related topics.

The educational mission is accomplished through four colleges: Medicine, Graduate Studies, Nursing and Health Professions. The College of Medicine educates students to be medical doctors. The College of Graduate Studies prepares students to be investigative research scientists in the biomedical sciences. The College of Nursing offers advanced education to registered nurses. The College of Health Professions prepares students for careers in seven health care fields.

Patient health care is offered through University Hospital, its ambulatory sites, satellite sites, specialty treatment centers and clinics. As the region's only Level-1 trauma center and burn unit, the hospital routinely treats the most critically injured. Services will be greatly expanded by 2009 when a 6-story addition to the Hospital is completed. Treatment for young patients will be especially enriched because two floors will encompass the Golisano Children's Hospital, a state-of-the-art pediatric care facility.

Community service is an integral part of Upstate Medical University and includes dozens of advocacy, education and outreach initiatives. As one of Onondaga County's largest employers, Upstate has a powerful and positive impact of the quality of life in the region.

SUNY Upstate Medical University attracts more than $20 million annually to support research efforts of scientists like Edward Shillitoe, PhD, of the department of microbiology and immunology.

VISITING NURSE ASSOCIATION OF CENTRAL NEW YORK

Each day, hundreds of homebound patients rely upon Visiting Nurse Association of Central New York, Inc. (VNA) for critically needed home health care services. Over the years the agency's role and contribution to the community has remained consistent and essential.

VNA has been in continuous operation since 1890. Its history begins in the late 1880s when a group of local women visited the "destitute sick" in the community and employed a "trained nurse" for the more serious cases. From this group, three public-spirited members, Miss Aria Huntington, Dr. Juliet Hanchett and Mrs. Laura Mills Marlow, formed the organization that we know as VNA. These early leaders recognized the needs of people in the community and set down the purpose of the association. Since its inception, VNA has cared for the sick in the comfort of their own homes, taught families how to care for their ill loved ones, and provided nursing supervision for maternity patients, infants, and young children. Today, more than ever, this historic legacy continues as VNA's clinicians deliver an unprecedented level of care specifically designed to meet the needs of those who mean the most to them—their patients and the community.

Today, the mission and goals of VNA reflect the same commitment to the health of local residents expressed by its founders. VNA is dedicated to providing quality health care and related services in a timely and cost effective manner to individuals, families and organizations. The goal of maintaining, restoring and promoting the health and independence of those they service is achieved by using the resources that are available, by working cooperatively with other organizations and by providing the proper environment for development and retention of caring, competent staff.

More than five million Americans receive health care services at home for both acute and long-term needs. As Americans live longer, this figure will continue to rise and caring for the sick at home will continue to assume a significant place in the nation's health care delivery system. Home health care remains the most cost-effective segment in our system. To meet the increasing demands for services in Syracuse and Onondaga County, VNA continually strives to meet the needs of its patients by program development, implementation and evaluation in much the same way as our founders did in 1890.

Dr. Julia E. Hanchett (1856–1921), a Syracuse native and founding member of VNA, practiced medicine in the city for over 30 years.

VISITING NURSE ASSOCIATION OF CENTRAL NEW YORK, INC.

A Tradition of Caring

CXtec

The self-made man is an American icon, and Bill Pomeroy is one such individual. However, he is quick to point out that the success of the company he founded should be attributed to "some good ideas that lasted, lots of luck, and the hard work and determination of many employees who helped me grow the business."

The Born Salesman

At an early age, Pomeroy was quickly recognized as a born salesman. Growing up in Binghamton, New York, his mother, Grace, has fond memories of his early entrepreneurial days, setting up and selling soda and doughnuts from his Radio Flyer wagon when he was 11. After completing a B.S. at Rensselaer Polytechnic Institute and an MBA at the University of Pennsylvania's Wharton School of Finance, he rose quickly in the world of corporate America. Pomeroy progressed through several important positions at General Electric in Charlotte, North Carolina; Proctor and Gamble in Cincinnati, Ohio; IBM® in Palo Alto, California; and finally to Syracuse, New York, for CIS, an entry into the mainframe brokerage business.

Prospering in Central New York since 1978 — William G. Pomeroy is shown here in 2001 at his World Headquarters in Syracuse, New York. He started the business in his LaFayette, New York, home and recently learned his ancestral roots are in Pompey, New York, just a few miles from his home. Today, CXtec has 325 employees and revenues exceed $100 million annually. The value proposition of the company explains that "CXtec helps customers reduce the cost of their networking infrastructure, allowing for greater investment in profitable applications."

Comfortable at CIS, Pomeroy had no active intentions of starting his own business until one fateful day in 1978 when office politics claimed his job. That day, he developed the idea that would become CABLExpress Technologies®. Pomeroy saw an opportunity to begin a business that would target an underserved and emerging market. Most IBM 360/370 mainframe owners had a problem acquiring or disposing of mainframe add-ons, known as features, channels and memory. Pomeroy used his product and marketplace knowledge to match buyers and sellers of used mainframe add-ons, creating the only centralized market in the world for these items.

A Solid Plan Does Not Ensure Instant Success

Pomeroy was dealt an early setback when New York State would not allow him to name his new company International Used Business Machines. He was allowed his second choice, Reliance Used Computer Corporation, a name taken from his grandfather's old used machine tool business in Pittsburgh. Pomeroy slowly built a steady set of accounts across the United States while working in his LaFayette, New York, home. The assistance of his then-wife, Mareta, was an essential element of the early days of CABLExpress. Mareta did everything from answering the phones to keeping the books to writing company correspondence, allowing Pomeroy to focus on development and growth.

Starting a business in the bleak Upstate New York economy of the late 1970s was a difficult proposition. Thankfully Pomeroy had a specific strategy for his vision. He was able to develop

customers across the country by targeting prospective companies with large mainframes. This allowed the business to not become dependent upon the local economy. Additionally, he perfected his telephone-based sales model, eliminating travel costs, saving time and improving productivity. He envisioned specific direct mail promotional ideas to support his telephone calls, and Bill Padgett of Erieville created the professional logos and layouts.

After a successful first year and continued growth, Reliance Used Computers ended in the black. Pomeroy recognized that the business had outgrown his modest home. Upgrading to more spacious quarters on Erie Boulevard East in Syracuse, Reliance Used Computers acquired the space needed to inventory more equipment. With a reputation for solving unusual problems, Pomeroy soon expanded the business into sidelines such as computer room equipment, chillers, air handlers, raised flooring and underfloor cabling. Despite a sluggish economy and high interest rates, Reliance Used Computers continued to prosper partly due to the fact that customers found used IBM mainframe equipment an appealing solution for stretching their downsized budgets.

As his business grew, Pomeroy's entrepreneurial instincts led him into an interesting side business. In 1978 IBM decided to stop providing replacement parts for its older transistor-based 7090 mainframes built in the 1960s. This decision left the U.S. Air Force in trouble as it was still

using the older mainframes to operate its over-the-horizon Ballistic Missile Early Warning System (BMEWS) sites in Alaska, Greenland and England. Pomeroy initiated a new business venture and decided to become the supplier of the spare parts for those units. With no commitment from the Air Force, he bought, at scrap prices, old mainframes found across the country and transported them to his Syracuse warehouse. Pomeroy then studied IBM parts manuals and tracked down IBM's parts vendors. His investment paid off, and Reliance became the sole source for

193

(Above right) Sandra Crellin, shown here in 1999, was the first employee of CABLExpress. She handled the accounting from manual entry to computer automation.

(Above center) Mareta Pomeroy, shown here in 1984, provided her invaluable assistance in the early days of CABLExpress.

(Above left) Pomeroy's mom, Grace Pomeroy, visiting CABLExpress in 1999. In 1955 she provided the coffee that he sold, in addition to lots of encouragement.

spare parts for the Air Force computers that monitored incoming Soviet missiles, (until those older mainframes were finally replaced in 1983).

In 1980 Pomeroy created the CABLExpress division of Reliance to identify the company's growing business in IBM 370 mainframe cables. By 1985 the company was exclusively providing a variety of IBM underfloor cabling to a majority of Fortune 500 companies, with Michele Tampa-Hoag directing sales. The company again outgrew its surroundings and relocated to E. Brighton Avenue after an extensive renovation handled by Brian St. Laurent and contractor Walt Gardner. A breakthrough in the way things were done in the CABLExpress office provided Pomeroy some insight in how to grow the business even more. He replaced the old Apple and Televideo computers and implemented an in-house IBM token-ring

network with IBM PS/2 computers and a PS/2 Model 60 server. Chuck Oelsner implemented the inventory, accounting and e-mail applications. Productivity increased so dramatically that Pomeroy was convinced that his customers would eventually want to install similar networks. As this became a reality, he expanded the business again to include network cable products. Peter Belyea joined the staff in 1988 and really got the networking business going.

In 1989 catalogs became an essential component of CABLExpress. The first of the legendary CABLExpress catalogs was produced by Jay LaBarge. The initial mailing brought a noticeable increase in both incoming calls and sales. Sandra Crellin managed the finances for many years, starting with the manual ledger system, transitioning to Oelsner's SBT system on an IBM AT and then to the IBM network. Gard McLean joined in 1992 and, with Cindy Daley's help, he built the accounting and financial systems to accommodate future growth.

The rapidly exploding customer base required additional space, and Pomeroy bought the 8,000-square-foot building adjacent to the main offices for the warehouse processing operation. Simultaneously, the sales and customer service staff grew to fill the existing 10,000 square feet. The business grew so rapidly throughout the 90s that pressure mounted through the decade to find a "final home" for the company. Pomeroy settled on a vacant 66,000-square-foot building near Syracuse's Hancock International Airport. The building was a unique structure in itself; it had previously been designed and built as a one-of-a-kind retail business: Switz's, which sold specialty crafts and costumes. After Brian St. Laurent and Walt Gardner's extensive renovation, the new CABLExpress World Headquarters was ready for occupancy in 1997. With space for up to 500 employees, the structure is a facility that will be able to serve the needs of the company well into the 21st century.

Early marketing material promoting the IBM mainframe cable business — catalogs began in 1989. Michael Cariglio, co-creator of the "Pappyland" TV series, provided the eye-catching original art and humor that was always used on the front cover.

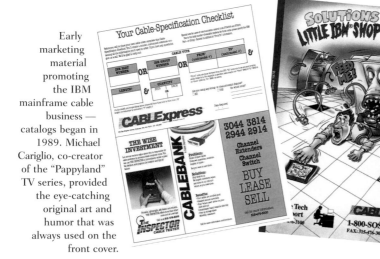

In the mid-1990s, as Cisco®, 3Com®, Cabletron® and Nortel™ shortened their product life cycles, a vibrant market emerged as users upgraded and needed to dispose of used technology. Well positioned to take advantage of this upturn, Pomeroy re-entered the used equipment business with the direction of Lisa Ross and Frank Kobuszewski Jr. by creating the equal2new® brand, differentiating CABLExpress' used equipment from its competitors. Before certifying equipment equal2new®, the company fully tests and, in many cases, upgrades pre-owned hardware and networking equipment at its Technology Certification and Distribution Center on Ainsley Drive. The brand carries a lifetime warranty, a first in the used equipment market. Pomeroy's creative ingenuity, matched with his unerring sound instinct for the marketplace, enabled the company to expand even further.

As technology progressed, CXtec's business in copper bus and tag mainframe cables transitioned to the fiber optic cables used in modern data and communications applications. The company's expertise is in a variety of network cables for both local and wide area networking applications. The addition of a new equipment business unit (which offers products from such companies as Cisco, Nortel, HP® and 3Com) enables the offering of new equipment alongside the equal2new® brand. This gives CXtec a unique edge on the competition, allowing the company to present lower-cost total solution proposals with both new and used equipment.

What started as selling soda and doughnuts out of a little red Radio Flyer wagon has become the CXtec of today. Supported by a team of outstanding employees, Bill Pomeroy's vision, courage and dedication have resulted in CXtec — a company that efficiently serves the needs of many of the largest corporations worldwide.

Bill Pomeroy's and CXtec's success is portrayed in Pomeroy's favorite quote: "A man is only as good as his word. I'll do what I say I'll do. I'll deliver on time."

Pomeroy started Reliance in his LaFayette home in 1978. It was equipped with four phone lines, a telex line, Xerox copier, an IBM Mag Card Selectric, an early word processing machine.

By 1980 his LaFayette home was overwhelmed by the office, so he relocated to Erie Boulevard East. It seemed spacious, with 1,000 square feet of office space and 3,600 square feet of warehousing space, plus a loading dock.

In 1985 CABLExpress outgrew Erie Boulevard and moved to East Brighton Avenue (left). The 10,000 square feet was quickly used, so the building on the right, with 8,000 square feet, was added in 1989.

CXtec's World Headquarters since 1997 — the digital time and temperature displays replaced the analog clocks on the towers. The roof structure contains Pomeroy's Thinkpad, accessible by a circular iron stairway from his office, and the Area 51 Room containing his historic computer collection and family history archives.

INFIMED INC.

InfiMed Inc. has become a worldwide leader in the medical imaging industry by providing the most advanced and easy-to-use digital X-ray imaging systems for medical diagnosis. The company designs and manufactures an array of products for X-ray image

capture, storage and connectivity for numerous clinical applications including urology, radiology, vascular imaging and cardiology.

InfiMed is a privately held ISO 9001 certified company based in the Syracuse suburb of Liverpool, New York. For over 20 years, it has pioneered medical imaging technology and provided cost-effective solutions for hospitals and imaging centers around the world. Today, InfiMed has over 4,000 systems installed.

Known as a technical innovator, InfiMed creates products that provide dramatic improvements in productivity and image quality. Its digital X-ray imaging replaces film-based images and reduces the time necessary for routine examinations. Also the need for X-ray image retakes is decreased because it has established instant availability and verification of image quality.

InfiMed introduced its chief product, the FC1000 Fluoroscopic Computer, at the 1985 Radiologic Society of North America meeting — medical imaging's largest congress. It was the first digital videofluorography (DVF) product in the general X-ray market. By 1987 the FC1000 was installed in several leading health care institutions in the United States, Canada and Japan. The company also branched into a new market with its development of the Theraview system for patient position verification during radiation therapy.

A major milestone was reached in 1995 when InfiMed's quality systems were ISO 9001, BS EN 9001, EN 46001 and ANSI/ASQC Q9001-1994 assurance certified. These world-recognized certifications reinforced to the medical industry as a whole InfiMed's commitment to quality standards.

The next year brought the premiere of the GoldOne product line, the "new gold standard"

InfiMed Inc. corporate headquarters, where since 1989, employees have designed and produced quality digital X-ray sensors for use around the world.

for medical imaging. The GoldOne product was designed for the 21st century using a custom-designed, high-resolution digital camera, remote-access, and software-driven quality and system diagnostics.

InfiMed's family of products currently includes the most advanced flat panel, direct digital X-ray machine — the Stingray DR — operating totally in a filmless environment; and the PlatinumOne Cardiac — a system that allows cardiologists to measure, analyze and archive to compact disc patient images taken during cardiac and vascular catheterization. The current cardiac software product offerings also embrace the convenience of the Internet providing a Web-based Cardiac PACS Viewing Software program called the CV™ series.

InfiMed began as S&S Inficon, the medical products division of another Syracuse-based company, Leybold Inficon, Inc. With its device advancements quickly reaching around the world, the company further solidified its identity in the medical imaging market by changing its name to InfiMed in the fall of 1992. Its parent company, S&S X-ray of Brooklyn, New York, was founded in 1945 and is one of the top X-ray accessory manufacturers in the United States, with annual sales of $50 million.

The focus of research and development at InfiMed is to integrate leading-edge technologies into its products to deliver systems that set new standards for image quality and productivity at a price that meets market needs. In addition, InfiMed continually evaluates new markets where its products and technologies may be used to meet specific customer needs. The in-house research and development team partners with a worldwide service organization to provide around-the-clock customer care. All product lines are designed and manufactured locally at the Liverpool facility.

An integral part of Syracuse's high-technology employer base, InfiMed provides jobs for software and hardware design engineers and manufacturing technicians. InfiMed's product successes are a

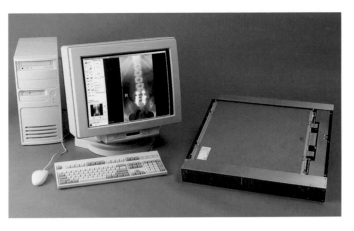

InfiMed's Stingray product line uses a revolutionary flat-panel X-ray detector to capture and display X-ray images instantly — a major inroad to a filmless environment where data can be shared and stored more cost effectively.

direct result of its talented employees. Each person strives to provide the type of service that will exceed customers' needs. InfiMed President Brian Fleming leads the team of nearly 100 employees in its efforts to build on product successes and technical innovations in a responsible, worker-friendly environment.

Many out-of-state employees are attracted to the company by its commitment to groundbreaking technologies and its upbeat and culturally diverse atmosphere. Company members are rewarded with continued professional development opportunities, an extended benefits package, flexible work schedules and tuition reimbursement through several local colleges and universities.

The city of Syracuse provides employees with year-round beauty and many cultural activities while the company's suburban location offers affordable housing with shopping and entertainment close by. Numerous community and sports activities abound, and employees take full advantage of the many parks and trails near the InfiMed site.

InfiMed is a member of several professional organizations including the Central New York Chamber of Commerce and the Manufacturers' Association of Central New York. In addition, employees participate in various local and national charity events, including school fundraisers, the annual United Way Giving Campaign, the Syracuse Corporate Challenge road race and more. The people at InfiMed feel privileged to be part of the community at large.

LOCKHEED MARTIN
MARITIME SYSTEMS & SENSORS

Lockheed Martin Maritime Systems & Sensors (MS2)-Syracuse, a world leader in radar and sonar technology and development, employs over 2,000 Central New Yorkers at its tradition-rich Electronics Park campus. Today's engineers and technicians are

continuing the Electronics Park legacy as they design, manufacture and test products for a wide range of strategic and tactical applications around the world. MS2-Syracuse is an operating unit of Lockheed Martin Corporation, a global leader in the aerospace and defense industries.

Electronics Park itself has a long and stellar history of global leadership and technological innovation. In 1944 at the height of World War II, the management team of General Electric (GE) was seeking to provide a new type of work atmosphere in the post-war era where a higher level of productivity could be achieved. Their vision was to become the first of its kind, combining research, engineering and production into a single facility on a 150-acre tract of farmland about five miles northwest of downtown Syracuse. They called it Electronics Park, and it was destined to be the home of the GE Electronics Department for many successful years. In his book, *Progress in Defense and Space*, M.A. Johnson said the Syracuse area was chosen "...because of its available, diversified labor force, its transportation, community facilities including Syracuse University, and its nearness to material suppliers, markets and GE research facilities."

For more than a year, 100 engineers and draftsmen worked on the design for Electronics

Electronics Park under construction, prior to the building of the New York State Thruway.

Park and in the process produced 500,000 blueprints. Initial clearing and grading of the land began in 1944. The official groundbreaking ceremonies were held on September 11, 1945. The first steel was erected in April 1946 and the Transmitter Building (Building 7), was completed in April 1947. The remaining original buildings were finished by the middle of 1948, all in a harmonious architectural style.

In April 1947 the 1,800 employees of the Transmitter Division began moving into the Building 7 from the older Thompson Road Plant. Just 10 days later, the first product, a radio broadcast transmitter, was shipped from Electronics Park. Production began in the Receiver Building (Building 5) in August 1947. Its first products were radio-phonograph combinations. Limited production of black-and-white television receivers began in March 1948. Television picture tube production began in 1949 when the 8-1/2-inch metal tubes were produced. In subsequent years, as the medium exploded in popularity, Electronics Park was to become known as the "Television Capital of the World." The first testing for color picture tubes was done on-site, with television production continuing throughout the decade of the 1960s. In Building 6, the Specialty Building, first production included toy phonographs, crystals, special contract radios, vending machines and "multi-weave" metal grilles.

Over the years, Electronics Park has seen many changes. While still manufacturing televisions, for example, GE became a leader in radar and acoustic technology.

One of the original businesses in Electronics Park was land- and ship-based air defense radars, as well as weapon location radars. GE supplied about 1,000 air defense radars in the 50s and 60s to be deployed all over the world. The advanced engineering department was formed in the mid-1950s, and during the late 50s and early 60s phased-array antenna techniques key to ballistic missile defense were developed, along with over-the-horizon bi-static, digitally beam-formed radars operating in the HF frequency band. This was followed by the development of solid-state radar systems. Today, the Radar Systems business, as it is called, designs and builds solid-state, ground-based and airborne radar for air surveillance, air and missile defense, battlefield surveillance and weather monitoring.

In 1955 the Heavy Military Electronics department (HMED), demonstrated its technological superiority with the development of the first long-range underwater object locator sonar, followed by the longer-range hull-mounted anti-submarine warfare sonar. In the 1970s and 1980s, the company further established itself as a leader in naval technology with the development of towed arrays and the U.S. Navy's first AN/SQQ-89 undersea warfare system. Today, the Ocean Systems business, part of MS2-Undersea Systems in Manassas, Virginia, serves the U.S. Navy with leading mine countermeasure systems, electronic and undersea warfare systems and sensors.

In 1993 Martin Marietta Corporation acquired GE Aerospace and in 1995, Martin Marietta merged with Lockheed Corporation to

The TPS-117 Tactical Transportable Radar, for long-range air defense.

form Lockheed Martin. As defense budgets declined in the 1990s, the direction of emphasis began to include commercial business as well as government contracts.

Over the years, Lockheed Martin has consolidated its operations in Electronics Park. In a sale-lease back arrangement, Lockheed Martin has a 99-year lease from the Empire State Development Corporation for its three major buildings (EP-5, EP-6 and EP-7) containing 1.4 million square feet. The remaining eight buildings, consisting of some 400,000 square feet, are leased to Electronics Park, LLC, for 30 years.

MS2-Syracuse continues to design, develop and integrate complex, software-intensive electronic systems throughout the world. Every day, its employees continue to build on the leadership and the innovative technological traditions of Electronics Park.

A 1948 GE publicity photo shows one of the first TV set series produced at Electronics Park, the Model 810.

BIBLIOGRAPHY

Published Sources

Alsever, John N., ed. *When Syracuse was a Village*. Syracuse: City Clerk's Office, 1915.

Baldwin, E. Howell, ed. *Trading Post to City*. Syracuse: Central High School, 1912.

Beauchamp, William M. *Past and Present of Syracuse and Onondaga County*, New York. New York: The S. J. Clarke Publishing Company, 1908.

Bradley, James W. *Evolution of the Onondaga Iroquois: Accommodating Change, 1500-1655*. Syracuse: Syracuse University Press, 1987.

Brewster, Arthur Judson. *Life Was Never Dull*. Syracuse: Syracuse University Press, 1953.

Bruce, Dwight H. *Memorial History of Syracuse*. Syracuse: H. P. Smith & Company, 1891.

Bruce, Dwight H., ed. *Onondaga's Centennial*. Boston History Company, 1896.

Buckenberger, A.C., Kingsley, M.J., Knauber, J.C., and Neville, J.J. *The Political Blue Book of Syracuse*, N. Y. Syracuse: E. M. Grover, Printer, 1902.

Calkins, Carroll C., ed. *The Story of America*. Pleasantville, New York: The Readers Digest Association, Inc., 1975.

Cathers, David and Vertikoff, Alexander. *Stickley Style: Arts and Crafts Homes in the Craftsman Tradition*. New York: Simon & Schuster, 1999.

Chase, Franklin H. *Syracuse and Its Environs*. Chicago: Lewis Historical Publishing Company, 1924.

Child, Hamilton. *Gazetteer and Business Directory of Onondaga County, N. Y., for 1868-9*. Syracuse: Hamilton Child, 1868.

Clark, Joshua V. H. *Onondaga or Reminiscences of Earlier and Later Times*. Syracuse: Stoddard and Babcock, 1849.

Colles, Christopher. *A Survey of the Roads of the United States of America 1789*. Cambridge, Massachusetts: The Belknap Press of Harvard University Press, 1961.

Connolly, Alethea. *God Love Ya: A Biography of Father Charles J. Brady*. Syracuse: Catholic Diocese of Syracuse, New York, 1989.

Connors, Dennis J. "Echoes of Our Past: The Historic Landscapes of Syracuse's Cemeteries." *Portraits of the Past #6*. Syracuse: Onondaga Historical Association, 1994.

Connors, Dennis J. and Neville, Lee. "Springs, Lakes and Reservoirs: A History of Syracuse's Water Systems." *Portraits of the Past #8*. Syracuse: Onondaga Historical Association, 1994.

Connors, Dennis J. "Bottoms UP!: A History of the Brewing Industry in Syracuse." *Portraits of the Past #12*. Syracuse: Onondaga Historical Association, 1997.

Connors, Dennis J. and Reap, John. *A Guide to Sites and Related History: Society for Industrial Archeology, Fall Tour 2001*. Syracuse: Onondaga Historical Association, 2001.

Connors et al. *Onondaga: Portrait of a Native People*. Syracuse: Syracuse University Press and Everson Museum of Art, 1986.

Cornwall, Zoe. *Human Rights in Syracuse: Two Memorable Decades: A Selected History from 1963 to 1983*. Syracuse: Human Rights Commission of Syracuse and Onondaga County, 1989.

Emilio, Luis F. *A Brave Black Regiment: The History of the 54th Massachusetts, 1863-1865*. New York: Da Capo Press, 1995.

Farrell, William R. *Classical Place Names in New York State: Origins, Histories and Meanings*. Jamesville, New York: Pine Grove Press, 2002.

French, J.H. *Historical and Statistical Gazetteer of New York State*. Syracuse: R. Pearsall Smith, 1860.

Galpin, W. Freeman. *Central New York: An Inland Empire*. Chicago: Lewis Publishing Company, Inc. 1941.

Gaska, J. and Mosher, E. *A Brief History: The Typewriter and Smith-Corona*. Cortland, New York: Smith-Corona Group, 1976.

Geddes, George. "Survey of Onondaga." *Transactions of the N. Y. State Agricultural Society*, Volume XIX. Albany, 1859.

Gersbacher, Ron.: "Play Ball! A History of Early Organized Baseball in Syracuse." *Portrait of the Past #7*. Syracuse: Onondaga Historical Association, 1994.

Gokey, Edward. *The Changing View: Selected Paintings from the Onondaga Historical Association*. Syracuse: Onondaga Historical Association, 1989.

Gordon, Thomas F. *Gazetteer of the State of New York*. Philadelphia: T. K. & P. G. Collins, 1836.

Hand, M.C. *From a Forest to a City: Personal Reminiscences of Syracuse, N.Y.* Syracuse: Masters & Stone, 1889.

Hardin, Evamaria. *Syracuse Landmarks*. Syracuse: Onondaga Historical Association / Syracuse University Press, 1993.

Hauptman, Laurence M. *The Iroquois Struggle for Survival: World War II to Red Power*. Syracuse: Syracuse University Press, 1986.

Hauptman, Laurence M. *Conspiracy of Interests: Iroquois Dispossession and the Rise of New York State*. Syracuse: Syracuse University Press, 1999.

Hedrick, Ulysses Prentiss. *A History of Agriculture in the State of New York*. Albany: New York State Agricultural Society, 1933.

Hirsch, Foster. *The Boys from Syracuse: The Shuberts' Theatrical Empire*. Carbondale and Edwardsville, Illinois: Southern Illinois University Press, 1998.

Hunter, Carol M. *To Set the Captives Free: Reverend Jermain Wesley Loguen and the Struggle for Freedom in Central New York 1835-1872*. New York: Garland Publishing, Inc., 1993.

Jones, Barbara L. *Nature Staged: The Landscape and Still Life Paintings of Levi Wells Prentice*. Blue Mountain Lake, New York: Adirondack Museum, 1993.

Kallfelz, et al: *Railroads in the Streets of Syracuse*. Marcellus, New York: Central New York Chapter National Railway Historical Society, 1979.

Kenney, James E. *History of Le Moyne College: The First 25 Years*. Syracuse: Le Moyne College, 1973.

Klein, Milton M., ed. *The Empire State: A History of New York*. Ithaca: Cornell University Press, 2001.

Mau, Clayton: *The Development of Central and Western New York*. Rochester: The Du Bois Press, 1944.

May, Samuel J.: *Some Recollections of Our Antislavery Conflict*. Boston: Fields, Osgood & Co., 1869.

Meyer, William B. "Why Did Syracuse Manufacture Solar Salt?" *New York History* 86 (Spring 2005): 195–209.

Mullins, Michael A. *Syracuse University Football: A Centennial Celebration*. Norfolk, Virginia: The Donning Company, 1989.

Munson, Lilian Steele. *Syracuse: The City that Salt Built*. New York: Pageant Press International Corporation, 1969.

O'Brien, William: *Forty Years on the Force*. Syracuse: Syracuse Herald, 1926.

Palumbo, George and Sacks, Seymour. *Syracuse and its Black Community: The Historical Development of the City as a Prologue to the 21st Century*. Syracuse: Syracuse University Maxwell School of Citizenship and Public Affairs, 2000.

Quigley, John P. *A Century of Fire Fighting: The History of the Syracuse Fire Department*. Syracuse Herald, 1926.

Ramsey, David. *Nats: A Team. A City. An Era*. Utica, New York: Pine Tree Press, 1995.

Rivette, Barbara S. "This is a Beautiful Country of Land..." *Portraits of the Past #5*. Syracuse: Onondaga Historical Association, 1994.

Roseboom, William F. and Schramm, Henry W. *Syracuse: From Salt to Satellite*. Woodland Hills, California: Windsor Publications, 1979.

Rudolph, Bernard G. *From a Minyan to a Community: A History of the Jews of Syracuse*. Syracuse: Syracuse University, 1970.

Schmitz, Marian K. *The Hollow and The Hill*. Parsons, West Virginia: McClain Printing Company, 1983.

Schramm, Henry W. *Empire Showcase: A History of the New York State Fair*. Utica, New York: North Country Books, 1985.

Sernett, Milton C. *North Star Country: Upstate New York and the Crusade for African American Freedom*. Syracuse: Syracuse University Press, 2002.

Smith, Ray B., ed. *The Red Book of Syracuse and Onondaga County*. Syracuse: The Syracuse Press, Inc., 1923.

Smith, E. Reuel. *Notes on the Vredenburgh and Burnett Families*. New York: The Knickerbocker Press, 1917.

Smith, Edward. *A History of the Schools of Syracuse*. Syracuse: C. W. Bardeen, 1893.

Spafford, Horatio Gates. *A Gazetteer of the State of New York*. Albany: H. C. Southwick, 1813.

Spafford, Horatio Gates. *A Gazetteer of the State of New York*. Albany: B. D. Packard, 1824.

Strong, Gurney S. *Early Landmarks of Syracuse*. Syracuse: The Times Publishing Company, 1894.

Trigger, Bruce G., ed. *Handbook of the North American Indian, Volume 15: Northeast*. Washington: Smithsonian Institution, 1978.

Tuck, James A. *Onondaga Iroquois Prehistory: A Study in Settlement Archaeology*. Syracuse: Syracuse University Press, 1971.

Webb, Stephen Saunders, ed. *Essays on the Renaissance in Syracuse: 1961-1981*. Syracuse: Onondaga County Public Library, 1981.

Wright, Kenneth W. *Foundations Well and Truly Laid: The Early History of SUNY Health Science Center at Syracuse*. Syracuse: Alumni Association of the SUNY Health Science Center, 1994.

Zellers, John A. *The Typewriter: A Short History, on its 75th Anniversary 1873-1948*. New York: The Newcomen Society of England, American Branch, 1948.

Archival Sources

Holdings of the Onondaga Historical Association Research Center:
- Vertical Files
- Manuscript Collection
- Map Collection
- Photographic Collection

INDEX

Abolitionism 47–51
Adanti, Paul 115
Adirondack 63
Ainslie, Adam 28
Albany 14, 39
Alcazar Theater 106
Alderman, Gordon 115
Alexander, Lee 86, 126, 132
Amboy Airport 101
AME Zion Church 48, 86, 128, 130
American Legion Post 41 109
Americanization League of Syracuse 85
Anthony, Susan B. 51
Appomattox 51
Archbold Stadium 135, 136
Archbold, John 119
Arlen, Harold 105
Arluck, Samuel 105
Armory Square Historic District 26, 44, 130, 143, 144
Auburn, New York 39
Avery, B. Austin 55
Avon Theater 106
Babcock, Edward C. 105
Baker, Art 135
Baker, Charles Ashley 47
Baker, James and Mary 50
Baldwin, Charles 73
Baldwin, Harvey 52
Ball, Lucille 115
Barnum, Phineas T. 60, 61
Barrow, John D. 63
Bartels Brewery 102
Barton Theater 62
Basilio, Carmen 135
Bastable Theater 62
Battery Wagner 52
Baxter, Blanche Weaver 82, 83
Bayberry Development 118
Belden, James 73
Benedict Billiard Factory 65
Berle, Milton 115
Bernardi, Roy 132
Bethany Baptist Church 86, 127
Biasone, Danny 133
Binghamton, New York 42
Blodgett Vocational High School 134
Board of Education 53, 72
Boeheim, Jim 136
Bogardus Corners 26
Bogardus, Henry 26
Booth, Edwin 60
Borden Company 80
Boston Celtics 134
Bradford Hills 99
Bradley & Company 77
Bradly, Dan 20
Brady, Monsignor Charles 130
Bray Hall 119
Bristol Laboratories 118

Brooklyn Dodgers 65
Brown, Alexander T. 76
Brown, Jim 136
Brown, John 51
Brown-Lipe Gear 76
Brown-Lipe-Chapin Company 109
Buckingham, James 96
Burnet Park Zoo 132
Burnet, John B. 75
Burnet, Moses DeWitt 46
Burpee, William 78
Cadwell, Matthew 28
Cameo Theater 106
Caesar, Sid 115
Cahill, Edward 89
Cahill, William 89
Calder Cup Championship 106, 135
Calthrop, Samuel R. 100
Cambria, New York 21
Camillus, New York 24, 25, 101, 123
Cananda Lake (Onondaga Lake) 17
Canandaigua, New York 95
Canastota, New York 135
Cantwell, James 63
Captain Henry's Show Boat 106
Carnegie Library 72–73
Carnegie, Andrew 72
Carrier Corporation 104, 118, 154
Carter, Fernando A. 75
Carter, George and Phebe 50
Carter, Jacob 52
Catholic Interracial Council 130
Cayuga Lake 24
Cayuga, Iroquois nation of 14
CBS 114
Central Baptist Church 59
Central High School 74
Cervi, Al 134
"Chain Gang," The 57
Chamberlain, Wilt 135
Chappell's, Department Store 89, 114
Chippewa, Battle of 27
Chittenango, New York 24
Cholera epidemic 37
Cicero, New York 16, 25, 114, 123
Civic Morning Musicals 75
Civil War 39, 51–52, 75
Clarke, Frances Amelia 61
Clarke, William 48
Clay, New York 123
Cleveland, Grover 73
Clinton Square 26, 35, 73, 120, 124–26, 144
Clinton-Sullivan campaign 15
Cody, William F. (Buffalo Bill) 60
Collins, Minnie 59
Columbus Circle 72, 124, 144
Columbus Monument 85
Comfort, George Fisk 75
Commonweal Club 82

Company C, 108th Infantry Regiment.....108
Comstock, Bessie.....82
Connoisseurs, The (painting).....63, 64
Corcoran High School.....32, 132
Corcoran, Thomas J......132
CORE.....130
Corinth.....33
Corinthian Club.....141
Cossitt, Sterling.....26
Costello, Larry.....134
Cotton Bowl.....136
County Board of Supervisors.....46, 131
Courthouses.....25, 45–46, 54, 73, 124–25, 145
Cousy, Bob.....134
Crosby, Bing.....105
Crouse Irving Hospital.....120
CSS *Alabama*.....52
Culp's Hill at Gettysburg.....52
Cultural Corridor.....144
Culverhouse, Johann.....36
Daggett's Saloon.....57
Danforth, Asa.....16, 47, 55
Darby, Golden.....82
Daugherty, Jean.....115
Davis, Ernie.....135
Davis, Thomas.....56
Day, James Roscoe.....119
DeForest, Andrew.....52
DeGroat, James.....25
DeGroat Family.....16
Delaware, Lackawanna & Western Railroad.....39, 42
DeLine, Jim.....114, 115
DeMarco, Tony.....135
Denman's Midwifery.....28
DeWitt, New York.....100, 118, 137
DeWitt, Moses.....16, 19
DeWitt, Simeon.....14, 17
Dey Brothers Department Store.....89
Dickens, Charles.....61
Dietz Company.....77
Dimond, Lillie Belle.....45
Docksteder, Harry.....21
Dodge, Bert.....80
Douglass, Frederick.....47, 82
Douglass, Lewis.....49
Doust camera store.....109
Dowdell, Dennis.....130
Driscoll, Matthew.....128
Driving Park.....66
Dunbar Center.....82, 128
Duncan, John.....25
Duval, Dennis.....128
Dwight, Colonel Augustus.....51
Earhart, Amelia.....101
Early, General Jubal.....52
Eastern Hockey League.....135
Easy Washer Company.....109, 110
Ecker, Herman.....96
Edge, Herman.....128
Edwards, E.W. Department Store.....89, 125
Edwards, Daniel M......93, 141
Edwards, O.M......79
Eisenhower Administration.....122
Elbridge, New York.....24
Electronics Park.....116
Elliott, Charles Loring.....31
Ellis Island.....134
Ellis, George.....63
Elmwood Neighborhood.....99–100
Empire Stateway Highway.....122
Engleberg-Huller Company.....76
Erie Boulevard.....100, 121, 124
Erie Canal Museum.....53, 144
Erie Canal.....18, 33, 36, 37–39, 42–44, 76, 100
Evans, Sheriff William.....58
Everson Museum of Art.....68,128,130–31, 144
Everson, Helen.....128
Fabius, New York.....25,123
Fairmount Fair Plaza.....123
Fayette Park.....43,75
Fayetteville, New York.....24
Federal Housing Administration.....105
Fiesta Bowl.....136
Fifteenth Ward.....126–31
Fillmore, Millard.....50
First Ward Methodist Church.....44
Fitch, Ursula Ann Elliott.....31
"Flum Num, Eddie".....115
Foery, Bishop Walter A......120
Foley, Jasena.....141
Foote, Hiram.....51
Forman Park.....33, 75
Forman, Joshua.....24, 32–33
Forman, Samuel.....24
Forrest, Edwin.....60
Fort Stanwix.....17
Fort Wayne Pistons.....134
Foster, Stephen.....63
Fralich, Henry.....58
Franklin Manufacturing Company.....72, 76, 102
Franklin Square.....78–79, 143
Franklin, Herbert H......76
French Catholic Church (St. Joseph's).....69
Fugitive Slave Law.....50
Gage, Matilda Joslyn.....61, 82
Gait, Paul.....136
Gait, Gary.....136
Garland, Benjamin.....86
Garrison, William Lloyd.....48
Gas Light Company of Syracuse.....55
Geddes, New York.....18, 36, 76, 94, 96
Geddes, James.....18, 50
Geddesburgh.....18
General Electric Company.....116, 118–119
General Motors Company.....84
Genesee Street.....24, 82, 96, 140–41
Genesee Theater.....123
Geneva, New York.....24, 120
George, Samuel (Sowenona).....14
Gere Building.....125, 126
Getreu, Sanford.....123
Gettysburg, Battle of.....52
Gibson, Margaret.....80
Gifford Street.....38, 104
Gifford, Henry.....38
Gifford, Luther.....58
Gillette, King.....98
Godfrey, Arthur.....115
Gonzalez, Bethaida (Bea).....136
Grace Episcopal Church.....131

Grand Opera House 62
Great Depression of 1929 ....74, 101–06
Great Genesee Road 24
Greater Syracuse Sports Hall of Fame 133
Greeley, Horace 44
Green Street 65, 73, 142
Greenway Brewery 102
Gridley Building 43, 125–26
Griffin, Joseph 93, 102
Gunpowder Explosion 58–59
Haberle Brewery 67, 102
Hall of Languages 119
Hall, Calvin 27
Hall, Hosea 28
Hancock Airport 122, 166
Hanna, Charles 101
Hanover Square Historic District 36, 42, 43, 51, 75, 125, 126, 143
Hanson, Vic 135
Harpers Ferry 51
Harrison Street 80, 126
Hawley, S. P. 28
Hazard, Dora Sedgwick 82, 107
Hazard, Frederick R. 107
Heiman, Celia 84
Heiman, Marcus 84
Heimann, Issac 84
Heisman Trophy 136
Hendricks, Francis 73, 119
Henry, William "Jerry" 50
Herkimer County 19
Herr, Merrilyn Hubbard 115
Hiawatha Lake 55
Hier, George 67
Hier, J.P. 80
Higgins, Robert 65
Highgate, Charles 52
Hills Building 102
"Hindenburg Line" 108
Hobart College 120
Holden, Hendrick S. 141
Holy Trinity Church 85
Hopps Memorial Methodist Church 86, 128
Horner, Frederick 25
Hotel Syracuse 89, 93
"Howdy Doody" 115
Howlett Hill 106
Hudson River School 14
Hudson River 14, 16
Hudson Valley 67
Hudson, A.A. 59
Hulin, Lovinia 38
Hunter-Tuppen Store 89
Huntington, Aria 82
Hutchinson Family Singers 61
Hutchinson, Lucia 22
Hutchinson, James 22
Intercollegiate Rowing Association 135
International Baseball League 65, 105, 133
Iroquois Confederacy 9, 13, 14
Iroquois League 14
Iroquois lacrosse 136
Jacobus, J.S. 105
James Street 43, 79, 140–41
Jamesville, New York 16, 58
Jay's Treaty 26

Jefferson School 53
Jefferson Street 39, 43, 72, 101, 128, 144
Jefferson, Thomas 16
Jerry Rescue 50
Jersey City 105
John Deere Company 76
Johnson, Caleb 28
Johnson, John 22
Journeymen Horseshoers Union 80
Justice Center 129
Kanoono Karnival 97
Keble School 82
Keene, Christopher 131
Keith, Benjamin Franklin 93, 94
Kellogg, Captain Leonard 27
Kemp & Burpee Company 76, 78
Kemp, Joseph S. 78
Kemper Building 114
Kerr, Johnny 134
King & King Architects 124, 178
King, George 134
King, Martin Luther 130
Kirk Park 66
Kirkpatrick, William 75
Knapp, George Kasson 23
Labor Day Storm 133
Lacrosse, Syracuse University 136
Lake Ontario 14, 37, 132
Lamb, Thomas 90, 142
Landmark Theater 90, 142
Lautz, Henry J. 105
Leavenworth Circle 74
Leavenworth, Elias 50, 141
Leland Hotel 59, 60
LeMoyne College 120, 141
LeMoyne Heights 120
LeMoyne, Simon 120
Leonard, Thomas 48
Ley Creek 105
Library Circle 72
Liederkranz 68
Lincoln, Abraham 51
Lind, Jenny 60
Lindbergh, Charles 101
Lipe, Charles E. 76
Lipe, Willard C. 76
"Little Italy" 85
Liverpool 18, 38, 116
Livingston, William H. 48
Lloyd, Earl 134
Lockheed (Lockheed Martin) 118, 198
Lockport, New York 36
Loew Building 102, 106
Loew's Strand 90
Loguen, Caroline 48
Loguen, Helen Amelia 49
Loguen, Jermain 48–51
Long Branch Resort 94–95
Long Island 30
Longstreet, Cornelius T. 121
Lowe Art Gallery 119
Lower, Conrad 22
Ludden, Patrick 66
Lum & Abner 106
Luminism 63

Lyman Hall 119
Lysander, New York 16, 25, 123
MacArthur Stadium 105, 132
Magic Toy Shop 115
Mainelli, Thomas 85
Malcom, William 59
Manlius, New York.......................19, 25, 61, 123
Mann, James 28
Maple Bay Resort 94
Marcellus, New York 16, 19, 20, 25
Mardi Gras 97
Marsellus, John 76
Marsellus Casket Company 76
Marshall Hall 119
Martin Marietta Company 118
Marvin, Rollie..104
Maxwell School, Syracuse University..............119
May Memorial Unitarian Church 100
May, Samuel J. 48, 50
McCarthy's Dry Goods................................87, 89
McGuire, James Kennedy 72, 73
Melvin, Crandall Sr. 102
Memorial Hospital 82, 120
Mercury Theater Radio Show 106
Meredith Company 114
Merrell-Soule Company 80
Merrick, Asa...93
Mickles, Nicholas 20, 27, 28
Midtown Plaza 120
Mill Pond 26, 37
Mills Brothers Restaurant 86
Mills, Harriet May 82
Minneapolis Lakers 134
Minstrel shows 60
Mohawk River 24
Mohawk Valley 16
Monarch Typewriter Company 78
Montgomery Street 44, 72, 129, 144
MONY Plaza 100, 124
Moore & Quinn Brewery 102
Moyer Carriage Company 76
Mulroy Civic Center 131
Mulroy, John 120, 131, 132
Municipal Stadium 105
Murphy, Conny 65
Murray, Heman 21
Myers, Carl 96
Myrtle Hill Cemetery 58
National Basketball Association 133–35
National Grid/Niagara Mohawk...................57, 170
National Guard Armory 133, 143
National Hockey League 135
National League 65
National Register of Historic Places 56, 143
National Theater 60
National Women's Rights Convention 61
NCAA Final Four..136
Nera Car 98
New York Central Railroad 39, 42, 88, 103–04, 116
New York City 21, 36, 114
New York Knicks 134
New York State Fair 66, 94, 96, 133
New York State Forestry School 119
New York State Office of General Services 19
Newhouse School, Syracuse University 119

Niagara River 19, 21
Nine Mile Creek 20
Northern Lights Shopping Center 123
Noxon, B. Davis 50
Oakwood Cemetery 58, 133
Oberdorfer Foundries 84
Oberdorfer, Moses 84
O'Brien, Billy 57
O'Connor, Fred 129
O'Hara, James 69
Oh Susanna 63
Oneida Lake 24, 94, 122
Onondaga Academy 32, 36
Onondaga Community College 120–21
Onondaga County Savings Bank 35, 43, 89
Onondaga County 19–20, 26, 36–37, 46, 123, 131–32
Onondaga Creek 15, 25–26, 37, 65, 76, 130, 143
Onondaga Furnace 20
Onondaga, New York 16, 25, 46, 99
Onondaga Historical Association.......7, 11, 19, 51, 75, 133, 144
Onondaga Hollow 23, 28, 36, 47
Onondaga Hotel...89–92
Onondaga Indian Nation 9, 13, 14, 15, 17, 28
Onondaga Lake Park 95, 102
Onondaga Lake 14, 17–19, 24, 33, 39, 42, 94–96, 102, 114, 143
Onondaga Park 15, 55
Onondaga Polka 105
Onondaga Pottery.....................................76, 90
Onondaga Register 17, 20, 28
Onondaga Salt Company 38
Onondaga Salt Springs Reservation 17
Onondaga Valley.......................................13, 121
Onondaga War Memorial.........................128, 134
OnTrack rail shuttle 39
Orangemen, Syracuse University 136
O'Reilly, Rev. 65
Oswego Canal 36–38, 42, 74, 76, 102
Oswego River 18
Our Lady of Pompeii 85
Owen, Joel 65
Owen, John 48
Paramount Studios 89
Paramount Theater 89
Paulus, Philip 68
PBS 116
Pearl Harbor 107
Pei, I.M. 130
Penn State 135
Percy Hughes Elementary School 84
Phoenix buildings 43
Pickwick Papers 61
Pioneer Homes..105, 129
Pirro, Nick 132
Planning Commission, Syracuse 75, 123, 128
"Play Lady" 115
Pleasant Beach Resort 94
Pompey Academy 32
Pompey, New York 16, 25, 26, 121
Post, Wiley 101
Post-Standard, The 124, 125, 129
Potter's Field (Rose Hill Cemetery) 59
Poughkeepsie, New York 25
Powell, Harriet 48
Prentice, Levi Wells 65
Price, Milton 66

205

Index

Primex Building 124
Prospect Hill 54
Prospect Hill Brewery 54
Putnam Grammar School 72
Putnam, Hiram 50
Quaker Road, Battle of 52
Queenston Heights 27
Randall, James 93
Rawson, Albert L. 14
Red Mill 26
Redfield, Lewis 28,75
Remington Rand Company 79, 104, 109
Renwick, James 121
Rice, Samuel 20
Robinson, Charles 86
Robinson, Edward 86
Robinson, Jackie 65
Robinson, John 76
Robinson, Sugar Ray 135
Rochester, New York 51, 105
Rockaway Beach Resort 94
Rockefeller, John D. 119
Romer, British Colonel 17
Roof Garden restaurant 90
Roosevelt, Franklin D. 102,106,119
Roosevelt, Theodore 96
Rosamond Gifford Zoo 132
Rose Hill Cemetery 58, 59
Rosenbloom's Shul 86
Rucker, Henry 60
Rudolph, Paul...129
Russell, Bill 134
Sackets Harbor, New York 26
Sacred Heart Parish 85
Saints Peter and Paul Russian Orthodox Church...86
"Salina Blues"...59
Salina Street 23, 26, 43, 44, 46, 47, 55, 70, 75, 89, 90
Salina, Town...25, 122–23
Salina, Village 18, 19, 29, 33, 38, 42, 44, 46–47, 56
Salt City March 105
Salt Point Baseball Club 63
Salt Point 18, 19
Sanderson Brothers Steel Company 76
Sarette, Dave 135
Schaffer, Peter 58
Schayes, Dolph 133
Schenectady, New York 30
Schwedes, Gerhard 135
Scotholm Residential Development 96
Sedgwick Farm Residential Development 96
Seneca Falls, New York 61
Seneca River 24, 95
Seneca Turnpike 22, 24, 27, 36
Seward, William 44
Seymour, Paul...134
Sheridan, General Philip 52
Shoemaker, Jack 16
Shoppingtown Plaza 123
Shubert, Sam 62
Shubert Family...62, 84
Simmons, Roy Jr. 136
Sisco, William 25
Skaneateles Lake 55, 74
Skaneateles, New York 21, 30
SkyChiefs Baseball Club 105, 133

Smith College...82
Smith Premier Typewriter Company 79, 120
Smith, Edward 28
Smith, Gerrit 50
Smith, Hurlbut 79
Smith, Lyman C. 66, 79
Smith, Monroe 79
Smith, Stephen 38
Smith, Wilbert 79
Sniper, General Gustavius 75
Society of Concord 29, 84
Soldiers and Sailors Monument 75, 126
Solvay, New York 55, 72, 76
Spafford Gazetteer of 1813 (Population of Towns) ...25
Split Rock Quarry...107
Sprague, Captain John 26
St. Agnes Cemetery 52, 58, 73
St. Cecilia's Foresters Baseball Team 63
St. John the Baptist Church..................................46
St. John the Baptist Ukranian Church 86
St. Joseph's Hospital..54
St. Mary's Circle...72
St. Mary's Church 69
St. Peter's Church 84
St. Peter's Kirche 68
St. Sophia's Greek Orthodox Church....................86
St. Stephen's Catholic Slovak Church 86
Stanton, Sidney 42
Star Park..63
State Agricultural Society 96
State Barge Canal 102, 124, 143
State Fair Coliseum 106, 133
State Theater 90, 93, 102
State Tower Building 101, 102
State University of New York 119, 120
Stearns, E. C. Company 76, 77
Stickley, Gustav 99
Straight Line Engine Company 76
Sugar Bowl 136
Swan, Joseph 28
Syracuse & Utica Railroad 39
Syracuse Arms Company 77
Syracuse Blazers..135
Syracuse Board of Education 53, 82, 128
Syracuse Chamber of Commerce 129
Syracuse Chiefs Baseball Club 105
Syracuse Chilled Plow Company 76, 77
Syracuse China Company 76
Syracuse City Water Works Company 55
Syracuse Common Council 47, 136
Syracuse Crunch Hockey Team 135
Syracuse Developmental Center 53
Syracuse Electric Light & Power Company 56
Syracuse Herald Journal 120
Syracuse Herald, The 96
Syracuse Home Association 31, 184
Syracuse House 48
Syracuse Journal 56, 63
Syracuse Liederkranz 68
Syracuse Mall 125
Syracuse Memorial Hospital 120
Syracuse Museum of Fine Arts 75
Syracuse Nationals Basketball Team 133, 134
Syracuse Stage 119
Syracuse Star..46

Syracuse Stars Baseball Club..63, 65
Syracuse Stars Hockey Team 106
Syracuse Stove Works Company 77
Syracuse Symphony 131
Syracuse University College of Engineering............................86
Syracuse University College of Fine Arts 63
Syracuse University Drama Department 119
Syracuse University 72, 118–120
Tallman Park 66
Teall, Oliver 56
Technology Club 75
Temple Adath Jeshurun 86
Temple Adath Yeshurun 84, 105
Temple of Concord 68, 84, 86
Temple Theater 89, 93
Thayer, Sanford 63–64
Third Ward Railway 55
Thompson Road 84
Thornden Park 75
Time Warner Cable 116
Tipperary Hill...47, 68
Trimm, G. Lee 120
Tucker, James...52
Tully, New York...25
Turn Verein 68, 69
Tyler, Comfort 16, 19, 23
"Typewriter City" 79
Uncle Tom's Cabin 60
Underground Railroad 48
Unitarian Church of the Messiah 48
United Technologies Corporation 118
University Hill 118–121
UPN Television Network..116
Upstate Medical University 120
USS Kearsarge 52
Utica, New York..19
Valley Cemetery 58
Valley High School..32
Van Heusen, Jimmy 105
Van Schaick, Colonel Goose 15
Vanderbilt Square...42, 108
Vanderbilt, Commodore Cornelius...42
Veterans Park 75
Vredenburgh, Evelina..30
Vredenburgh, Mary 30
Vredenburgh, William 21, 30
WAGE 106
Walker, Moses Fleetwood 65
Walrath, John 132
Walton, Abraham 26
Ward, Ward Wellington 99

Warr, Robert 128
Washington Park 19, 63
Water Street Burying Ground 58
WCNY 116
Webster, Daniel 44, 50
Webster, Ephraim..28
Welles, Orson..106
Wells, Ernest G...15
Wells, H.G. 106
Welsh, Walter..131
Wesleyan Methodist Church 50
Westvale Plaza 123
WFBL 106
WHEN...106, 114–115
White City Resort 94
White, Hamilton S. 59, 75
White, Horatio Nelson...54
Whitesboro, New York 19
Wieting Hall...51, 61
Wieting Opera House 62
Wilbur, Hervey 53
Wilkinson Reservoir 55
Wilkinson, John 33, 39, 50
Wilkinson, John (grandson) 76
Will, Anton 76
Willis, Charles 52
Wilson, Edward 86
Witherill's Department Store 89
Witney, Noah 28
WIXT 115
WNYS 115
WOLF 106
Woman Suffrage Association 82
Women's Political Union 82
Wood Creek 24
Woodlawn Cemetery 58, 96
World War I 51, 101, 107–108, 109
World War II 1105, 106–109, 111, 113
WPA (Works Progress Administration)...............................104–05
Wright, Frank Lloyd...124
WSPX..116
WSTM 114
WSYR...106, 114
WSYT 116
WTVH 115
Yates Castle 121
Yates Hotel 89
Yates, Alonzo...121
YMCA 74
Young, Henry 37

INDEX OF PARTNERS & WEB SITES

ABC Refrigeration &
Air Conditioning Inc. 152
www.abcrefrigeration.com

Bristol-Myers Squibb Company 160
www.bms.com

CXtec 192
www.cxtec.com

Carrier Corporation 154
www.carrier.com

Cathedral Candle 161
www.cathedralcandle.com

Comfort Inn & Suites
Syracuse Airport................................164
www.tramzhotels.com

Costello, Cooney & Fearon, PLLC 172
www.ccf-law.com

Dal Pos Architects, LLC. 174
www.dalpos.com

Department of Aviation,
City of Syracuse 166
www.syrairport.org

Hal Silverman Studio 186
www.silvermanstudio.com

Hardy Construction Services...............148
www.hardyconstruction.com

Harrison Industrial Supply, Inc. 162
www.harrisonind.com

InfiMed Inc. 196
www.infimed.com

Jaquith Industries, Inc. 158
www.jaquith.com

JCM Architectural Associates 176
www.jcm300.com

King & King, Architects LLP................178
www.kingarch.com

Le Moyne College..............................187
www.lemoyne.edu

Lockheed Martin Maritime
Systems & Sensors 198
www.lockheedmartin.com/syracuse

National Grid/Niagara Mohawk..........170
www.nationalgridus.com/niagaramohawk

New York State Fair 188
www.nysfair.org

Onondaga Historical Association 179
www.cnyhistory.org

Pastabilities......................................165
www.pastabilities.com

Stickley, Audi & Company 163
www.stickley.com

Syracuse China Company 156
www.libbey.com

Syracuse Convention &
Visitors Bureau 189
www.VisitSyracuse.org

Syracuse Home Association 184
www.syracusehomeassn.org

The Post-Standard 171
www.syracuse.com

The State University of New York
Upstate Medical University 190
www.upstate.edu

Visiting Nurse Association
of Central New York...........................191
www.vnacny.org